CAMBRIDGE LIBRARY COLLECTION

Books of enduring scholarly value

History

The books reissued in this series include accounts of historical events and movements by eye-witnesses and contemporaries, as well as landmark studies that assembled significant source materials or developed new historiographical methods. The series includes work in social, political and military history on a wide range of periods and regions, giving modern scholars ready access to influential publications of the past.

The Navy of the Restoration

Arthur Tedder's 1916 study of the Royal Navy during the seventeenth century describes the Navy's cautious support for the restoration of the monarchy, its position as protector of commerce in the Mediterranean and its role in the Anglo-Dutch wars. It chronicles the constant struggle to staff, feed and equip the Navy and the challenges of plague, poor discipline and frequent skirmishes with the Dutch. It explores in detail the tactics of individual battles in the Anglo-Dutch wars as well as the practical difficulties that often hampered the English war effort. The author served in the RAF in WWI and became a member of the British high command during WWII; his tactical flair informs his analysis of the Royal Navy's progress during a turbulent period. His account also includes fascinating details of wage disputes, embezzlement of funds and the work of the infamous press gangs.

The Navy of the Restoration

From the Death of Cromwell to the Treaty of Breda

Its Work, Growth and Influence

ARTHUR WILLIAM TEDDER

CAMBRIDGE
UNIVERSITY PRESS

CAMBRIDGE UNIVERSITY PRESS

Cambridge, New York, Melbourne, Madrid, Cape Town, Singapore,
São Paolo, Delhi, Dubai, Tokyo, Mexico City

Published in the United States of America by Cambridge University Press, New York

www.cambridge.org
Information on this title: www.cambridge.org/9781108013147

This edition first published 1916
This digitally printed version 2010

ISBN 978-1-108-01314-7 Paperback

Additional resources for this publication at www.cambridge.org/9781108013147

Cambridge Historical Essays

THE NAVY OF THE
RESTORATION

CAMBRIDGE UNIVERSITY PRESS

C. F. CLAY, Manager

London: FETTER LANE, E.C.

Edinburgh: 100 PRINCES STREET

New York: G. P. PUTNAM'S SONS

Bombay, Calcutta and Madras: MACMILLAN AND CO., Ltd.

Toronto: J. M. DENT AND SONS, Ltd.

Tokyo: THE MARUZEN-KABUSHIKI-KAISHA

THE NAVY OF THE RESTORATION

FROM THE DEATH OF CROMWELL
TO THE TREATY OF BREDA;
ITS WORK, GROWTH AND INFLUENCE

BY

ARTHUR W. TEDDER, B.A.

MAGDALENE COLLEGE, CAMBRIDGE

Cambridge:
at the University Press
1916

INTRODUCTION

" OUR historians," said Sir J. Knox Laughton at
the recent International Historical Congress,
"have considered, and therefore people in general have
considered, that the navy is merely an engine for
fighting battles." That is an attitude which it is
becoming increasingly easy to avoid, because its fallacy
is being ever increasingly exposed ; though, until our
present standard naval history is superseded, there
remains in being a monumental example of that prime
fallacy.

It is that fallacy, or rather, that lack of true proportion, which it is particularly necessary to avoid
in this study of the Navy of the Restoration. The
Restoration period is one of vital interest and importance regarding the development of the Navy as a self-
containing, independent service, and as a part of the
nation. It is not too much to say that it is during this
period that there is the first dawn of a service consciousness—*esprit de corps.* That "very calme and
good temper" with which the fleet as a whole took
any and every political change that came along was
not mere stolid indifference, nor a stupid dull obedience
resulting from thick brains ; there was as much live

interest in questions of the day in the Navy as in the
Army, but it scarcely ever became so uncontrolled as
to gain the upper hand of discipline ; though once, in
February, 1660, it rose perilously near the danger
point. The naval captain rarely forgot that he was
not a mind himself, but a part of a unit, of a squadron
or a fleet. The precision of the English ships when
manœuvring drew applause from friend and foe alike,
and that at a time when tactical manœuvres were
in their infancy : no mere letter-of-the-law discipline
could have enabled them on the third day of the great
Four Days' Fight, when they were shattered and torn
by a three days' losing fight against superior odds, to
have retired in the perfect order in which they did,
one line covering another like a bulwark, a splendid
example of a well-ordered retreat. Nothing but
loyalty, loyalty to fellow-captains, to the admiral,
loyalty to the service, could have compassed such a
feat. It is true the fleet was honeycombed with petty
personal spites and quarrels but—a contrast to those
in the Dutch fleets—they were not indulged in to the
service's detriment. Even in the notorious case of the
division of the fleet in June, '66, the crime was committed—supposing the story is true—by one man, to
curry favour : and the storm of complaints, of abuse,
that arose from all ranks of the fleet, was too unanimous
to be but the wailings of Englishmen weeping for their

country ; it was the deep and bitter resentment of the professional seaman who sees his profession disgraced by a blunder criminal to him—to the true professional it were better to die than blunder.

The attitude of the Navy towards the Restoration is specially interesting, for then the new spirit was already born but not yet conscious, it could be used, not understood.

Thus, in trying to treat of things in their true proportion, I have given a comparatively small space to the actual fighting, and have endeavoured rather to give space to the things that matter now, to treat of things at that time, not as events between 1658 and 1667, but as threads of a pattern that is still being weaved, spans of a bridge that is still being built. There lies one great danger in the way of such an attempt, one great difficulty ; the danger of looking at the past *as* the past, the difficulty of looking forward from the past to the present instead of merely the reverse. In all cases of naval operations it is as essential to appreciate what the various commanders did not know, as it is to know everything : more so. And to carry the point further, to the question of ideas, there seems to be a great danger in the unconscious assumption of the existence and comprehensibility at that time of ideas which are commonplace axioms at the present day. The most striking case in point

during this period is that of the Mediterranean ' policy '
which, though to the modern eye it was clearly practised
then, was, with equal definiteness, to them a meaning-
less, pointless incident or turn of chances.

I have, where possible, gone to original sources for
every point; the exceptions to this rule have full
references, the most extensive being to the important
Sandwich papers brought out by Mr F. R. Harris in
his *Life of Mountagu*; not having had access to the
originals I have been compelled to take them second-
hand; I have given full reference in each case. I have
also been unable to see the Dutch MSS. at the Rijks-
museum. For the rest, my main authorities have been
the Pepys MSS. at the Pepysian and Bodleian Libraries,
and the Admiralty papers at the Admiralty Library
and the Public Record Office. I have been compelled
to limit the scope of the essay to naval operations in
European waters, and consequently to omit the ex-
peditions of Holmes and Harman in the West. I have
also but barely touched on the particular questions
of ' shipbuilding,' and ' the Flag and the right of
Recognition and Salute.' Lest the size of the Bibliography seem disproportionate with the essay itself, I
should explain that I have considered the compilation
of a comprehensive bibliography one of the most
important parts of my work.

My thanks are due to Dr J. R. Tanner, of St John's College, to Mr S. Gaselee, Librarian of the Pepysian Library, Magdalene College, who kindly gave me every facility for access to the Pepys MSS., and also to Professor C. H. Firth, and Mr R. G. Perrin, Librarian of the Admiralty Library, for doing me a like service at the Bodleian and Admiralty Libraries respectively. I am greatly indebted to Mr F. R. Salter, my History Tutor at Magdalene, who, during my absence in Fiji, undertook entire charge of the proofs; also to Mr H. R. Tedder, Librarian of the Athenaeum, who has given me invaluable assistance in the correction of proofs of the Bibliography.

A. W. T.

January 1915

P.S. The difficulties attending the correction of proofs under active service conditions, which have greatly delayed publication, will, I trust, at least partially excuse the more palpable faults and omissions which under happier circumstances I should have hoped to correct and repair.

April 1916

CONTENTS

CHARTS

CHAPTER I

THE NAVY BEFORE THE RESTORATION

" THE credit of your navy is so greatly impaired that having occasion to buy some necessary provisions, as tallow and the like, your minister can obtain none but for ready money [1] " : so wrote the Admiralty Commissioners to the Council of State two months before the death of the Protector ; nor was it the first time that they had written in that strain. The reins of government were indeed already loosening in Oliver Cromwell's grasp, and the Navy early felt the change. The all too small assignments to the Navy had been diverted in part to the Army, and to pay the salaries of the Protector, the Judges and others. A naval administrator without money is like a sower without seed, and at a decent interval after the death of Oliver the Commissioners again wrote a bitter complaint to the Council giving a vivid picture of the financial condition of the Navy. They wrote, " we have several times laid before you the great straits and necessities of naval affairs and hoped something would have been done.... The late sad change has constrained us to silence, but the need becoming more pressing, and no whit provided for, we must remind you thereof, the

[1] *Cal. S. P. Dom.* July 6th, 1658.

rather that the receipts assigned to the Navy are again
in part diverted and diminished, though falling very
short of the charge. We have struggled to keep off
clamours, but ships have to be kept abroad upon dead
wages, contracts and debts are unpaid, the stores are
unsupplied, and contracts for the ensuing year have to
be disannulled. We beg that the Navy income may
not be diverted, and that some course may be taken to
carry on the service[1]."

On September 3rd, 1658, Oliver Cromwell died, and
on the 4th his son Richard was proclaimed Protector
of England : " the Vulture died, and out of his ashes
rouse a Titmouse[2]." The trouble anticipated with so
much eagerness by the Royalists seemed to be very far
off. The proclamation was peacefully accepted throughout the country : the fleet under Rear-Admiral Bourne
" made bold to manifest the truth of its affection by the
expense of some powder from the several ships in the
Downs[3] "—a proceeding for which Bourne was severely
reprimanded[4] : which did not, however, prevent him
from ' making bold ' once again, on this occasion " to
expend some powder to solemnize the funeral of his
late Highness[5]," precisely 14 days before that ceremony
took place. Apart, however, from such small contre-
temps, the fleet adapted itself very readily to the change
of government ; and, with one or two exceptions in
the Mediterranean squadron, there were no objections
raised by the commanders against subscribing to an

[1] *Cal. S. P. Dom.* October 14th, 1658.
[2] Heath's *Chronicle*, p. 409.
[3] *Cal. S. P. Dom.* September 8th, 1658.
[4] Rec. Off. *Adm. Sec. In Letts.* September 10th, 1658.
[5] *Cal. S. P. Dom.* November 9th.

address, which Mountagu prepared, swearing fidelity
to the "undoubted rightful Protector[1]" as against
royalist and republican. Indeed the fleet showed at
this juncture the same loyalty towards its admiral that
made it so important a force a year and a half later.
The change of government did not mean improved
administration or finance so far as the Navy was concerned. A spasmodic attempt was made to remedy
some of the abuses of absenteeism among the dockyard
officials, but there was no alteration made at the root
of the evil ; the shortness of supply continued and,
inevitably, its consequences developed and worsened.
The political split that was growing, between the sup-
porters of Richard and Fleetwood and his republicans,
had a twofold result, in increasing the neglect of the
Navy and in still further weakening the credit of the
government : a strong healthy debtor is a more reliable
person than one who is constitutionally weak. When
it became necessary to set out a fleet, in November and
again in February, the cry of the Navy Commissioners
was for ready money. "Unless there be a present
supply of money to provide necessaries," they write
on February 14th, "there will be a full stop to your
affair, for our credit is gone....The hemp merchants
deliver not what they have, because not paid for the
former ; timber, plank, cordage, and the like, not to
be gotten because no compliance with bills....Although
we know that of late we have given good price for several
provisions, yet now—men's stocks and credit being
drawn out who have usually dealt with us—other men

---

[1] *Brit. Mus.* E. 999, 12, "A true Catalogue."

will not deal upon any terms[1]." Contractors, seamen
and dockmen alike suffered from this intolerable
neglect. Some ships had already gone 2½ years unpaid
at Richard's accession—some actually being still unpaid
in the spring of 1660, a period of 4 years without pay[2].
Some contractors were bankrupt, others had paid the
State's debts with their own money, others borrowed to
pay them. An estimate of the debts of the Navy to
November 1st, 1658, gives the total as £541,465. 14s. 7d.,
of which £160,000 is due on bills already signed, £266,257
due for wages of seamen, £25,000 for wages in dockyards[3]. Eight months later the total has risen to
£703,703. 16s. 3d., £210,000 due on bills, £317,600 in
wages to seamen, £38,000 in wages in dockyards : the
growing charge to December 1st is estimated at £549,490,
making a total of £1,253,193. 16s. 3d., " towards which
the provision already made exceeds not the summe of
£260,000...," the remainder " falls much short of
answering the pressing occasions of the Navy unto
which they are applyed." " Present action " needs
£20,000 a week and upward, while since May 31st
" there has not been received £8,000 a week[4]."

The following pathetic little series of letters is
typical of the ever increasing volume of entreaties and
complaints with which the Navy Office was inundated :

"Dover, *July 2nd*, 1659.

Our need at Dover is so exceeding great that we are
constrained to cry out to you to help us to the money due

---

[1] *Cal. S. P. Dom.* February 14th, 1659.
[2] *S. P. Dom. Int.* ccxxii. f. 28.
[3] *Adm. Lib. MSS.* 8, Orders and Warrants, 1658–60.
[4] *Ibid.* July 8th (" Report touching money for supply of Navall
occasions ").

to this poor town. Our condition is so bad that we are
weary of making known our wants...3 quarters account
due to us....

August 6th.

Is so much out of pocket, and so much engaged, that he
cannot remain silent, but must still be begging a supply.

August 10th.

Hopes pity for their condition at Dover and an order
for some money, as they are always in action, and as speedy
with dispatch of business as any port in England[1]."

etc., etc.

" Let me be an humble petition," writes Major Bourne,
a commissioner, "in ye behalfe not only of many
hundreds of poore seamen and their distressed wives
and children who are ready to starve (having their
just pay kept back) and in ye name of many poore
widdowes and families who are in danger of utter ruine
for want of due payment for their goods ; But also in
behalf of divers other persons who tho' their estates are
larger yet suffer extremely both in reputation and loss
of Trade by a non compliance wth them in point of
payment, who have given a vast creditt to the Nation
for supply of Navy stores...[2]."

With shortness of money came also the inevitable
shortage and badness of victuals, and the State Papers
contain numerous complaints against both quantity
and quality. " At Woolwich," writes Vice-Admiral
Goodson, " I find the men are victualled with fiery salt,
old and rusty meat, and this not only by report but
have seen and tasted some of it myself. At this place,

---

[1] *Cal. S. P. Dom.* 1658-9, 1659-60 *passim.*
[2] *Rawl. MSS.* A. 187. f. 1.

when men have been at their labour all day, they cannot
get their provisions till night[1]."

In the face of such facts as these in the administration of the Navy, it is not a little surprising to find quite
a considerable activity on the part of the State ships.
It was probably the inertia of Cromwell's naval energy.
He had initiated a naval policy which necessitated, and
made use of, an effective permanent fleet : and even
though the idea of a fleet as a purely diplomatic argument was not yet appreciated, the principle that a fleet
was a unit that was usable for other things besides a
battle *mêlée* was already deeply set. The new government acted on, if it did not understand, the principle,
and the year following the death of Oliver is one of
a naval activity that is extraordinary, in the light of
the financial difficulties, when it is remembered that
England was not at war and had no specially warlike
thoughts against any of her neighbours.

Since 1657 there had been war in the Sound between
Denmark and Sweden : in the summer of 1658 the
Netherlands, after remaining neutral for some time,
joined to support the Danes, and early in November
they gained a hard-won victory. In the meantime the
English government had decided to interfere with the
object of ensuring a reasonable balance of power in
those waters : neither a Dutch nor a Swedish supremacy was likely to favour the English trade. Sir George
Ayscue was to go out and endeavour to mediate between
Denmark and Sweden. The original idea was that
wo " fit vessels[2] " should accompany him. Early in

[1] *Cal. S. P. Dom.* February 10th, 1659.
[2] *Ibid.* October 25th. 1658.

November, however, a fleet[1] was ready to sail for the
Sound under the command of Goodson : Ayscue was to
go with it. On the 17th Goodson sailed from the
Downs. Winter had already set in, and the English
fleet, meeting some very rough weather, was forced to
put in at Sole Bay. There Goodson was kept until the
beginning of December. He made use of the time to
supply the fleet with pilots or their substitutes :
originally he had only one pilot. After " rummaging
the fleet, according to the sea phrase," he found six
mates and midshipmen somewhat " acquainted with
the Sound," whom he distributed amongst the ships[2].
At length, early in December, he got clear of the coast
and made for the Scaw, meeting with winter gales and
heavy seas, and being " hurried to and again by the
foul weather." Not until the 15th did the fleet arrive
off the Scaw, and then " on account of the ice and
violent cross winds[3]," it being impossible to get into the
Sound, it was decided at a council of war to return to
England. The following day the fleet was scattered by
a violent snowstorm and gale, and when the whole of
it had reached the English coast by December 30th, it
was found that no less than 12 ships had more or less
serious defects, one being entirely dismasted.

This unfortunate experience did not, however, deter
the Parliament from preparing a still larger fleet to
go to the Sound in the following spring. For a time
the question was in doubt as to whether it should be
sent: news of the Dutch preparations settled it. "It is a

---

[1] List in *S. P. Dom. Int.* cxcv. ff. 72–3.
[2] *Cal. S. P. Dom.* November 30th, 1658.
[3] *Ibid.* December 21st.

shame," writes a news-letter, "that wee should sitt still at home with our hands in our pocketts, and to let the Dutch goe with so great a fleete into the Sound, and so probably have it delivered up by the Dane unto them, and we sit still at home, and not to come and interpose by way of mediation to keepe the balance equall betweene those two Princes, that the Dutch may not take it from them both, and give a law to us as to our navigation, the woodden walls of the nation[1]." At the end of February, Parliament decided to send a fleet. On March 12th, Mountagu, having been appointed 'General-at-Sea,' went on board his flagship, the *Naseby*, on the 22nd he set sail with a fleet of 51 sail including 18 of 50 guns and over, 13 between 40 and 50, and 8 between 40 and 26. On April the 6th the vessels anchored in Elsinore Roads. He had arrived before the expected Dutch reinforcement, and immediately made precautions against their arrival, setting guards in the entrances to the Sound while he himself lay before the town and castle of Elsinore. He sent a letter to Opdam, the commander of the incoming Dutch fleet, explaining his mission; he desired Opdam's "assistance in promoting the peace" and asked, "that you will not suffer the fleet or fleets under your command to act in hostility against, or give any further assistance to either side, or act in such a way as may occasion jealousy between England and the United Provinces, whilst these endeavours are on foot[2]." In the meantime Goodson was given orders that if the Dutch attempted to relieve Copenhagen he was to

[1] *Clarke Papers*, III. 183.
[2] *Rawl. MSS.* A. 64, f. 43, printed in *Thurloe S. P.* VII. 645.

engage them " and fight with, sink, take or destroy
such of them as shall proceed to pass through as afore-
said ; the which myself and the rest of the ships of the
fleet...shall second and stand by you in[1]."
At the same time that he wrote to Opdam, Mountagu
had written to the Kings of Denmark and Sweden also
explaining his mission, " a common friend to you both,
contributing what in me lyes to remove those difficulties, that may be in the way of the peace[2]." The
term ' common friend,' however, was not one that was
true in any but a very superficial sense. The one
constant factor in the negotiations was the utter distrust that the Dutch and English had of each other :
Mountagu's feeling was best illustrated by his precautions ; De Ruyter wrote home " that the English, as
far as he was able to judge by their manner of Proceeding, seemed ill intentioned, notwithstanding all their
fair Protestations, and that he believed they turned
Affairs in that manner, with Design to favour Swede-
land[3]." Mountagu had corresponding suspicions concerning the Dutch and the Danes. Consequently it
was almost inevitable that his good relations with
Sweden should prosper rather at the expense of his
' common friendship.' Then came the news that the
two Dutch divisions under Opdam and De Ruyter
intended to unite—which would have given them a
united fleet of over 80 ships. In a council of war it
was decided to berth the ships " in the most advantageous manner to hinder the conjunction[4]." Before

---

[1] *Sandwich MS. Journal*, i. 67 in Harris, *Life of Mountagu*, i. 124.
[2] *Thurloe S. P.* vii. 645.　　　[3] *Life of Tromp*, p. 215.
[4] *Sandwich MS. Journal*, i. 87–90, in Harris, *op. cit.* i. 128.

even this plan could be put into execution there came
the news which changed the whole face of matters so
far as Mountagu and the English were concerned.
Richard Cromwell had been deposed. His last instructions to Mountagu show how much the whole policy of
the English towards the Dutch was changed : " you
shall carry yourself friendly towards them and use your
endeavours that by consent they may not give their
assistance to the Dane, until the issue of the treaty be
known, but not engage with them unless it be in your
own defence[1]." The fleet accepted the new political
change with the " very calme and good temper[2] " that
characterises it through the recurring changes at this
time ; at a council of war it was decided, in the light of
the new instructions, to withdraw northward to the
Scaw, and from that time the English fleet is of interest
merely as the focus for the intrigues that finally won
over Mountagu to Charles, and through him, the fleet.

The other scene of active naval action was the
Mediterranean. In July, 1658, it had been resolved in
council, " on consideration of the Mediterranean trade,
that a fleet be continued there of the same strength as
formerly[3] " : consequently Capt. John Stoakes remained out in those waters doing useful work in the way of
pirate-catching[4], of which the most noteworthy incident

[1] *Thurloe S. P.* VII. 666.
[2] *Public Intelligencer*, May 31st–June 6th, 1659.
[3] *Cal. S. P. Dom.* July 27th (Council Proceedings, 5).
[4] Piracy was not by any means confined to the Mediterranean :
the Irish Sea was a favourite haunt of pirates, a large number of whom
were Spanish. " There are great complaints by merchants of pirates
being on the coast and none of the state's ships to look after them.. ..
There are no less than 5 pirates now upon the coast, some carrying
22 guns apiece...if some course is not taken to secure the coasts all

was the capture of Victorio Papachino, " the prince of
Spanish pirates." " He was so confident as to give us
chase, taking us for three Baccallas men," writes Capt.
Bonn of the *Phœnix*. " We chased him for nearly
seven hours before we could bring him by the lee, and
would not have effected it then had not his sails been
all shot to pieces. The force of his vessel is ten guns
and some pedereros. She sails well, on which account
Papachino always kept her full of men for the purpose
of boarding.... The news of his being in our hands is
very welcome in this place, and the French are no less
joyful than ourselves[1]." Successes such as this, a peace
with Tunis, and the quietening down of the sea-rovers
in the Mediterranean, gave an opportunity for Stoakes
and his squadron, as being no longer necessary, to be
recalled and " the public charge eased[2]." At the
end of July the English squadron left the Mediterranean
once more at the mercy of the Corsairs. Not yet was
it realised that for a Mediterranean policy to be effective,
to be a policy, it must essentially be continuous and
without gaps of time or force.

trade will be spoilt." (*Cal. S. P. Dom.* July 29th, 1659.) Such is an
official report from the Lancashire coast. Another official account
from Ireland tells of worse things, 14 vessels lost in a week off London-
derry, from Coleraine : " there are 17 vessels, great and small,
ordered to ply this coast, so that it lies under a universal ruin," off
Carrickfergus 28 vessels have been lost in eight days. (*Cal. S. P.
Dom.* July 13th.) It is probable these stories are exaggerated ;
however, in May, 1660, it was noted in council " that there are
now at present ten Pyrats which ly upon that coast " (Barnstaple)
Add. MSS. 22,546); in March, 1659, the only warships in the Irish
Sea at all were the *Guift Prize*, 16 guns, and the *Fox*, 14 guns.
(*Carte MSS.* 73, f. 227.)

[1] *S. P. Dom. Int.* CLXXXIII. 96.
[2] *Cal. S. P. Dom.* February 18th, 1659.

The following list will give a better idea of the real condition of the Navy before the Restoration than pages of description. There seems no reason to doubt its fundamental accuracy.

" A List of the fleete of this Commonwealth both at Sea and in harbour, with accompt of their respective stations and present condition and the time they have been unpaid. March, 1659.

				Months
			Guns	*unpaid*
	James (V.-Ad. Lawson)		56	10
	Worcester		48	14
	Yarmouth		40	10
In the Hope being	*Portland*		38	25
foule and out	*Centurion*		44	19
of victuall and	*Maidstone*		40	33
unfitt for ser-	*Dover*		40	27
vice till they be	*Dragon*		40	22
repair having	*Taunton*		40	25
laide there	*Elias*		38	38
since 20th Dec.	*Dartmouth*		22	38
last.	*Pearle*		22	41
	Nightingale		24	39
	Convert		26	37
	Kentish		38	10
	Winsby		40	14
	Nampturch		40	25
	Hampshire		36	10
	Foresight		36	32
	Marmaduke		36	16
	Bradford		22	24
	Forrester		22	32
In the Downes and	*Norwich*		22	12
sent forth upon	*Wakefield*		22	19
severall occa-	*Grantham*		24	3
sions of con-	*Cheriton*		20	30
voy, etc., many	*Lizard*		16	14
of them being	*Weymouth*		16	16
foule.	*Drake*		12	39
	Martin		12	8
	Nonsuch (Ket.)		8	9
	Eaglett		8	25
	Larke		10	20
	Roe (Ket.)		8	33
	Swallow		6	37
	Lilly		6	13
	Cignett		6	13
	Hart		6	37
	Total men			4565

	Gainsborough	.. ..	40	26
	President	.. ..	34	11
Plyeing to the	*Saphyre* ..	.. ..	32	28
W. t. in the	*Const. Warwicke*..	..	28	10
mouth of the	*Sonlings* ..	.. ..	28	44
Chan. sound-	*Oxford* ..	.. ..	22	43
ings, most of	*Litchfield*	.. ..	20	24
them being	*Fagons* ..	.. ..	22	44
foule and out	*Colchester*	.. ..	22	32
of victualls and	*Mermaid*	.. ..	22	27
want repairs.	*Greyhound*	.. ..	20	35
	Wolfe ..	.. ..	16	50
	Griffin ..	.. ..	12	52

Bristoll..	.. 40	10	Gone convoy to Portugall.
Successe	.. 38	16	„ „ „ Helena Is.
Satisfaction	.. 30	13	„ „ :, Hope.
Fame ..	.. 22	18}	Minding N. Sea fishery.
Bryer ..	.. 22	13}	
Providence	.. 30	10	Ply on N. coast.

4 Ketches plying nr. Thames Mouth.
2 „ „ bt. Maze and Yarmouth.

Portsmouth	.. 36	29}	Ply bt. Portland,
Hindketch	.. 8	25}	Aldern. etc.
Paradox	.. 12	26	G.c. to Jersey.
Guift Prize	.. 16	8}	Coast of Ireland.
Foxe ..	.. 14	17}	
Truelove			
Henrietta }	..	12	16	Guard of Medway.

In Port cleaning and victualling.

Lamport	54	23}	Woolwich	*Nonsuch*	32	2}	Ports-
Tredagh	54	14}		*Bateing*	26	17}	mouth

2675 men.
Total 7240.

Ships lately come into Port and intended to be paid off.

			at *Portsmt.*	*Torrington*	54	25}	*Chatham*
Rubye ..	40	19	having ben				etc.,
			there almost	*Fairfax*	54	32}	3 months
Phœnix ..	36	35	4 mon. and				
			their whole	*Newly in.*			
Tiger ..	36	22	coy. borne	*Advice*	40	14	Woolwich
			on them.	*Expedition*	28	23}	Deptford
				Selby	22	27}	

1410 men.

Shipps now refitting and victualling.

As additional guard for the Channele	*Richard* 66 *London* 64 (Sr. Ri. Stayner) *Speaker* 54 *Plymouth*	} Chatham	
Swiftsure *Essex* *Newcastle* *Guift* *Pembroke* *Paul*	} Woolwich	*Reserve* *Convertine* *Assistance* *Adventure* *Rosebush*	} Deptford

3210 men.

Ships gone convoy to the Streights.

Leopard	50	13
Preston	40	16
Jersey ..	40	15
Elizabeth	40	14

710 men.

Ships at Jamaica.

Diamond	36	22
Coventry	22	23
Hector ..	20	32
Chestnutt	10	25
Cagway	8	38
Pearle ..	4	48
Dolphin	4	36

495 men.

Shipps in Harbour.

Portsmouth		Chatham		Woolwich		Deptford	
Andrew	56	*Soveraigne*	100	*Newbery*	54	*Amity*	30
Moncke	54	*Resolution*	80	*Bridgwater*	54	*Assurance*	34
Lyme	54	*Naseby*	80	*Indian*	48	*Sophia*	26
Marston		*Dunbarre*	64	*Gt. Charity*	42	*Halfemoone*	30
Moor	54	*Triumph*	64	*Beare*	36	*Wexford*	18
Gloucester	54	*George*	56	*Augustine*	26	*Cornelion*	12
Mathias	46	*Rainbow*	56	*Westergate*	26	*Vulture*	12
Welcome	36	*Victory*	56	*Rose*	6	*Blackmore*	12
Guinny	30	*Unicorne*	56			*Kinsale*	10[1]
Francis	10	*Vanguard*	56				
		Lyon	56				
		1 gt. galley					

[1] *Carte MS.* 73. 227.

CHAPTER II

THE NAVY AND THE STUART RESTORATION

NEGLECTED as was the history of the Navy until the
latter end of the last century, ignorance had
resulted in an almost absolute non-recog-
nition of the influence of the fleet upon the
Restoration and the intrigues and negotiations accompanying it. The more modern refusal
to recognise that influence is, however, less comprehensible. It is possibly true that merely as an
armed force the fleet " could only apply pressure by
intercepting trade and cruising outside ports,"—by
blockade " in circumstances which made effective
blockade impossible[1] "; but as a moral force the Navy
was far from being negligible on either side of the
Channel. There were simple reasons for this. In
England after the death of Cromwell every party, every
political force, had lost half its power through divisions
and dissensions ; there was the Army against the
Parliament, Lambert against Monk, the Rump against
the ' Secluded Members,' minor sect against minor
sect, petty faction against petty faction, until no man
knew where to turn for authority and there was no
' power ' in the land. The one exception to this rule

[1] Hannay's *Royal Navy*, I. 298; cf. also *Camb. Mod. Hist.* IV.
485.

*Power of
the fleet.
Naval
discipline
and its
results.*

of chaos and disunion was the Navy. There were of
course differences of opinion, of belief, among officers
and men ; there are plenty of signs that all shades of
opinion, from royalist to republican, were represented
in the fleet ; but the important fact is that opinions
seem to have had no effect on discipline as regards the
fleet as a whole. In that sense it is true that the Navy
followed and ' did not lead[1] ' at this critical time ; it
did follow its commander—a unique discipline and
obedience which at that time gave it a special prestige
and power. The fleet had no politics beyond those
of its commander. It was the royalist tendencies of
Mountagu that brought it back in haste from the
Baltic, the—apparent—parliamentarianism of Lawson
that took it up to Greenwich to demand a free parliament, and again the royalism of Mountagu that took it
over to Scheveling to meet Charles.

Across the Channel the prestige of the Navy had an
added importance. The position to which Cromwell
had raised the English Navy still claimed a healthy
respect from the European powers and they were
closely interested—possibly more so than the English
themselves—to see which party was to have the control
of the one reliable force the country owned. According
as to whether he could show the Navy on his side or
not, so would be the provision or the lack of that
financial support and diplomatic toleration which were
so essential to the practical working of Charles' schemes.
" I am to tell you by his Majesty's command," writes
Clarendon, " that if any impressions could be made upon
the Navy, or a part of it, that five or six ships would

<hr>

[1] Hannay's *Royal Navy*, I. 298.

betake themselves to his service, the consequence and
reputation of it would be so great that all would be done
from hence and from France that could be wished[1]."
20,000 pistoles were to be promised to the officers and
men of these ships. " You may think," he continues,
" that such a sum of money if it be in our power, might
hire ships to do our work as well, and it may be it would
do so, but the money can be in our power to no other
purpose, nor upon any other terms, than upon getting
off part of the English Navy, which would persuade
those who would assist us that the rupture and divisions
are in truth as great as we report it. Whereas, while
they see the Navy entire and against us, they will not
be persuaded that we can make a prosperous attempt."
It would indeed have been a vivid proof of the greatness
of the divisions if the fleet had caught the general
contagion and become divided against itself—though
the fiasco of the royalist revolt in the fleet in 1648
scarcely offered good prospects for the success of such
a split. But with the conversion of Mountagu and
Lawson to royalism the fleet became *ipso facto* a royalist
weapon and when the long-wished-for fleet came to
fetch Charles back, it was not merely ' five or six
ships,' but over thirty of the pick of the English Navy.
By the end of April public opinion tended almost
universally towards Restoration, largely because it
was the obvious and apparently inevitable outcome of
events—inevitable because it was widely believed that
Monk and Mountagu aimed at restoring Charles and in
their hands was a powerful and willing instrument in

---

[1] *Clarendon S. P.* III. January 12, 59–60, Hyde to Wright
(Rumbold).

the form of the fleet. Because the influence of the
fleet during the time between Mountagu's appointment
to the command and his arrival at Scheveling is not
calculable in any concrete way, is no reason for assuming
that it was really negligible. The mere passive presence
of that force, believed to be in royalist hands, in the
Thames, probably acted as a very liberal royalist
education to many waverers.

The process of gaining control of the fleet was on
Conversion of the whole a less unedifying spectacle than
Mountagu. such an intrigue might be expected to be—
possibly because a great part of it is hidden from our
view. Mountagu was the most important person to
catch and even before he left England for the Sound in
1659, hopes were entertained of him, and it was thought
that "there might be application made to him of no
small hopes[1]," and it was not long before Charles
opened negotiations. "I am assured by so many who
believe they know much of your mind and purposes,"
wrote Charles, "that you have much affection for me,
and a resolution to do me all the service you can, that I
think it necessary you should know from myself, that I
am very willing to be served and obliged by you,... and
you may be confident I shall never expose you upon
any rash undertaking for the vindication of it, but
concur with you in such councells as are most proper,
and shall give you all evidence of my beinge heartily
your most affectionate friend[2]." But Mountagu was

---

[1] *Clarendon MSS.* 60, f. 465.
[2] *Clarendon MSS.* 60, f. 436, May 9th, 1659, a Draft in Hyde's
hand.

"withall extreme cautelous[1]," and he had besides a
real regard for Richard Cromwell : it needed more than
tactful or flattering letters from Charles or his followers
to make him royalist. The republicans at home soon
provided the necessary impetus. The deposition of
Richard left the government in the hands of a republican militarism particularly distasteful to Mountagu,
and from him they received " no assurance, only
compliment[2] " ; so, " as if resolved to declyne all the
precepts and examples of Policy in the Christian
world, by aggravating a malcontent in supreme command so far out of reach[3]," they deprived him of his
lodgings at Whitehall, his regiment of cavalry and pay,
sent out as Vice-Admiral, John Lawson, a man who had
few reasons[4] for being well disposed towards him[5],
and, as a final proof of their petty inability either to
trust or to dismiss, they sent out three new commissioners, Honeywood, Boone and Algernon Sidney, to
act as joint plenipotentiaries with Mountagu—in other
words, to act as a check on his actions.

The royalists were more clever, and Mountagu
now became the centre of secret intrigues of which he
was a more or less passive subject, Whetstone and

[1] *Clarendon S. P.* III. 488, June 15th, Mr Herbert's report on M.
to King.
[2] *Cal. S. P. Dom.* July 10th, 1659.
[3] *Clarendon MSS.* 61, f. 172, June 10th.
[4] In January, 1656, Mountagu, then young, inexperienced,
absolutely ignorant of the sea, had been appointed joint commander
of the fleet with Blake over the head of Lawson, an experienced
seaman and fighter. Lawson resigned.
[5] " Lawson's fleet, appointed to guard the Narrow Seas, is rather
to bring Montague to reason." *Cal. S. P. Dom.* July 10th, 1659.

Edward Mountagu[1] the go-betweens, and Charles and
Clarendon the authors : everything that tact, persuasion and bribery could do was done, down to the offering
of an earldom, the Garter, any command or office he
might desire[2]. But Mountagu's caution was only
equalled by his secrecy, he was not to be enticed into
any immature or rash attempts, and the King got
scarcely anything more satisfactory or tangible than the
' compliments ' that had annoyed Parliament. It is
evident, however, that by August the Admiral was a
virtual, if not a confessed convert, for in that month
there came an opportunity for him to prove his good
or ill will towards the King without at the same time
unduly endangering his own skin.

It was an opportunity after Mountagu's own heart
and he made full use of it, both defensively and offen-
sively.

As we have seen, the fleet had been originally sent
Return of   to the Sound to maintain the balance of
Baltic fleet.   power in that quarter, to balance the Dutch
support of Denmark by affording Sweden the moral
support of a large fleet : it was, in other words, a
natural continuation of the Cromwellian policy of
hostility to the Netherlands. The change of government in England, however, brought a change of official

---

[1] Ed. Mountagu was the Admiral's cousin ; Whetstone, O. Cromwell's nephew.

[2] *Clarendon MSS.* 61, ff. 291 (Whetstone's instructions), 303 (to
Mountagu), 335 (to Morland) ; 62, f. 30 (to Hyde). In *Clarendon S.
P.* III. 497 (Hyde to Ed. Mountagu) there is even a suggestion that
Gen. Mountagu should take any ships that would follow and appear
off some good harbour in the King's name.

policy; republican ascendancy put republican sym-
pathies in power, and republican Holland became, in
the eyes of Fleetwood and his friends, the natural
ally of a republican England. Consequently the new
commissioners were given instructions favouring Denmark rather than Holland, and between July 25th and
August 4th an agreement was come to between Holland
and England that their combined fleets should force
a settlement and compromise upon the combatants[1].
The King of Sweden protested at this arrangement,
" telling the English lords, 'I accept of you for my
mediators, not for my arbitrators, for as much as you
continue in the terms of good friends; and for you'
(turning himself to the lords Netherland commissioners),
'I refuse you for my mediators, since you are my
enemies[2]'"; and in this protest he had the sym-
pathies of Mountagu with whom he had been on the
best of terms throughout the negotiations. A policy
thus in itself distasteful to Mountagu was made but
little less so to him by its chief upholder, Algernon
Sidney, one of the new commissioners. It is unnecessary here to trace the story of the antagonism and
inevitable quarrel between these two men, the one
capable, inquiring and republican, the other clever,
secretive and royalist[3]; it is only the final stage of it
that has a direct bearing on the movements of the
fleet. Up to the time of the change in English policy

---

[1] Manley, *Late Warres*, p. 82.
[2] *Thurloe S. P.* VII. 736.
[3] Harris in his *Life of Mountagu*, vol. I. pp. 142–157, gives a
detailed account of it, quoting largely from the *Sandwich MSS.
Journal.* I. 109–128.

the English and Dutch Fleets had acted as armed
sentinels on each other, manœuvring to obtain strategic
positions ; and late in July Goodson had written from
the Sound : " the change of government hath putt a
longe stoppe to affaires here, the Dutch not well
knowing how to deale with their old antagonist our
present Parliament. Their fleete and wee have bin
long facing one another in this and the Belt[1]." But
now that they were to act in combination there was no
need for the continuance in the Sound of such large
fleets, while with the English the victualling question
was becoming serious. A proposal was set on foot that
proportional number of ships from each fleet should be
withdrawn to return to their respective countries.
Sidney trusted the Dutch to carry out their side of
such an agreement, Mountagu—rightly as it proved—
did not, and he came to a decision, on which he promptly
acted, to return with the whole fleet. He described the
whole proceeding to Richard Cromwell a few weeks
later : " when ye victualls of ye Fleete was spent to a
months proportion at whole allowance the consideration
of sending ye whole or a part of it home became neces-
sarye, and after much discussion amongst ye plenipotentiaries at last wee resolved to send it all home, 3
of us beinge for it and only Coll. Sidney against it....
Two very powerful reasons were ye Dutch would send
away none of theire Fleete whereby if wee had left
fifteen shipps behind it would have beene useless and
at theire mercye, and ye other ye absolute necessity^e
for want of victualls, wee could not have been supplied

[1] *Clarke Papers*, IV. 29.

in any way wee could devise[1]." In other words
Mountagu was quite determined to return home : he
knew that a royalist rising in England was imminent
and he fully appreciated the effect that the proximity
of the fleet under his command would be likely to have.
The delay caused by Sidney, however, proved fatal to
any royalist hopes Mountagu may have had. The
sporadic risings throughout the country had fizzled out
before the fleet reached England, and Mountagu,
helpless and yet suspected as he was, went into retire-
ment and the command of the fleet passed to the yet
unconverted Lawson.

Thus it looked as though Mountagu and the fleet
had failed, as though the time and trouble, tact and
promises, expended on his 'conversion' had been
wasted. In reality, however, a big step towards
ensuring final success had been taken ; Mountagu's was
the bigger one of the two names the fleet would follow,
and, the leader secured, it only remained to supply a
safe and favourable opportunity for him.

Mountagu's caution had led him to a right appreciation of the weakness as well as the strength of the
fleet in this question of Restoration. No fleet could
lead the nation in an unpopular direction, it could force
obedience to no unwished-for government ; and in
September, 1659, the nation as a whole (if that can be
spoken of as a whole which is split and torn into
innumerable squabbling sects and factions) did not yet
want the Stuarts back. The nation knew not what it
wanted—a mystery that was finally solved partly by

[1] Bodl. Libr. *Carte MSS.* 73, f. 312, cf. also *Tanner MSS.* 51,
ff. 69–127.

elimination, by experience, of things it did not want, partly by an admixture of tact and bluff on the part of three men using the fleet as their instrument[1].

It was not until the early part of December that the Navy took any concerted or decisive action with regard to the civil disturbances and changes[2]. By that time England, and especially London, was heartily tired of the vagaries of military rule under the name of the "Committee of Safety"; notice was made of "strange discontents growing in the City and other places[3]," and on December 13th, Lawson, in the name of the fleet in the Downs, wrote to the Mayor and Aldermen of London enclosing a declaration "in order to the removal of the interruption that is put upon the Parliament the Thirteenth of October last[4]."

Navy v. Army.

---

[1] A tabulated summary of the whole process is contained in a MS. list of the "Ten Changes of Government in England : from May 1659 to May 1660, viz. : 1. In May 1659 Richard Protector. 2. In the same month Wallingfordhouse. 3. In June following the Rump restored. 4. In October a Committee of Safety. 5. In December the Rump againe. 6. In January Genll. Monk. 7. In February ye secluded Members. 8. In March a Councell of State upon ye dissolution of ye secluded members. 9. In Aprill a parliament convened. 10. In May ye King Lords and Commons." This is on the fly-leaf of "An Exact History of the several changes of Government in England" (1648-60). Brit. Mus. E. 1917 (2).

[2] On November 4th, a party of naval officers, including Stayner and Wm. Goodson, had written a letter to Monk remonstrating with him for his opposition to the English army (printed in Whitelocke's Memorials, p. 687) : the ineffectiveness of which proceeding is a good example of the futility of any attempt of any part of the Navy to act as an independent power instead of merely as an instrument in the hands of a leader.

[3] Monthly Intelligencer, December, 1659. (Brit. Mus. 669, f. 22 (51).)

[4] The Declaration is printed in the Mercurius Politicus for December 22-29, p. 975; and Lawson's letters in the Public

This, however, had no effect and received no answer, so
Lawson took a more practical method of showing the
firmness of his intentions, and on the 17th he was
sailing up the Thames, much to the alarm of the existing
authorities. Sir Henry Vane and some military
officers went down the river to meet him and endeavoured their utmost to persuade him not to come further
up the river, but Lawson was quite firm and irre-
sistible, and the same evening he came to anchor off
Gravesend with his fleet of some 24 ships. Vane and his
companions made feverish, futile attempts to win over
Lawson, or even to obtain the removal of part of the
fleet down the river : but Lawson had the whip-hand
and kept it. On the 21st he sent a second letter to the
Mayor and Aldermen enclosing the declaration and a
copy of the previous letter : and as, on this occasion,
the fleet was near enough to lend point to their resolve
—" if it cannot be done by Christian and friendly
means... to use our utmost endeavor for the removal
of that Force " (put on Parliament by the army
officers[1])—the effect was immediate, and success rapid :
the plans of the army officers fell to pieces at the
touch :

Intelligencer for December 19–26, p. 967 (*Brit. Mus.* E. 773), also
in Granville Penn's *Memorials* (Penn wrongly dates the second
letter the 29th), with a *Narrative of the Proceedings of the Fleet*,
II. 186.   The declaration is an interesting and noteworthy exception
to the usual navy attitude of no interest and non-interference in
civil matters ; it " disclaimed the interest of Charles Stuart," and
advocated the maintenance of the " maimed or dismembered," and
of widows and orphans of sailors, the abolition of tithes, excise, and
of impressment " in any military employment either by land or sea,
otherwise than in the defence of his country."
   [1] See previous reference.

" December 17th. The Council took care to issue
forth immediately the writs for the election of a Parliament, and it is thought they had proceeded vigorously
therein, but for Vice-Admiral Lawson his declaring
(this day) for the Old Parliament, which began to put
the council of officers at a stand[1]." So complete was
the ' stand ' to which they were put, that by the 24th
their rule was a thing of the past, and Parliament
House again open and clear of guards : on the 26th
the Rump of the Long Parliament sat once again.
In spite of appearances there were not wanting people
to say that the Navy action was all part of a royalist
plot[2], and it was probably that fact and also a certain
undesirable restlessness in the City, which led Lawson
to send a third letter to the Mayor and Aldermen on
December 28th, speaking of "Charles Stuart's party "
and suggesting the advisability of a " total, absolute,
and publicke disowning and discountenancing of
them[3] " : and on January 7th he was " still in the
Thames, to awe the City which talks high[4]."

Affairs in England at this moment were in an extraordinary state of ferment : " truly," writes Hyde to
Bennett[5], " the People there (in England) are so

---

[1] *Monthly Intelligencer*, No. 1, December, 1659 (*Brit. Mus.*
669, f. 22 (51)).

[2] Baker's *Chronicle*, p. 698. How little truth there was in
this suspicion may be gathered from *Clarendon S. P.* III. 628
(Broderick to Hyde, December 16th). "Lawson with his two
squadrons attempted the Tower, and negociate in all parts of the
Nation, never considering themselves embarked in the same ship
with us....They say the King offers nothing."

[3] *Brit. Mus., Thomason MSS.* 669, f. 22 (43).

[4] *Clarendon S. P.* III. 640, Lambourne to Hyde.

[5] *Ibid.* p. 647, January 17th, 1660.

fantastical and change their minds so often, that I believe they who live within twenty miles of London, and receive letters thence every day, know as little what will be done the next day as we do," and again, "I believe if you did at this instant receive twenty letters from London of the same date with our last, you would receive so many several opinions of the state of affair there, according to the constitutions of the persons who write[1] ": any attempt to detail the course of all these changes would fortunately, however, be out of place here ; they may be briefly summarised.

Apart from Lawson, the one force, the one man in the country was George Monk, commander of the Army in Scotland, a man of action, to be frightened neither into tears like Fleetwood, nor into supercautious inactivity like Mountagu. Until he heard of Lawson's declaration and move up the Thames, Monk had contented himself with improving the fitness and discipline of his army and with keeping up more or less futile negotiations with Fleetwood and Lambert : on the receipt of the news from the Thames and from London he started on his march south to London. Lambert's army in the north of England melted before Monk who made a slow unopposed progress through England : it was not until the end of January that he came as near as St Albans. There Lawson and his captains " presented their Acknowledgments to Gen. Monck at St Albans, who gave them a very courteous reception[2]." On February 3rd, with 5600 men Monk entered London, his forces " in very good plight and

[1] *Clarendon S. P.* III. 641.
[2] *Public Intelligencer*, January 23rd–30th, 1660, p. 1052.

stout officers[1]." A week later he declared against the
Rump and for a fully representative Parliament, a
death-knell to the Rump which caused universal joy
—that night, says Pepys, " Bow bells and all the bells
in all the churches as we went home were a-ringing...
and at Strand Bridge I could at one view tell thirty-one
fires[2]." It was the beginning of the end : the whole
attitude towards Charles had altered in a week or two :
" Everybody now drinks the King's health without any
fear, whereas before it was very private that a man
might dare do it[3]."

And now it was that the Navy again became a vital
Navy and   factor—not as an independent force, but as
the Stuarts.   an all-important instrument in the hands of
Monk, Mountagu and Lawson. The nation no longer
hated the idea of the Restoration but was still in a
doubtful, touchy mood : both tact and bluff were
needed if the King was to be restored without a hitch.
Monk had the necessary qualities and means for both.
Though neither he nor Mountagu, who had been
appointed joint General-at-sea with him, showed their
hands, there is no doubt that by the beginning of
March they were determined in their own minds as
regards the Restoration. On March 6th Mountagu
told Pepys that " he did believe the King would come,"
though he thought he " would not last long...unless
he carry himself very soberly and well[4] " : and by

---

[1] Pepys' *Diary*, February 3rd, 1660.
[2] *Ibid.* February 11th. There are a number of letters from
Pepys to Mountagu describing events in London from October
onwards in *Carte MSS*. 73, f. 320 and foll.
[3] Pepys' *Diary*, March 6th.
[4] *Ibid.*

March 18th Monk was in definite negotiation with the King.

With Mountagu and Monk converted there remained Conversion one important person to be made sure of. of Lawson. In spite of the command he had held, Mountagu was no true seaman, and, though his tact might soothe some opposition, he was not the man whom the seamen would follow naturally : but Lawson was. Sailor born and bred, he was a sailors' leader, a man whom they would follow with less question than any. His conversion then was necessary if the fleet was to be a reliable instrument of Restoration. As early as December 16th, Broderick had written, "if the King would find some means to treat with Lawson it is not improbable but he may in some measure be wrought upon[1] " : Broderick's next notice of him on December 30th speaks volumes of the intervening fortnight, " Lawson...a Sea-Fairfax, so sullen, so senseless, of so obstinate a courage and so wayward an animosity...[2]." Lawson was evidently a hard nut to crack ; during December and January he took, as we have seen, every opportunity to disclaim the interests of Charles Stuart, but after Monk's arrival in London he seems to have adapted himself to changing circumstances. We hear of no protest from him against Monk's treatment of the Rump—though he was still in the Thames with his fleet; later on he sent his congratulations to Mountagu on his appointment to command of the fleet[3], an appointment whose outcome he must have foreseen

---

[1] *Clarendon S. P.* III. 629 (Broderick to Hyde).
[2] *Ibid.*
[3] Bodl. Libr. *Carte MSS.* 73. f. 355.

and on March 23rd he welcomed Mountagu on board
the *Swiftsure* and stepped down to second in command.
" The Fleet is now secured to your Majesty's service,
by Lawson's proffer to do what Mountagu shall direct
him," writes Lord Mordaunt to the King on the 24th,
" Mr Bremes has wrought him so to it[1] " : and that
is all that appears of the process of Lawson's conversion.

It remained to convert the fleet itself in order to
Conversion   ensure success. Pepys, who was with the
of the fleet.   fleet as Mountagu's secretary (and incidentally remarks, " I pray God to keep me from being
proud or too much lifted up thereby "), gives vivid
glimpses in his Diary of the gradual preparation of the
fleet for royalism. On March 29th he gives a hint of
what a difficult task Mountagu and the royalists
would have had with the Navy unaided by Lawson :
on that day he writes : " this evening was a great
whispering of some of the Vice-Admiral's captains that
they were dissatisfied, and did intend to fight themselves, to oppose the General. But it was soon hushed,
and the Vice-Admiral did wholly deny any such thing,
and protested to stand by the General[2] " : an incident
which rather gives the impression that even Lawson
had had some difficulty in controlling some of the
officers. Mountagu, however, was determined to have
his fleet as thoroughly reliable as possible. " After
dinner " (April 1st), says Pepys, " My Lord did give me
a private list of all the ships that were to be set out
this summer, wherein I do discern he hath made it his

[1] *Clarendon S. P.* III. 706.
[2] Pepys' *Diary*, March 29th.

II] THE STUART RESTORATION 31

care to put by as much of the Anabaptists as he can[1]."
Lists of commanders and officials were also drawn up
by Pepys and Creed, and against any doubtful characters notes were made, such as " distracted," " use-
lesse, and in matter of attendance," " querie his
affection," " Anabaptist," etc.[2] ; further procedure was
as follows : " At night he (Mountagu) bid me privately
to get two commissions ready, one for Capt. Robert
Blake to be Captain of the *Worcester*, in the room of
Capt. Dekings, an anabaptist, and one that had
witnessed a great deal of discontent with the present
proceedings. The other for Capt. Coppin to come out
of that into the *Newbury* in the room of Blake, whereby
I perceive that General Monk do resolve to make a
thorough change, to make way for the King[3]." On
April 8th, Mountagu and the fleet sailed from the
Thames and anchored in the Downs on the following
day : London needed overawing no longer ; and the
Straits of Dover being the highway of the ever-increasing
stream of intrigue and negotiation between Charles
and his would-be subjects, the presence of the fleet in
the Downs had a special strategic importance. Pepys
with his exceptional advantages is again the best
chronicler of events in the Navy at this time : " April
17th. He " (Mountagu) " told me clearly his thoughts

[1] Pepys' *Diary*, April 1st.
[2] *Carte MSS.* 73, ff. 264, 402 ; 74, f. 490.
[3] Pepys' *Diary*, April 15th. M. wrote to Monk complaining of
Dekings and Captain Newbury—the former had " designed in the
river very weake and undutifull thinges "—but with characteristic
caution asked that " if any thinge be done towards them, a motion
by any member of the Councell may doe it, and take off any unkind-
nesse from mee towards them." *Carte MSS.* 73. f. 399.

that the King would carry it, and that he did think himself very happy that he was now at sea, as well for his own sake, as that he thought he might do his country some service in keeping things quiet[1]." "21st. This day dined Sir John Boys and some other gentlemen formerly great Cavaliers, and among the rest one Mr Norwood, for whom my Lord give a convoy to the Brill, but he is certainly going to the King. For my Lord " (cautious ever) " commanded me that I should not enter his name in my book. My Lord do show them and that sort of people great civility. All their discourse and others are of the King's coming, and we begin to speak of it very freely[2]." Now too, after years of stern Puritanism the spirits of the fleet began to rise : on the 23rd " the first time that we had any sport among the seamen " ' my Lord ' himself " fell to singing of a song made upon the Rump, with which he played himself well[3]." " Every man begins to be merry," and supper parties with music after them became the fashion : "...to supper, where...we had very good laughing, and after that some musique " not quite satisfactory to the critical Pepys—" Mr Pickering beginning to play a bass part upon the vial did it so like a fool that I was ashamed of him[4]." On May 1st, " the happiest May-day that hath been many a year in England," " they were very merry at Deal, setting up the King's flag upon one of their maypoles, and drinking his health upon their knees in the streets

---

[1] Pepys' *Diary*. M. was evidently not at one with present day opinion that the influence of the Navy was insignificant.
[2] *Ibid.*   [3] *Ibid.*
[4] *Ibid.* March 26th.

and firing the guns[1]." Two days later Mountagu made
public to the Fleet the King's Declaration[2]. " This
morning my Lord showed me the King's declaration
and his letter to the two Generals to be communicated
to the fleet.... Upon receipt of it this morning by an
express, my Lord summoned a council of war, and in
the meantime did dictate to me how he would have
the vote ordered which he would have pass this council,
which done the Commanders all came on board, and
the council sat in the coach (the first council of war
that hath been in my time), where I read the letter and
declaration ; and while they were discoursing upon it,
I seemed to draw up a vote, which being offered, they
passed. Not one man seemed to say no to it, though
I am confident many in their hearts were against it.
After this was done, I went up to the quarter deck
with my Lord and the Commanders, and there read
both the papers and the vote ; which done, and de-
manding their opinion, the seamen did all of them cry
out, ' God bless King Charles ! ' with the greatest joy
imaginable." This form was repeated throughout the
fleet, Pepys going from ship to ship reading the Declaration to vote, " not one through the whole fleet showing
the least dislike of the business[3]." The next day
Mountagu sent, simultaneously, an account of the proceedings to the King[4], and an application to Parliament

---

[1] Pepys' *Diary*, May 1st.
[2] " *King Charles II. his Declaration to all his loving Subjects, dated
from his Court at Breda in Holland* 4/14 *of April*, 1660." London,
1660, 4º, pp. 8.
[3] Pepys' *Diary*, May 3rd.
[4] *Clarendon MSS.* 72, f. 165, also printed in Lister's *Life of
Clarendon*, III. 104.

for permission to send that account to the King. He had something about which to be satisfied, he had justified his extreme caution and tactfulness in gradually educating the fleet up to royalism, in accustoming them to the idea of Restoration, by the success with which his ultimate appeal met ; and though he thought Monk " but a thick-sculled fool " he was willing " to let him have all the honour of the business[1]," knowing that the King himself knew the due proportion of merit to be assigned to each. Then followed a week of gay bustle in the fleet ; ordering of alterations, of music and flags, pulling down " all the State's arms in the fleet," setting up the King's, and all the other multitudinous preparations necessary for what was a change not merely of rule, but of national spirit.

Parliament and its commissioners were now the

Fleet at Scheveling.

only cause of further delay of the King's return—delay which the King begged Mountagu to cut short by crossing to Holland. Monk too wrote to Mountagu " that the King's friends thought his Majesty's present repair to London was absolutely necessary, and therefore he wished mee (Mountagu) to sail and waft the King over as soon as I could[2] " : this Mountagu, after " a high debate with the Vice and Rear-Admiral[3] whether it were safe to go and not stay for the Commissioners[4]," decided to do without waiting for the Commissioners, and on the 12th he sailed for Holland, arriving off

---

[1] Pepys' *Diary*, May 3rd.
[2] Quoted from *Sandwich MSS. Journal* by Harris, *op. cit.* vol. I. p. 182.
[3] Lawson and Sir Rich. Stayner.
[4] Pepys' *Diary*, May 11th.

Scheveling on the 14th. On the following day the
Court moved to the Hague, and there were gay times
there in which most of the fleet joined as opportunity
allowed. Pepys for instance, as his habit was, did
himself well ; and in the experience he had one morning,
" being not very well settled," of mistaking " the sun
rising for the sun setting," he was probably far from
unique in the fleet[1]. The King too had his joys :
when he received the money that had been brought
over for him he was " so joyful, that he called the
Princess Royal and Duke of York to look upon it as
it lay in the portmanteau before it was taken out[2]."

In the meantime several days very rough weather
prevented the King from visiting his fleet. But on the
16th he appointed his brother, James, Duke of York,
Lord High Admiral of England[3], and on the 22nd the
new Admiral went out to his fleet amidst general
salutes, Mountagu offering " all things to the pleasure
of the Duke as Lord High Admiral." "Nothing in the
world but going off of guns almost all this day[4]."

The fleet of which James then took command
numbered 32 ships of war of all sides, of which the
principal were :

Naseby,	Gen. Mountagu, Capt. Cuttance	80 guns,
London,	Vice-Adm. John Lawson	64 guns,
Swiftsure,	Rear-Adm. Sir Rich. Stayner	60 guns,
Richard,	Capt. Jno. Stoakes	70 guns,
besides four other ships of over		50 guns.

---

[1] Pepys' *Diary*, May 14th–26th, contains a full and vivid account
of the festivities before and during the King's crossing to England.
[2] *Ibid*. May 16th. [3] The patent only dates from June 6th.
[4] Pepys' *Diary*.

On the following day the King himself came on
board with the rest of the Court amidst
"infinite shooting off of the guns, and that
in a disorder on purpose, which was better than if it
had been otherwise." After dining in great state Charles
purged the fleet of the more obtrusive of the unpleasant
memories by rechristening a number of the ships :
the *Naseby* became the *Charles*, the *Richard* the *James*,
the *Speaker* the *Mary*, the *Dunbar* the *Henry*, the
Winsby the *Happy Return*, the *Lambert* the *Henrietta* ;
some lower rate ships also changed their names.
" That done," says Pepys, " the Duke of York went
on board the *London* and the Duke of Gloucester[1] the
Swiftsure. Which done, we weighed anchor, and with
a fresh gale and most happy weather we set sail for
England." The voyage was short and prosperous; all,
from the King downwards, very merry. On the 25th
the fleet arrived off Dover and the general spirits rose
still higher. At breakfast the King and the two Dukes
paid a tactful compliment to the seamen to whom they
owed so much ; " there being set some ship's diet
before them, only to show them the manner of the ship's
diet, they eat of nothing else but pease and pork, and
boiled beef[2]." Gifts of £50 for Mountagu's servants
and £500 for the officers and men of the King's ship
were an earnest of the practical nature of the gratitude
to the fleet Charles felt and meant to demonstrate.
The reward of the rest of the fleet and of Mountagu in
particular was yet to come, and in the meantime the

Restoration.

---

[1] Charles I's youngest son : died of smallpox in September of
that year.
[2] Pepys' *Diary*, May 25th.

King and Court landed at Dover and set off for London
to the accompaniment of enthusiasm that was almost
hysterical in its fervour.

The fleet had done its work ; it remained for the

Rewards.   country to do due honour to the King who
had been brought back to them. The
combination of tact, patience and bluff had proved
successful : tact with the seamen, patience and bluff
with the nation : it is not surprising that Mountagu
was pleased with himself for his share in the proceedings.
" My Lord," says Pepys[1], " almost transported with
joy that he had done all this without any the least blur
or obstruction in the world, that could give an offence
to any, and with the great honour he thought it would
be to him."

He had not long to wait for the expected reward.
The day after the King's departure a letter arrived
from the Lord Chancellor announcing to Mountagu that
he had been created an Earl and asking what style he
would take so that the patent might be prepared[2] : on
the following day came Sir Edward Walker, Garter
King-at-Arms, with the George and Garter, and in the
presence of all the commanders Mountagu was forthwith installed as Knight of the Garter. The rest of
the fleet had longer to wait : but anticipation—the
King had promised a month's pay all round—kept
them merry ; Pepys tells of Cuttance, Stayner and
Lawson " drinking all day," and perhaps it was to
check the exuberance of spirits that on the 4th " the
King's Proclamation against drinking, swearing and

---

[1] *Diary*, May 25th.
[2] *Carte MSS.* 223. f. 210.

debauchery, was read to our ships' companies in the fleet[1]." It was not until July that the ships received the promised 'gratuities,' of which the principal were— the *Charles* (late *Naseby*), £801. 19*s.* 6*d.*, the *London*, £580. 13*s.* 6*d.*, the *Swiftsure*, £444. 13*s.* 6*d.*, and the *Royal James* (late *Richard*), £369. 4*s.* 3*d.*[2]   Lawson and Stayner were knighted on September 25th.

[1] Pepys' *Diary*, June 4th.
[2] Brit. Mus. *Add. MSS.* 9311.

CHAPTER III

ADMINISTRATION

1. *Civil. Navy Office.*

THE restored Stuarts had every reason for having a due regard for the Navy and its importance. During their exile Cromwell's effective naval policy both in home waters and in the Mediterranean, and the prestige it had gained for the English Navy, pointed a moral of the truth of which they had had practical experience before their restoration, when they found how necessary for them was some sound naval support. The effectiveness of that support once gained gave added point to the moral. Fortunately for the Navy, however, inclination and interest, as well as strategy and diplomacy, were present to encourage the Stuarts to a practical care for Naval affairs ; not only was there Prince Rupert, the enterprising leader of the forlorn royalist squadron of 1649–50, but James, Duke of York, the King's brother and now Lord High Admiral, had been destined for that post from boyhood, and if ever personal interest and administrative skill could compensate for lack of practical experience, they did so in his case.

It was no easy task that James took up when he

became head of the Navy. The Commonwealth and the
Protectorate had bequeathed two things to him: a
policy, and a debt. The policy was, briefly, that of a
large and effective fleet both for political and commercial purposes ; and herein lay the sting of it for the
new rulers ; it was a compulsory policy. Had James
been inclined to neglect or reduce the fleet public
opinion, or rather commercial opinion, would soon have
made itself effectively felt through Parliament. Divine
Right was no longer a working doctrine in practical
politics ; petitions out of Parliament and resolutions
in it, neither could be ignored without risk of unplea-
santness, unpleasantnesses might be dangerous, and
the dominating principle of Charles II's rule was his
determination not to go on his ' travels ' again. Cromwell's regard for the protection of trade, and the further
increase of that trade, had led to a far higher standard
of expectation on the part of merchants, and the
political consciousness which no amount of ' loyal '
declarations or the like could destroy, gave that
expectation a practical power.

It was the irony of fate that, at the same time that
he inherited an unavoidable policy, James
Initial Debt. also inherited with it a heavy debt that
could not but dog any efforts he should make towards
securing increased efficiency. As we have already
seen, the political chaos that followed on the death of
the Protector, the weak and changing governments, the
general sense of insecurity, had had their inevitable
effect on the Navy ; mismanagement and neglect had
left the department practically bankrupt. In February
of that year the wages debt to seamen alone amounted

to nearly half a million[1], some ships having gone
unpaid for as much as four years, and the total debt of
the Navy in June must have amounted to over three
quarters of a million[2].

It was organisation rather than reorganisation that
the Navy needed. Cromwell had made a practical
weapon of the fleet and had demonstrated some of its
uses, but the machinery behind it had been personal
and individual rather than official and departmental :
and, despite its drawbacks, departmental administration is absolutely necessary to give reliability and
permanency to a great service. In other words, the
Navy had to be officialised and formalised into the
shape of one of the public services.

James recognised what was necessary, and the best
test of what he did to meet that need is the fact that the
structure he set up lasted without any vital changes
until the beginning of the 19th century.

In the meantime, however, the Navy could not stand
still while new arrangements, new organisations were
being devised. It was like building a coach on a chassis
already and continually in motion—a process having
both its advantages and disadvantages, the advantages

---

[1] *S. P. Dom.* ccxxii. 23.

[2] Tanner in *Camb. Mod. Hist.* v. 170, says they amounted to
" more than a million and a quarter " : but by ' debt ' he apparently
means the total charge, which was being continually though inade-
quately met. According to the official report of July, 1659, the charge
of the Navy (including all debts) up to December 1st was estimated
at £1,253,193. 16s. 3d., " towards which the provision already made
exceeds not the summe of £260,000," " present action " needed
£20,000 a week and upward, but " since May 31 has not been
received above £8000 a week." (Admiralty Lib. MS. 8. *Orders
and Warrants*, 1658-60.)

of evolution and the disadvantages of patchwork. The first step was, on May 31st and June 2nd, to order the provisional continuance of all the standing arrangements with regard to the Navy, the issuing of " monies for the necessities of the Navy " and of " victuals and all things necessary for the Navy, as formerly, until further orders[1]," and in the respite thus given a definite scheme of establishment was drawn up in the form of proposals by Sir Wm. Penn in the name of the Duke of York. On June 27th a committee of eight, including the Duke, Monk and Mountagu—now Earl Sandwich—was appointed " to meet on...the 30th of this instant, at eight of the clock in the morning, to consider of a Paper delivered in by his Royal Highness touching the regulation of the Navy, this day read at the board ; and...to make report unto His Majesty of what they conceive fit to be done thereupon[2]." And on July 2nd, upon consideration of that report, the existing commissions were ordered to " forbear to act from henceforth[3]," and four " principal officers " : Sir George Carteret (Treasurer), Sir William Batten (Surveyor), an unnamed comptroller[4], and Samuel Pepys (Clerk of the Acts), were appointed, to be assisted by three " commissioners for the navy "—Lord Berkeley, Sir Wm. Penn, and Peter Pett, esquire. Two days later the salaries of the new officials were fixed : the Treasurer £2000 per annum, the Comptroller £500 (including former allowances), Surveyor

New officials.

[1] Penn, *Memorials of Sir Wm. Penn*, II. 241.
[2] Penn, II. 242; the Proposals are printed in Appendix T. pp. 589-92.
[3] *Ibid.* II. 243.
[4] Sir Robert Slingsby was subsequently appointed.

£490 (including allowances), Clerk of the Acts (including allowance) £350, and £500 per annum to each of the commissioners. Thus the new form of administration was a compromise between the systems of the Commonwealth and pre-Commonwealth times; the offices of Lord High Admiral and the principal officers had been revived only to be part of a commission which came to be known as the Navy Board, and the Commonwealth system of a fixed salary had been combined with the older one of fees and allowances. The choice of new officials afforded on the whole a good omen for the future management of the Navy : with one exception the new men were all men of experience[1] in some branch of military service : the exception was Pepys. Sir George Carteret had already served as Comptroller in 1659, having been brought up to the sea. The testimony of his enemy Sir Wm. Coventry is telling: "he is a man that do take the most pains, and gives himself the most to do business of any man about the court, without desire of pleasure or divertisements," "which," remarks Pepys, "is very true[2]." Sir Robert Slingsby was "almost the eldest sea captain surviving[3]." Sir Wm. Batten had already been Surveyor of the Navy from 1638 to 1642, besides having seen considerable active service. Sir Wm. Penn was a seaman born and bred, "bred up under Sir Wm. Batten[4]"; the debt which the Restoration Navy owed

[1] There are short biographical notices of most of Pepys' colleagues at the Navy Office in Wheatley's *Pepysiana* (companion volume to the *Diary*), chap. IV.
[2] *Diary*, October 30th, 1662.
[3] *Cal. S. P. Dom.* 1660–61, p. 16.
[4] *Diary*, August 21st, 1660.

to him was almost incalculable, he was the best English commander whether of a ship or a fleet, and he was a seaman who could turn his practical experience to use in an administrative office ; as we have seen, he was the chief framer of the new naval constitution. Lord Berkeley had served in active service under Turenne for over three years ; while Peter Pett had already served nearly thirteen years as commissioner at Chatham Dockyard, and though his loyalty to the shipbuilding family of which he came made him unpopular with those not related to him, it is questionable whether it seriously lessened his value to the State as an experienced shipwright. And finally Samuel Pepys, though he had acted as Mountagu's secretary with the fleet in the Baltic and at the Restoration, can have known little or nothing of the Navy, and " so little of accounts that apparently he learned the multiplication table for the first time in July, 1662[1]."

Nor was the principle of utilising experience neglected in the following years. Sir John Mennes, who succeeded Slingsby on the latter's death in 1661, had had wide experience of naval service, though it vexed Pepys " that so great a trust should lie in the hands of such a fool[2] " : and when in 1664 two additional resident commissionerships were created, at Portsmouth and Harwich respectively, the appointments went to men of practical experience ; while in the case of the two other additional commissioners appointed, lack of experience once again notably justified itself in the person of William Coventry, who became one of the

---

[1] Wheatley's *Life of P.*, prefixed to vol. I. of *Diary*, p. xxvii.
[2] *Diary*, April 7th, 1663.

most capable officials in the Navy Office, and ranked very high in Pepys' estimation[1].

Such was the machinery for the reorganisation and regulating of the Navy. How far the work that ensued was that of one or two men it is very difficult to estimate with any certainty of justice. There can be no doubt that the official head of the Navy, prince though he was, was far from being a mere figure-head : Pepys frequently refers to his practical interest in his office, " he do give himself up to his business[2]," and a mere glance through his official letters[3] will show into what details he went. Beyond that it is impossible with justice to ascribe merit to him, since in his position as Lord High Admiral orders, reforms, and suggestions come above his name though they might be the work of his subordinates : Pepys, Coventry, and especially Penn, were undoubtedly the originators of many of the alterations and improvements in naval administration during the period preceding the Treaty of Breda.

The most pressing question to be dealt with was that of the debt of the Navy which was,

Retrenchment
and reform.
Debt.

says Pepys, " in very sad condition, and money must be raised for it[4]." By the end of August an estimate of the debt had been drawn up and submitted to the Council, at the same time that Parliament received a message from the King " hoping that care would be taken to raise moneys for paying the debts of the Navy[5]." It was not, however, a process to

---

[1] *Diary*, October 30th, November 20th, 1662 *et passim.*
[2] *Diary*, January 20th, 1664 *et passim.*
[3] *Adm. Libr. MS.* 24, *Duke of York's Letters*, 1660–67.
[4] *Diary*, July 31st, 1660.
[5] *Cal. S. P. Dom.* August 31st, 1660.

be completed in a month or two, though immediate
measures were taken in the form of paying off twenty-
five ships then in harbour and provision of £70,000 per
mensem for eight months[1]. On November 12th, an
estimate was presented to the Commons which set the
Navy debt[2] at £1,300,819. 8s. 0d., of which £670,868.
8s. 0d. was needed for " present supply and advance-
ment " : " all his Majesty's stores," it was also stated,
"are now empty both of victual and all other necessaries
for the fleet[3]." It is not surprising therefore to find,
more than a year later, the Navy Board complaining to
the Duke of " the bad condition of the Navy for want
of money[4]," and, still later, Pepys exclaiming : " God
knows ! the King is not able to set out five ships at
this present without great difficulty, we neither having
money, credit, nor stores[5]." Nevertheless the strenuous efforts made to extinguish the debt met with fair
success in the end : on December 3rd, Pepys records :
"this day Sir G. Cartaret did tell us at the table, that
the Navy (excepting what is due to the Yards upon the
quarter now going on, and what few bills he hath not
heard of) is quite out of debt ; which is extraordinary
good newes, and upon the 'Change to hear how our
creditt goes as good as any merchant's upon the

---

[1] *Commons Journal*, September 13th, November 6th ; also
Parl. Hist. IV. 143, 149.

[2] *i.e.* current charge including unpaid debts.

[3] *Parl. Hist.* IV. 143.

[4] Pepys' *Diary*, November 13th, 1661.

[5] *Ibid.* June 28th, 1662. On March 14th, Albemarle wrote to
the Duke entreating " a hearing in council for the petition of the
hundreds of poor people concerned in the debts incurred for the
Navy. He wished to see so many families whom he had a hand in
engaging, freed from ruin." *Cal. S. P. Dom.* March 14th, 1662.

'Change is a joyfull thing to consider, which God continue[1] ! "

The Navy Board, although it was a primary necessity with them to clear off the debt, did not, however, fail to realise that the truest retrenchment is that which is founded on increased efficiency, and though ships were paid off and establishments reduced[2], special care was directed against unnecessary or wasteful expenditure. As early as October, 1660, an order was given against the excessive use of pilots, it having been found " by dayly experience, that his Majestie's ships of all rates, have gotten a custome not to stir out of the Downes, unto any place without an extra Pilott[3]." Another item of wasteful expenditure was " unnecessary and unfitting expense of Powder " by " unusuall salutes[4]," which was to be put an end to by means of

---

[1] *Diary*, December 3rd, 1663. It is questionable how far Sir G. Carteret's statement may be considered reliable when we consider an entry Pepys makes in April, 1665 : after speaking of " money to be got for the Navy, or else we must shut up shop," he complains " how Sir G. Cartaret do order business, keeping us in ignorance what he do with his money " (*Diary*, April 7th, 1665). There can, however, be no doubt that at the end of 1663 the debt was, for a short time, brought within control.

[2] Alterations in establishment (in March and October, 1660) (*Pepys' MSS.* 2873).

		March.		October.
		War.	Peace.	
Soveraine	..	700	600	500
Henry ..	..	380	340	280*
Victory ..	..	320	280	250
Dreadnought	..	240	210	180
Mountague	..	269	220	180

* Raised to 430 in 1664.

[3] Brit. Mus. *Add. MSS.* 9311.

[4] *Adm. Libr. MS.* 23, *Orders of D. of Y.*

the definite rules regulating salutes which the Duke
issued at the beginning of December : that this regulation may probably not have been, from a financial point
of view, the minor detail it appears, is evident when
one occasion, for example, is noticed on which each ship
of an English fleet of over 20 ships fired at least 43
guns—and that duly according to regulation[1].

The main process of reform and regulation can,
however, best be appreciated as the whole that it was
if it be considered along the three principal lines of
' Civil Administration,' ' Personnel,' and ' Discipline.'

The first essential towards any reorganisation of
Civil the civil side of the service was the purging
Administra-
tion.   out of the unnecessary, the impotent, or the
incapable ; and on January 28th, the Duke wrote to
the principal officers giving directions to that effect.
" I desire you," he wrote, " that your first care be to
discharge unnecessary workmen in the yards, and yᵉ
next to sett a mark on such who shall appear to have
served either deceitfully or negligently that they may
not hereafter be entered into his Majestie's yards upon
any occasion of work for the future " : " the ordinary
in H.M.'s yards " was to be examined, " who I am
informed is in some of them rather fit for an Hospitall
than the King's service " : report was also to be made
" if you find any to be prodigall," or " if yᵉ master
shipwrights have put yᵉ King to unnecessary charge in
repairs, if they have exceeded their estimate[2]." Apart

---

[1] Bodl. Libr. *Tanner MSS.* 296.
[2] Printed in Penn, II. 265, with error of " commanders " for
" commissioners " (vide Tanner in *Introd. to Cat. of Pepysian MSS.*
p. 21 n.). MS. copies in *Pepysian MSS.* 2867, p. 352 and 2611, p. 121.

from these preliminaries the real need, however, had
been truly summed up in 1660 by Sir Robert Slingsby ;
he then proposed that, for the regulation of the Navy
Office, "which by the frequent vicissitudes of form is
still in great confusion, whereby neither are accounts
exactly kept, nor sufficient order taken for the recti-
fying of known abuses, or preventing the like for the
future...his Royal Highness would vouchsafe...to
regulate the navy by his princely instructions, to be
preserved in the office in a book fairly written, as a
direction for every officer to walk by in the execution
of the duty of his place[1] " : and the Duke's letter
covered a set of instructions just such as Slingsby
had outlined.

These instructions were not new or original, and
James speaks of them as a ratification of instructions
issued by Buckingham in 1640 "with some small ad-
ditions and alterations[2]." They had been prepared by
Penn in 1660, but the issue of them had been deferred,
as the Duke says, "until the want (of money) and in it
the pretence of offending[3] " was removed. In one
point alone did the new regulations differ from the
previous ones in a matter of importance, and that was
in an attempt to remedy a serious abuse. In Article 9
the Navy Board and all inferior officers are "to take

---

[1] *Discourse of the Navy* (printed with Hollond's *Discourses* [Nav.
Rec. Soc. vol. VII.]), p. 342. MS. copy in Brit. Mus. *Add. MSS.* 11,602.

[2] Buckingham's instructions are in the Penn Collection at the
Brit. Mus., *Sloane MSS.* 3232. The instructions of 1662 in Brit.
Mus. *Harl. MSS.* 6287 and 7464, also in *Pepysian MSS.* 2867 and
2611 : an imperfect copy of them was printed in 1717 entitled
Oeconomy of H.M.'s Navy Office.

[3] Penn, II. 265.

T.　　　　　　　　　　　　　　　　　　　　4

care " that they do not " trade in any such commodities
as were used in the navy," "or go sharers with any
merchant in any way for commodities sold to the navy,"
lest way was made " for serving and receiving in unfit
commodities and at exorbitant rates[1]." In general,
however, there are two noteworthy points in connection
with these regulations. In the first place there was
what they lacked. The very fact that they were in all
vital points identical with those issued in 1640 is the
root of their insufficiency and consequent failure. The
Navy during Buckingham's tenure of office was very
different to what it was under James—just the difference between a small profession and a great national
service ; the increase in purely official business connected with the Navy in those twenty years was enormous. Even after the revival and growth under the
Commonwealth the increase was very large. Pepys[2]
gives some idea of the growth of the work of his office
when he compares the two Dutch wars :

Between May, 1652 and December, 1653
              Letters   390 ⎫
              Orders   288 ⎬ 678
              Contracts   — ⎭
Between September, 1664 and September, 1667
              Letters   5329 ⎫
              Orders   3113 ⎬ 8848
              Contracts   406 ⎭

The result of this growth was naturally that the old
arrangements were absolutely inadequate. One principal official could no longer do work that would occupy

[1] *Harl. MSS.* 7464.
[2] *Pepysian MSS.* 2242 in a marginal note.

a whole department, and yet, the subordinate officials
being given no power of initiative or responsibility, the
service fell between the two stools. The other noteworthy point is the spirit that the instructions attempt
to foster. Article 18 enjoins that the officials are " to
be able to trace one another in their distinct and severall
dutys." To know his neighbour's duty as his own was
to be each official's ideal; a process of mutual spying
which experience has seldom proved efficacious.

Six and a half years later the Duke issued to the
Navy Board some caustic " Reflections[1] " upon the
Instructions of 1662. These ' reflections ' were, from
beginning to end, entirely the work of Pepys[2], and,
since their truth was practically admitted by the officials
in question, form solid support to the opinion that has
been widely upheld that he was one of the keenest
and most efficient officials this country has had. The
work of each of the chief officials is criticised first
separately in detail and then jointly. As some idea
may be gained therefrom of the way in which the
higher administration of the Navy was carried on during
this period, a few quotations from them will not be out
of place. The Treasurer has "failed in the Annuall

---

[1] *Harl. MSS.* 7464, also 6003. *Pepysian MSS.* 2242 contains
these ' Reflections ' and a whole series of papers and notes concerning
the enquiry into the conduct of the Navy, 1660-8.

[2] On July 24th, 1668, Pepys " did long and largely show him
(the Duke) the weakness of our office, and did give him advice to call
us to account for our duties, which he did take mighty well and
desired me to draw up what I would have him write to the office "
(*Diary*). This Pepys did, " though I know," he says, " it will set the
Office and me by the ears for ever" (*D*. August 22nd), and on the
27th the Duke signed a copy of Pepys' letter "without alteration of
a syllable " (*Diary*).

4—2

makeing up of his accompts and presenting them to his
fellow officers...(they being seldome less then Two
yeares in arreare)." Concerning the Comptroller, the
muster books have been " kept undone many months
after, and then committed unto uncertaine hands and
many tymes to hands the least qualified for that trust " :
he " hath not to this day either in peace (when y^e
worke was more easy) or warr (when...it became the
more necessary) stated or examined the Accompt of
one storekeeper," and also " by the totall ommission
(as farr as I can understand) [of the 10th article] the
Treasurer's and victualler's accompts have att noe
tyme beene knowne to any but themselves[1]." " Soe
farr hath the surveyor beene from a Constant knowledge of the state of H.M.'s shipps...that I doe not
remember that I have ever hitherto upon my commands
of what shipps were most in Readynesse for this or
that Perticular Service received other Answer...then
that he would send downe to the yards to informe
himselfe " ; also, despite many loans of H.M.'s stores
" noe Regular Accompt thereof is knowne to have
beene kept. By which how wide a doore hath beene
opened to the defrauding his Majesty." Of Pepys'
own post as Clerk of the Acts, " there hath not as yet
occurred to me any perticulars wherewith to charge
him with failor[2]."

[1] Cf. *Diary*, April 7th, 1665 " ...Sir G. Cartaret do order business,
keeping us in ignorance what he do with his money."
[2] This was through no lack of effort on Pepys' part to find out
his own failings. Cf. *Diary*, August 15th, 1665, P. told Coventry :
" I did depend still upon his promise of telling me whenever he finds
any ground to believe any defect or neglect on my part, which he
promised me still to do ; and that there was none he saw...."

In other words the Instructions of 1662 had been
utterly ignored, and with such conduct in high offices
it is not surprising that the lower ranks of the service
became rotten with corruption and neglect of duty.
Apart from the structural weaknesses of the instructions in themselves—and their essential inadequacy
must continually be borne in mind when criticising
the Restoration official—the causes of this failure are
not far to seek. Pepys' keen eye towards efficiency
saw very near to the root of the trouble when, in the
course of conversation with Sir W. Coventry over
" the unhappy state of our office," he said " that,
though the backwardnesses of all our matters of the
office may be well imputed to the known want of
money, yet perhaps, there might be personal and
particular failings[1]." Those " personal and particular failings " were the failings that had become the
characteristics of England after the Restoration. Under
a King and a Court without honour to man or woman,
a King who regarded his kingdom as a source of income
and amusement to himself, a Court employed in appropriating that income to itself on every opportunity, it is
not surprising that official life was rotten with the
same rottenness that ran through the Court. Official
honesty was a thing unknown, incomprehensible ; to
steal from the State was not to steal; neglect of official
duty was too general to be even remiss. Even the
conscientious Pepys, though after a lapse he frequently
reproaches himself for neglect of duty and could on
occasion refuse a bribe, " resolving not to be bribed to
despatch business[2]," had no scruple in making a gain

---

[1] *Diary*, August 15th, 1665.   [2] *Ibid.* August 7th, 1665.

for himself provided he could set against that some
gain to the State also; as for example on one occasion
he makes note : "In one business of deales in £520
I offer to save £170 and yet purpose getting money to
myself by it[1]."

The financial embarrassment that dogged the Navy
Office from their assumption of office was
Renewed
Financial an obvious reason for many of the defects
Troubles.
in their administration. No sooner had
they got under hand the cumbersome debt which they
had inherited, than fresh shortage of supply met them
—accompanied by the hugely increased needs brought
on by the second Dutch War. Any collection of
naval papers covering the period 1663 to 1667 teems
with complaints from officials, entreaties from victims,
evidencing the criminal shortage of supply to the Navy.
The State Papers and Pepys' *Diary* are specially
eloquent on the subject. There are stories of merchants ruined, both great and small, of seamen and
workers starving or stealing. Constance Pley, a lady
merchant at Portsmouth, writes "beseeching speedy
reimbursement for the great sums expended ; is deeply
in debt ; the total amount owing is £17,234, her French
creditors, on rumour of war and plague tumble in their
bills all at once, and she has not 600 pence to pay with ;
she begs for money to keep the life in the poor men to
whom it is owing[2]." Her partner, Col. Reymer, also

[1] *Diary*, September 26th, 1664. Cf. also November 23rd : "Sir
G. Cartaret here this afternoon ; and strange to see how we plot to
make the charge of this warr to appear greater than it is, because
of getting money."
[2] *Cal. S. P. Dom.* 1664–5, September 3rd, 1665 ; 1665–6,
pp. xxxix, xl, November 5th, 1665 *et passim*.

writes that he " would have been aground long since
but for his woman partner[1]." One James Kember
writes that he " has served for two years as master,
mate, and gunner, without ever receiving one farthing.
Is utterly undone, not having a farthing in the world[2]."
The streets of London and the seaport towns were
filled with the unfortunate victims ; Pepys writes of
" the horrible crowd and lamentable moan of the poor
seamen that lie starving in the streets for lack of
money. Which do trouble and perplex me to the
heart ; and more at noon when...a whole hundred of
them followed up ; some cursing, some swearing, and
some praying to us[3]." The inevitable consequence
to the Navy Office of this lack of money was loss of
credit. When experience taught that the office could
neither pay its bills nor its men, men refused to serve
or to trade with it. Dealers refused to supply the
government with goods except for ready money.
Comr. Thom. Middleton writes from Portsmouth that
he " is put to his wits' end for want of masts and money :
he cannot procure broom, candles, timber, oars or any
necessaries[4]." Even when credit was obtained it had
to be paid for in hard bargains : Penn and Pett write
from Chatham that they " will contract for plank and
elm at the best terms possible, but for want of ready
money, must pay 4s. or 5s. a load extra[5]." " Reddy
money," wrote Middleton, would " save ye Kinge 2/6

[1] Cal. S. P. Dom. September 3rd, 1665.
[2] Ibid. September, 1665, vol. cxxxii. No. 81.
[3] Diary, October 7th, 1665.
[4] Cal. S. P. Dom. October 27th, 1665.
[5] Ibid. October 25th, 1665.

att least in ye pound...besides I finde men not willinge to sell for London pay, saying it cost them more tyme and expense to goe to London to beg it[1]." Appeals on the part of Pepys and his colleagues met with no success : Pepys gives a graphic account of one such interview where he had given " a large account of the charge of the Navy, and want of money. But strange to see how they held up their hands crying, ' what shall we do ? ' Says my Lord Treasurer, ' why, what means all this, Mr Pepys ? This is true, you say ; but what would you have me to do ? I have given all I can for my life. Why will not people lend their money ? Why will they not trust the King as well as Oliver ? ' And this was all we could get, and went away without other answer, which is one of the saddest things that, at such a time as this,...nothing should be minded, but let things go on of themselves, do as well as they can. So home, vexed[2]."

In short, the civil administration of the Navy of the Restoration, in so far as it was modelled by the Instructions of 1662, failed, and failed utterly. But it is a failure that must not be separated either from the ultimate success towards which it was a steppingstone, or from the great administrator who arose amidst the ruins and never forgot the lessons of experience he learnt there—Samuel Pepys.

---

[1] *S. P. Dom. Chas. II*, cx. f. 61.
[2] *Diary*, April 11th, 1665.

2. *Discipline. The Fleet.*

Money, or rather the lack of it in the right, and its presence in the wrong places, perpetually hampered if it did not ruin the Duke of York's disciplinary measures also. Yet, nullified sometimes, hampered always, as they were, in more than one case do his measures mark important developments in the Navy.

It was one of the charges most frequently brought

Personnel, 'Gentlemen Captains.' against the management of the Navy after the Restoration, that it had resulted in the appointment of ' gentlemen ' to commands in the fleet and that to them was due the slackened discipline, the immoralities, the mistakes and the failures from which the Restoration Navy was far from free. It is a subject offering opportunities of rhetoric that have been seized on by many, from Macaulay back to the gentleman whose " illiberal and improper observations[1] " shocked the author of *Marine Architecture.* To a certain extent a substitution of ' cavalier ' officers for others whose religious or political sentiments made them unreliable, was inevitable. As we have already seen there was a certain amount of weeding out done by Mountagu and Lawson previous to the actual Restoration, and no doubt that process was continued both by voluntary and compulsory resignation. One of the best known seamen who thus disappear from the Navy was Vice-Admiral Goodson, no gentleman

[1] Charnock, *Marine Architecture*, vol. I. pp. lxxiv–xcv, says " it might have been wished for the sake of decency and propriety " that he " had conveyed his animadversions in somewhat less vulgar terms." MS. of the pamphlet in Rich. Gibson's Collection at the Brit. Mus.. *Add. MSS.* 11.602.

sailor but a true old salt bred from cabin-boyhood up.
There is one article of the 1662 Regulations which gives
official recognition to the process and at the same time
shows the care James took to obviate its drawbacks as
far as possible. On the return and paying off of any
ship the Commissioners are to make a " strict enquiry
...of yᵉ ability and behaviour of all standing officers
dureing the voyage (because it hath been necessary
to remove and appoint divers warrant officers rather
upon presumption of their good affection than that
there could be any certainty of their ability) soe that it
will be necessary to have a reviewe of such as have been
so put in, after experience of them by a voyage[1]."
Complaints of " that great evill of putting our navall
strength into the hands of our gentry[2] " were plentiful,
and not always from the prejudiced or ignorant only ;
Pepys tells of Coventry referring to the " unruliness
...of young gentlemen captains[3] " : one ingenious
writer traces one disaster after another, including the
loss of St Christopher, back to the loss of the ship
Coventry, owing to the incompetence of its gentleman
captain, and from his elaborate chain of consequences
draws an equally elaborate chain of arguments[4]. All
these writers, however, seem to have been so struck by
the convenience of certain definite examples of their
case, that they have not looked further and have missed
the fact that the spirit they so much deplored in the

---

[1] *Supra,* p. 49.
[2] Brit. Mus. *Enquiries...relating to Safety and Strength at Sea.*
Add. MSS. 11,684, f. 26.
[3] *Diary,* July 27th, 1666, also June 2nd, 1663, January 10th,
1665, etc.
[4] *Add. MSS.* 11.602. ff. 36–46.

Navy was at the time pervading the whole nation.
When for instance we find John Lawson, the stern Anabaptist seaman born and bred, solid old Puritan if ever
there was one, when we find him broaching bottles of
wine for the King's health, or spending a whole day
drinking with a little company of his fellow-officers[1],
then we get some idea of the way in which the spirit
of the Restoration infected the whole Navy, puritan
as well as cavalier. It was the universal reaction from
puritanism more than occasional appointments of
' gentlemen captains ' that was largely responsible for
the sapped discipline in the fleet.

Nevertheless ' Gentlemen Captains ' there were,
and ' Gentlemen Captains ' there would be while there
was a cavalier government and the Navy as a service
was popular with the gentry. And James took steps
to utilise that popularity in a regular and reliable
manner. How far he realised the ultimate direction
of that step it is impossible to say ; but, deliberately or
accidentally, he laid the foundations of the present staff
of naval officers. On May 7th, 1661, Sir Wm. Coventry
'King's Letter   issued an order to the effect that " His
Boys.'   Royal Highness (being desirous to give
encouragement to such young gentlemen as are willing
to apply themselves to the Learning of Navigation, and
fitting themselves for the service of the Sea), hath
determined that one Voluntier shall bee entred on evry
shipp now goeing forth ; and for his encouragement
that hee shall have ye pay of a Midshipman[2] " ; he

---

[1] Pepys' *Diary*, May 7th and June 1st, 1660.
[2] *Adm. Lib. MS.* 24, *Duke of York's Letters*, 1660–8, May
7th, 1661.

was also to be shown "such kindness as you shall judge fitt for a Gentleman, both in the accommodating him in your Shipp, and in farthering his Improvement." These new arrivals into the fleet were the first of the modern midshipmen. Hitherto the 'midshipman' had been merely a petty officer, having to serve seven years before appointment, but with the appearance of this new class of gentlemen probationers the old office died out[1]. In other words James was determined that since gentlemen must join the Navy they should as far as possible be properly trained to the sea, and from that determination dates the birth of the modern naval officer. That is, briefly, the outline of the one reform during James' administration which had more far-reaching effects than all his other reforms put together.

There was in that connection one other order which again shows the endeavour to remedy the abuse of the 'gentry,' also of undue 'influence' generally, and incidentally gives a glimpse of the manner in which appointments were too often 'managed.' With regard to the filling of vacancies, order was given in November, 1664, that instead of the examination being held at Trinity House, "which is done perhaps formally and slightly and without any regard to the Courage, Prudence, Sobriety or Good Behaviour of the person," it was to be held at Portsmouth " by some of the able commanders, and certificate made in writing of the fittness of yᵉ men to be preferred to that charge " ;

---

[1] At the same time as the above order, order was given that one midshipman less per ship was to be carried : and in September, 1662, order was given " wholly to omit midshipmen in Ye Narrow Seas." (*Adm. Lib. MS.* 24, September 1st, 1662.)

enquiry was to be held into their qualities and skill :
for " this will be an encouragement to able men to come
into the fleet...when they know the preferrment is to
arise from (ability)[1] whereas now they have noe hopes
of those preferrments but by keeping at London to
bee in the remembrances and knowledge of the
office[2]."

The *laisser faire* policy, of which we have already
seen Pepys complaining in the Treasury, was in fact
very far from being the policy of James or the Navy
Office towards the discipline and management of the
fleet. It was one continual fight against two or three
main springs from which flowed innumerable abuses ;
yet it was a fight that was maintained with determination and imagination, against lack of funds and against
the spirit of the Restoration. The reform of abuses was
indeed of vital importance where the manning of the
fleet was concerned. In spite of the powers of the press-
gang the popularity or otherwise of the
Navy as a service and a profession made
all the difference both to the quantity and quality of
the men available. At the time of the Restoration
men were actually " solicitous to be admitted into the
service[3] " ; but after a few years of Restoration finance
there was a different tale to tell. In the meantime,
however, the Duke and his advisers were quite awake
to the need for encouraging a good temper among the
men, and one of the first acts of importance dealing
with the Navy was the institution of an enquiry into

Seamen.

[1] Word illegible in MS.
[2] Bodl. Libr. *Rawl. MSS.* A. 174, f. 478.
[3] Slingsby's *Discourse of the Navy.*

the Chatham Chest[1]. " Notwithstanding," wrote
James to the Navy Office, " that there are sevrall
persons who have received hurts and been maimed in
H.M.'s Navall Service, which are at present in great
want and necessity and cannot receive reliefs from the
Chest at Chatham (notwithstanding they have usually
contributed to the same) in regard of the great debt
at present lying upon the said chest, I desire you will
forthwith cause a strict enquiry to be made into the
business of the Chest[2]." On February 4th, 1661, he
wrote of it again, " having as yet received noe returne
from you concerning that business,...I have thought
fitt to remind you... [3]." The reminder had little
effect, and in July, 1662, Pepys discovers " what a
meritorious act it would be to look after " the Chest[4],
an act which lost none of its attractions when
he found it would " vex Sir W. Batten, which is one of
the ends (God forgive me) that I have in it[5]." As a
result of Pepys' endeavours a Commission was appointed
and met twice, but did nothing ; " unless I have time
to look after it," he writes nearly two years later,
" nothing will be done, and that I fear I shall not[6]."

[1] It was a fund for relief which had " from the year 1588 or 1590,
by the advice of the Lord High Admiral and principal officers then
being, by consent of the seamen, been settled, paying sixpence per
month, according to their wages there, which was then but 10s.
which is now 24s." Pepys' Diary, November 13th, 1663. (N.B.
In August, 1663, A.B.'s wages were 21s. and contribution to chest
1s. per month, cf. Rec. Off. Adm. In Letts., August 18th 1663.)
[2] Brit. Mus. Add. MSS. 9311, October 21st, 1660.
[3] Adm. Lib. MS. 24, Duke of York's Letters, 1660–8.
[4] Diary, July 3rd, 1662.
[5] Ibid. August 20th, 1662.
[6] Ibid. March 30th. 1664.

His fears regarding both lack of time and its results
were well founded, and throughout the second Dutch
War the conduct of the Chest remained a public scandal
and a crying injustice to those who depended on it.

Early in 1661 the grievance that was in a year
or two to assume alarming proportions, had already
appeared, and reverence and admiration for their
Royal Highnesses had so far been overcome by the
feelings aroused by systematic refusal to pay wages
with hard cash, that as early as February of 1661 the
seamen petitioned[1] for payment of overdue wages.
True to his policy the Duke did not ignore the matter,
and on February 21st he wrote to Lawson of it : " I
...chose to be silent in it, untill I had effected somewhat
which might bee of advantage to the persons agreived " ;
though full relief must wait till the next Parliament,
" the Commissioners are," in the meantime, " resolved
to use soe speedy a way for the Payment of the Ticketts
(the dilatory way for which seemingly prescribed in the
Act, I suppose was none of the least Grievances) as
that is wil bee as satisffactory to the seamen as if they
were paid at the same moment with the Shipps[2]."
Money due for short allowances was to be paid immediately out of royal treasure, and two days later the Lord
Treasurer was ordered to supply £7000 to pay the
latter[3]. That was, however, the merest palliation, and
bad finance soon resulted in a rotten fleet. Starvation
turned many men almost to madness, and mutinies
and riots were frequent at all the dockyards. In August,

[1] Copy of Petition in Bodl. Libr. *Carte MSS.* 73, f. 511.
[2] *Adm. Libr. MS.* 24, *Duke of York's Letters.*
[3] *Ibid.* February 23rd, 1661.

ADMINISTRATION

1663, we hear of Sir John Mennes being attacked by
starving workmen and lucky to escape " out of the
hands of so rude a multitude[1] " (though Pepys says he
" did act as much like a coxcomb as ever I saw any man
speak in my life[2] "), in September, 1665, of Pepys being
" set upon by the poor wretches[3]," whereon he remarks
that they "in good earnest are not to be censured if their
necessities drive them to bad courses of stealing or the
like, while they lack wherewith to live." In October,
1666, matters were so serious that we hear of " twelve
well fixed firelocks " being asked for " for the defence
of the Navy Office[4]." On board the fleet itself, mutinies
were less frequent since there the men were at least fed
and clothed[5]; grievances on the ships were rather
about another effect of bad finance—bad victualling.
The ' ticket ' which was the direct subject of grievance
was a kind of I.O.U., signed by the officers of the man's
ship, specifying his length of service, which, when signed
by the Navy Board, was in effect a warrant on the
Treasurer for payment of wages. At first the King
had opposed the adoption of the ticket system, " which
the King do take very ill[6]," Pepys tells us, but the
partial adoption of it—payment of wages " half in
ready money and tickets for the other half, to be paid
in three months after[7] "—soon developed until the

[1] Rec. Off. *Adm. Nav. Board, In Letts.* 1663.
[2] *Diary*, September 2nd, 1663.
[3] *Diary*, September 30th, 1665.
[4] Hist. MSS. Comm. *XV. Rep. App. Pt.* 2, *Hodgkin Papers*, f. 167,
quoted in Tanner's Introduction to *Pepys' Catalogue*, p. 119.
[5] They could get clothes on their tickets : *vide sub.*
[6] *Diary*, December 3rd, 1660.
[7] *Ibid.*

Navy was practically run on this paper credit. Had these tickets been promptly paid on presentation no harm would have been done and they would have been negotiable for the seamen at very small loss, but the delays and absolute uncertainty of payment depreciated their value and the seamen would lose as much as 25 per cent. or even more in exchange[1].

Impotent as he was to remedy the primary source of all the trouble, James did his best to meet the secondary difficulties. "I am," he writes in March, 1665, "soe sensible of the necessity of keeping the minds of yᵉ seamen in good temper in this tyme of service that I cannot but recommend...that as often as any shipps come into port which have been long out, you present the seamen's demand of Pay by giving them a fitting proportion of their pay for support of their Familyes[2]." The Duke, however, favoured more definite and practical remedies than the one so suggested and on December 8th he issued a " Remedy for the uncertain payment and consequent high rates " containing 14 articles[3]. The articles dealing with the ticket question ordered that any tickets " under yᵉ value of twenty pounds be paid when tendered without observation of time or order of payment " ; those over £20 were to have precedence ; failure on the part of

---

[1] *Cal. S. P. Dom.* 1666–7, p. 426; 1665–6, p. 75.
[2] *Adm. Lib. MS.* 24, *Duke of York's Letters*, 1660–8. Pepys makes a note in this connection of the " unreasonable hardship of yᵉ general practice of our Navy of paying those Ships off first where the least sume clears yᵉ most men : those who have served longest, and therefore need their pay most being postponed to those who have served least." (*Pepysian MSS.* 2866, *Naval Minutes.*)
[3] Bodl. Libr. *Tanner MSS.* 45, f. 41.

one man to tender his bill for payment was not to
" hinder the next to be paid before he come," and " his
money shall be reserved for him in the Treasury untill
demanded and then paid[1]." Eighteen days later
further Remedies were issued[2] which included the provision of a separate court for bills under £20 (except
Pilotage and Bills of Exchange)—that is to say, for
most seamen's tickets. The unavoidable saving clause,
however, effectually nullified these remedies : payment
was to be made " as fast as the state of his Maj[t]'s
Treasure shall permit[1] " ; the only real remedy was set
forth by the Navy Office in reply to the House of Commons Inquiry of 1667—" a supply of money in every
place, at all times, in readiness, where and when...any
...occasions of discharging seamen shall occur[3],[4]."

Systematisation and regulation were as much the
need of the military as of the civil side of the naval
service, and even during the first seven years of his
office some of the Duke of York's orders mark important stages in naval development. Curiously enough in
this, as in the case of the civil ones, the new Regulations were far from being original.

[1] Bodl. Libr. *Tanner MSS*. 45, f. 41.
[2] *Ibid*. 45, f. 51. The preamble is very typical of the careful and
practical nature of most of the Duke's reforms : " I omitted severall
particulars," he writes, " least in this time of action the introduction
of too many new Rules might obstruct other services untill the
practise of those then given being by use become easy should make
the addition of others more seasonable." Cf. also the opening of his
reply to the Seamen's Petition, February, 1661 *supra*.
[3] Penn's *Memorials*, II. 509.
[4] Another minor point showing the Duke's politic regard for the
rights of the seamen is an order of August 13th, 1663, for wages to
be paid to men who had been prisoners—their captivity to count as
service. (*Adm. In Letts*. 1663.)

The act of 1661 (13 Car. II. c. 9) " for the Regulating and better Government of his Majesty's Navies, Ships of War, and forces by sea " was founded directly upon the articles of war of 1652, which were an elaboration of the ordinances passed in 1647 for Warwick's fleet. They are directed mainly at discipline in the fleet, and set forth in detail the powers and limitations of the courts-martial. Though neither original nor novel in its articles this act remained as the basis of naval discipline for a century ; it was only repealed by 22 Geo. II. c. 33.

The duties of the captain were set forth and regulated by the " General Instructions to Captains" of 1663, and from them it is possible to gain some idea of the inside of naval life. The first instruction provides that " Almighty God be duly Served...twice every day by the wholle Ship's Company according to the Liturgy of the Church of England[1]." Nine articles deal with duties connected with the stores and provisions of the ship, and the check to be kept on the Purser and other persons dealing with them. Of the other articles, one provides for a daily muster of the whole ship's company, another that no man is to be employed as an able seaman unless he " hath continued seaven yeares at sea " and is 24 years of age, and no one as midshipman unless he " hath served at least seaven yeares and can navigate the ship " : the captain, in council with the master, boatswain, and gunner, has power to appoint inferior officers and enter them in the ship's book : in port he is to take care to keep officers and men together : he is to protect H.M.'s subjects and trade : he is to compel

New Instructions.

---

[1] *Adm. Libr. MS.* 23, *Orders of the Duke of York,* 1660–5.

ships to strike their flag, and to exact payment from
English ships for any shots that may have been necessary : prizes in war are to have their hatches ' spiked
up ' immediately : lights and fires to be out after
setting watch, no candles for ship's use except in lan-
thorns; no tobacco is to be taken except in the fore-
castle over a tub of water (if this regulation was kept
the spectacle of a huddled circle of seamen solemnly
smoking their pipes over the prescribed ' tub ' must
have been not without its humour); the top men are
not to be hazarded in ' blowing weather ' : any
foreign ship to be searched for any Englishmen serving,
but the master of such a ship is to pay such men their
due wages (note again the consideration for the seaman) : detailed instructions are given as to the occasion
and quantity of salutes and on no account is a salute
to be given unless a return of it is certain. The two
final instructions are of special interest, one because
it was rarely kept, the other because it shows us what
training in gunnery was considered necessary. Instruction xxx forbids the captain to take in any merchan-
dise except gold, silver or precious stones ; trading on
the part of naval captains was one of the chief of the
minor breaches of discipline, and throughout our period
this article was far more honoured in the breach than in
the observance. Instruction xxix orders that " for
the first month the men be exercised twice every week
to the end they may become good Fire Men, allowing
six Shott to every exercising. That the 2nd month
they may be exercised once every week, and after that
only once in two months allowing six shott to each
time of exercising."

A month earlier the Duke had issued another set
of instructions, which, though they were far from being
a deliberate imposition of a uniform, yet must have
resulted in more or less uniformity of dress among the
seamen. As a matter of fact they were primarily intended to relieve seamen from the extortion of the
'slopsellers' as the clothes vendors were called. Only
the " under-mentioned cloathes[1] " were to be sold on
board the ships ; and here again the ' council ' of the
captain, master, boatswain, and master gunner (or any
three of them) was to have decisive powers, in this
case to settle the rates, which were not to be higher
than the under-mentioned :

" Monmouth caps	..	..	2/6
Red caps	..	..	1/1
Yarn stockings p.	..	..	3/0
Irish „ „	..	..	1/2
Blew Shirts	..	..	3/6
White Shirts	..	..	( )[2]
Cotton waistcoats	..	..	3/0
„ drawers p.	..	..	3/0
Neat leather shoes	..	..	3/6
Blew neckcloathes	..	..	/5
Rugs of one breadth	..	..	4/0
Canvas suits	..	..	5/0
Blew suits	..	..	5/0 "

The sale of clothes was to be held " always above
decks at the Maine Mast in presence of the Captain,
officers and the whole Ship's company," largely in
order that " Tobacco, Strong Waters or other such like

[1] *Adm. Libr. MS.* 23, *Orders of the Duke of York*, 1660–5, March
2nd, 1663.
[2] No price set either in this or in other copy of orders in MS. 20.

comodityes be not sold as cloathes." Debts for
clothes could be put down on the seamen's tickets—
an unavoidable concession when the men received no
ready cash for their wages. The clothes of any deceased
seaman were to be sold " at the maine mast " and the
proceeds sent to his executors. Though it is evident
that these rules must have resulted in a certain uniformity of dress, the fifth article shows that such was
not the deliberate intention of them, for it orders that
" none of the said cloathes be permitted to be sold to
any of the ship's company two full months from their
entrance[1]."

The question of the division of prizes and prize-
money was another that needed regulation, for not
only did it nearly affect the temper of the men, but
also it was an important item in the income of the
Navy[2]. Embezzlement of prizes meant serious loss
to the revenue, and insufficient partition of them meant
further discontent among seamen and increased
difficulty in manning the fleet[3]. At the outbreak of
the war the matter became urgent, and in January,
1665, the Prize Court appointed local sub-commis-

---

[1] This was made void in November, 1664, owing to the filthy
state of many of the new men's clothes. (*Adm. Libr. MS.* 23,
November 22nd, 1664.)

[2] Arms and ammunition taken on prize ships formed no small
addition to the Ordnance; *vide* orders for delivery to Ord. Dept.
Harl. MSS. 1510, f. 660 *et passim.* There are two volumes in the
Brit. Mus. of *Proceedings of H.M. Commissioners for Prizes,* 1664–7;
Harl. MSS. 1509, 1510.

[3] The difficulties and abuses of the press-gang, though the outcome
of the financial muddle, are more properly connected with the preparations for war in 1664–5, and are treated of in that connection;
vide pp. 106–9 *infra.*

sioners " in the ports of London, Dover, Portsmouth,
Plymouth, Bristol, Hull, Newcastle, and other places
where it may be thought necessary[1] " (their work having
previously been entrusted to the local customs officials[2]),
and instructions were issued to them urging them " to
exact performance of their duties[3]." Two months earlier
than this the other side of the question had been dealt
with in order to meet and check the growing scarcity
of men : on October 28th, 1664, the King issued a
declaration for the " encouragement of seamen and
marines[4] " which settled their share of prize-money.
Seamen, whether serving on King's ships or merchantmen, were to receive 10s. per ton on all prizes, £6. 13s. 4d.
for each piece of ordnance, £10 a gun for every man-
of-war sunk or destroyed, and the pillage of all mer-
chandise on or above the gun deck.   In March, 1665,
the Duke of York diplomatically granted a wider
application of these regulations to the case where the
prize ship had not resisted, for, he said, " the restrayn-
ing yᵉ seamen from an indulgence formerly given them
would have a consequence too dangerous to be recom-
pensed by yᵉ value of those goods which wilbe (what
ever yᵉ order be) very hard to preserve[5]."

[1] *Cal. S. P. Dom.* 1664–5, January 21st.
[2] A class much despised by the naval officers.
[3] Brit. Mus. *Harl. MSS.* 1509, ff. 1–102.
[4] *S. P. Dom. Chas. II*, cᴍ. 145 (1).
[5] *Adm. Libr. MS.* 24, *Duke of York's Letters*, March 8th, 1665.

CHAPTER IV

THE MEDITERRANEAN

IT is difficult to estimate how far the Mediterranean
Cromwell and the Mediter- ranean. policy of Cromwell and his successors in the
government in England was the deliberate
piece of diplomatic strategy that it appears
to the latter day observer. To the Mediterranean
Powers whom it influenced so vitally it could not but
seem deliberate : it was so effective. But on the English side, on the other hand, there appears but the most
doubtful appreciation of the true inwardness of the
policy which later developments have made so distinct.
Blake, in 1654, by reason of a three weeks' wait at
Gibraltar—against which he and his men fumed—had
prevented the junction of the two parts of the French
fleet, frustrated Mazarin, and thus offered to modern
eyes the first practical example of the true significance
of the " Gibraltar defile[1]." His actions within the
Mediterranean also had had wide effects and had been
the cause of much discomfort and many fears to the
Italian powers and France. The convenience of the
position of Gibraltar had not escaped Cromwell's
notice, and, if we are to believe Pepys (on the authority
of Sir Robert Haddocks), " had not yᵉ ship which was
sent by Oliver with spades and wheelbarrows been

---

[1] Corbett, *England in the Mediterranean*, I. chaps. 7 and 8.

taken, he had certainly taken Gibraltar[1]." The domi-
nant idea in Cromwell's foreign policy, however, was
the war against Spain as a part of his religious policy
of Protestantism : and the opportunity of making
Dunkirk the base of operations against the Spanish
power soon put the idea of Gibraltar in the background,
and Mountagu with the largest ships was recalled.
Blake, however, remained on the station using Lisbon
and Tetuan as his bases, and his famous attack on the
Plate fleet in the harbour of Santa Cruz is the most
notable naval exploit of the century. But of Mediterranean policy there was now no sign. The two
ports mentioned acted as an efficient substitute for the
coveted Gibraltar : and at the end of that year (1657),
when it was learned that the much vaunted Spanish
fleet preparing at Cadiz was never likely to get to sea,
all but ten sail were ordered home[2]. The remaining
squadron was ordered to protect English trade from
the depredations of the pirates of Tunis, Tripoli, and
Majorca. It may be said that the continuation of even
so small a squadron in the Mediterranean was an up-
holding and continuance of the policy of a ' Mediterranean Fleet,' a part of a strategic plan. It is difficult
to believe that, had the home government actually
realised the strategic lessons of the preceding occurrences in the Mediterranean, they would ever have let

---

[1] *Pepysian MSS.* 2866, *Naval Minutes.* I have been unable to
trace any other reference to this ship : a note on the plan in Sheere's
Discourse concerning the Medit., however, gives some colour to the
story : it is placed beside the neutral ground and runs—" Oliver
Cromwell had a design on this place and would have cut this neck of
land to make Gibraltar an island."

[2] Corbett, *op. cit.* pp. 332-5.

loose their hold on the instrument whose power had been so strikingly demonstrated. It is true that the maintenance even of so small a squadron as the one under Stoakes in 1658 meant in effect the maintenance of the English influence. But it would seem rather far fetched to read such deep designs of policy and strategy into the simple orders with regard to pirates that were issued to John Stoakes as the commander of the squadron. The question of the protection of trade in those waters had become one of real seriousness. Algiers, Tunis, Tripoli and Majorca were the bases for the piratical raids of small flotillas of Turkish and Majorcan privateers which respected no flag and were indiscriminate regarding the nationality of those whom they sold into slavery[1]. " I wish something could be done against the Majorcans," wrote Blackborne to Stoakes in September, " there is a great cry here of the damage our English merchants have lately sustained from them[2]."

In the meantime, however, while Cromwell's policy was showing itself in its true light as a repetition of the Elizabethan one of attacking Spain in her Atlantic trade—with the addition of the local action round Dunkirk—Mazarin showed that he had, in a practical way, learnt the lesson of Blake's Mediterranean actions. In April, 1658, he asked for, and received, the co-operation of part of the English Mediterranean squadron. Capt. Whetstone was told off with six frigates to join the French at Toulon where he remained, much to his

---

[1] Playfair, *Scourge of Christendom*, and Poole, S. L., *Barbary Corsairs.*

[2] *Cal. S. P. Dom.* September 16th, 1658

disgust, for more than a month in enforced idleness. " All that hath been done," he wrote after three weeks of it, " has been nothing but the whole fleet making a show before Marseilles...and yet no appearance of the removal of this fleet, our merchants meantime not only suffering very much, but the enemy growing more and more numerous and insolent every day[1]." The junction of the fleets did, however, satisfy Mazarin's object, and there is no doubt that it formed in the end a very substantial addition to the persuasion towards peace that her reverses in the Netherlands were to Spain. In the meantime also, Stoakes had successfully contrived a treaty with Tripoli[2]. In other words, one of the last noteworthy events Cromwell had the opportunity of seeing during his lifetime was a striking demonstration of the Mediterranean policy in practice; yet within a week of his death, in an order which must have been planned by him, the Admiralty commissioners wrote to Stoakes—" The Council has now ordered that only 6 frigates be kept abroad this winter and that the rest be called home[3] " : the remainder were to receive victuals to " enable them to keep at sea, and protect trade, much annoyed by the Majorcans and other pirates in those parts."

Such were the antecedents of the Mediterranean ' policy ' at the death of Cromwell. It is in the light of them that the developments of Charles II's reign must be considered. The policy as it is known at the present day, the diplomatic use of the strategic power

---

[1] *Cal. S. P. Dom.* August 3rd, 1658.
[2] There is a copy of the treaty in *Rawl. MSS.* A. 185, f. 293.
[3] *Cal. S. P. Dom.* September 9th, 1658.

of a fleet in or at the mouth of the Mediterranean, had
been, almost unconsciously, demonstrated; but as a
potential weapon it was not yet understood by those
in whose hands it lay. Further demonstrations of the
principle in practice were needed before its possibilities
could be more than vaguely realised. Were it not
for that fact, not only Cromwell himself, but Charles
and all his advisers also, would lie under the charge of
blunders of omission and commission that would have
been inexcusable.

It was not long before the universal muddle that
followed the death of the Dictator began to have a
two-fold effect in the Mediterranean. The squadron
being so distant from home, and its importunities for
stores and money the less effective, it was the first to
feel the effects of the loosened rein, to suffer from
neglect. " I earnestly beg that you would seriously
provide for it in tyme," wrote Mountagu to Thurloe as
early as July, 1658, " the distance is so great to them
and the prejudice so intolerable if reliefe come not from
England ; and truly I give you an account of a neces-
sitye to change some of them[1]." The victualling ship
sent out in September was merely a stop-gap, and
Stoakes had a hard winter of it. The next spring he
writes, somewhat pathetically, of a small and almost
sinking vessel which he had "made shift to tow" to
Toulon, " being unwilling to lose anything, that may
make money, be it ever so little[2]."

The political effect also of the changes in England
was soon noticeable in the Mediterranean. France
appreciated the principle of the ' policy,' if England

---

[1] *Thurloe S. P.* July, 1658.   [2] *Ibid.* April 12th, 1659.

did not, and with the loss of Cromwell's name the
English fleet lost prestige, and with that its force as
a diplomatic weapon. Not merely was Whetstone's
small squadron no longer desired, but the English ships
began to find themselves no longer welcome at Toulon.
In the same letter as that quoted above[1], Stoakes
writes, " the different face wherewith I am now treated
from my last, makes me jealous these people have
already embraced the Spanish interest and do seek to
weary us off their port," a fact which led him to add " if
there be not a way thought of to procure a port in this
seas of our own, the squadron will not be very secure,
our interest being so small in these people." A further
example of the precarious position of the English influence in those seas comes from Tripoli in the plaintive
complaints of the English consul there, who, after
bewailing the lack of pay and begging the Admiralty
" to consider the remoteness of yᵉ place," says, " Here
are several who labour all they can to make a breach
by persuading the Bassha and others that the peace is
of noe force since the death of Oliver Lord Protector
in whose name it was concluded," and in the meantime he himself is treated with but little respect[2].

However, the home government was at this time
far too interested in its own domestic tangles to look
at the Mediterranean squadron from other than a
purely financial point of view : peace had been made
with some of the pirates, others had been suppressed,
the war with Spain was over[3], what further need could

[1] *Thurloe S. P.* April 12th, 1659.
[2] Brit. Mus. *Add. MSS.* 22,546.
[3] Peace was first made on May 3rd, 1659.

there be of a fleet in those waters? On June 17th
Stoakes was recalled with all the remaining ships.
No doubt the political unrest in the fleet itself had its
share in bringing about this withdrawal. Soon after
the death of Oliver, when the officers had been asked
to sign the general declaration expressing goodwill to
Richard, trouble had broken out. Capt. Whetstone,
who had already given Stoakes "just cause for complaint[1]," had to be sent home under arrest[2], and in a
kind of 'sympathetic strike' one of the other officers,
Capt. Saunders of the *Torrington*, deserted with his
ship and came home—to find himself imprisoned in
the Tower.

———

The first naval move made by England after the
Restoration, in the direction of the Straits
or Africa, was of a commercial and more
or less unofficial nature. As early as
October 3rd, 1660, the Duke of York was speaking
of a " great design " that he and a number of others
had " of sending a venture to some parts of Africa to
dig for gold ore there " : they intended " to admit as
many as will venture their money, and so make themselves a company, £250 the lowest share for every
man[3]." The project matured, and in the following
spring a small expedition was sent out to the Guinea
Coast of Africa under command of Captain Robert
Holmes. Details are lacking as to its operations, and

Mediterranean 'Policy' and the Straits 'defile.'

———

[1] *Thurloe S. P.* Adm. to Stoakes, July 29th, 1658.

[2] There is a collection of papers covering the whole incident in
Bodl. Libr. *Rawl. MSS.* C. 381.

[3] Pepys' *Diary*, October 3rd, 1660.

its interest lies principally in its position as the fore-
runner of the official expedition to the same coast in
1664. It sufficed, however, to irritate the Dutch who
considered they had a right to the monopoly of the
Guinea trade.

In the meantime, however, diplomatic negotiations
were in progress which were to bring the Straits once
more into prominence. Even before the Restoration
the Braganzas had opened tentative negotiations
regarding a marriage between Charles II and Catherine,
the King of Portugal's sister. Alliance with England,
the natural enemy of Spain, offered obvious advantages
to Portugal in their struggle to maintain their indepen-
dence, and she was prepared to pay a high price
for it. In return for a promise of military and naval
assistance the Portuguese offered a dowry of two
million ' crusados ' and the cession of Tangier and
Bombay[1]. Both these ports were valuable posses-
sions, but since Spain claimed the one and the Dutch
threatened the other, it was but a wise bargain to sell
them for a tangible return before they were lost for
nothing. The treaty was signed in June, 1661, and
England was embarked on an enterprise which she
neither understood nor valued at a fraction of its true
worth. Indeed it would have been foresight extraordinary had the full importance of the Straits been
realised at this time ; for the Mediterranean was still
eclipsed by the Atlantic in both political and commercial importance, and Louis XIV and Colbert had not
yet raised France to that position which made the
Straits a determining factor in European politics. On

[1] *Camb. Mod. Hist.* v. 105.

the whole it does not seem to have been considered in England as an especially good bargain, though for reasons of the Portuguese trade it was not unpopular. Tangier was much talked of by some, but then " as the foundation of a new empire[1]." Lawson, however, one of the few persons who seems to have had an inkling of the strategic possibilities of the Straits, speaking from personal experience, said those who possessed it could keep it " against all the world, and give the law to all the trade of the Mediterranean[2]." Sir R. Southwell speaks of Tangier making England " masters of the trade in the Mediterranean[3]," but then he was voicing the opinion of the Portuguese among whom he had lived; and they, in contemporary opinion, exaggerated the value of it as much as the English depreciated it. "Tangier," writes Fanshaw from Lisbon, "is as much over-valued in Cabales heer, as undervalued in England, and it must be only the improvement and enlargement thereof by changing master that can justify these and confute those[4]."

However, with the acceptance of these terms came immediate need for a fleet to take possession of the new ports, and also to fetch the future queen. There was also another matter that called for naval action. The withdrawal of the English from the Mediterranean had had a stimulating effect on the Algerines, and their fleet of corsairs had begun to assume large proportions. A list towards the end of 1659 gave its numbers as 7 ships of between 30 and 40 guns, 8 of between 16–30,

---

[1] Burnet, *Hist. of My Own Times*, I.
[2] Clarendon, *Life, etc.*, II. 151.
[3] Kennett's *Register*, p. 91.
[4] Bodl. Libr. *Carte MSS.* 73. f. 592.

and 3 galleys of 21–28 pairs of oars holding 400–500 men[1], a total of nearly 7000 men. Complaints of them from English merchants became more frequent; and early in 1661 their fleet must have numbered over 30 ships[2]. Later in the year, when Sandwich[3] was already in the Mediterranean he received a petition from some 160 British slave-prisoners in Algiers, also a list of ten small ships taken there in the course of two months[4].

On June 14th, Sandwich, with Lawson for his vice-admiral, sailed from the Downs with instructions[5] to obtain a peace treaty with Algiers which should include an undertaking not to search or molest English ships, and he was authorised to bombard Algiers if necessary[6]. Favourable weather brought him to Malaga early in July and to Algiers by the 29th. No time was lost in sending ashore the articles of the English proposals to the Governor. But "hee presently stumbled at ye second article y^t our shipps should be free from searching and without much considering ye rest sent me word y^t they would have noe peace wth me rather than Admitt ye Article[7]": and on the following day he suddenly opened fire on the fleet. "Wee resolved to veere in two or three cables nearer ye shore and bestowe our

---

[1] Bodl. Libr. *Rawl. MSS.* A. 185, f. 76.

[2] Bodl. Libr. *Carte MSS.* 73, f. 343.

[3] Mountagu had been created Earl Sandwich in the summer of 1660.

[4] Bodl. Libr. *Carte MSS.* 73, ff. 606, 7.

[5] Bodl. Libr. *Ibid.* 74, f. 338, draft copy of instructions, cf. also 74, f. 449 ; 274, f. 2 ; and 73, f. 512.

[6] At the same time the Earl of Marlborough was sent out with five ships and some troops to take possession of Bombay.

[7] Bodl. Libr. *Carte MSS.* 73, f. 520, let. fr. Sandwich, August 8th.

Broadsides upon them the w^h we did for two or three
houres together[1]." However, as the wind was contrary and would have made it difficult to reach the
Turkish ships it was decided to " warp off out of Shott
and waite for a fitting opertunitie of winde and weather
to carry in ye Fleete and Fireships." Sandwich's
characteristic caution was not repaid on this occasion
and no better opportunity arrived. The Algerines
made the most of the opportunity thus given them and
in a week had made " a Strong Boome of Masts from
ye Mouldhead to ye Fish Gate, and mounted more guns
and made that worke exceedinge more difficult and
hassardous." With somewhat more justification for
his caution Sandwich decided to give up the attempt.
He realised that the essential duty of the fleet was
" not ye performing one single attempt but to main-
taine themselves saileing in these Seas," and disposed
his force to "ye best advantage for anoyinge them at
sea." Patrols of two or three ships were sent eastward
and west to the Straits while Lawson with the main
body of 9 or 10 remained to ply in the vicinity. Sandwich himself sailed with the remainder of the fleet for
Lisbon, there to carry out the diplomatic part of his
duties, and arrange for receiving Catherine and as much

[1] *Op. cit.* There is a glorious printed account of this action in *Carte
MSS.* 223, f. 248 : the title is sufficient description : " *The Demands
of his G. Majesty the King of Great Britain* to the grand seignior or
Emperor of Turkey...with a true Relation of the great and bloudy
fight between the English and Turks, the dividing of his M.'s R. Navy
into several Squadrons by the Victorious Earl of Sandwich and ever
Renowned Sir Jno. Lawson, the battering down of half the City, and
all the Castle Walls, the dismounting of the Turkish cannon, the
sinking and burning of 18 Great Ships with above a thousand piece
of Ordnance, etc., etc." London. Printed for G. Horton, 1661.

of the money part of her dowry as he could squeeze
out of the reluctant and—according to his own account
—impecunious Portugee.

While Sandwich was performing these not altogether
pleasant duties Lawson was doing some effective service, and we hear of him keeping in " 25 sayle of those
Pirates that are fitted and ready to come out[1]," besides
taking one or two small prizes. But questions of far
wider import were now coming to the fore and the war
with Algiers sinks to insignificance before the threats of
a European war between the chief naval powers. The
Portuguese were not the only people to appreciate the
value of their concessions to England. As we have
seen, those precise ports were coveted by Spain and
Holland respectively ; but the prospect of such acces-
sions to England aroused still wider interests. The
Papal Powers were roused by the support given to
Portugal against the leader of the Catholic Powers—
Spain, while antagonism to her led Louis to give
Charles the secret support that finally decided his
acceptance of the offer. The main issue, however, lay
between Spain and Holland on the one hand, and England and Portugal on the other. In the spring of 1661
it had become known in England that a powerful
squadron under De Ruyter was preparing in Dutch
waters ostensibly to protect Dutch trade in the Mediterranean. Scepticism was general regarding this
alleged object, and many were the doubts concerning
the real aim of it. " What the intention of it may be
is uncertaine," wrote the Duke of York in October,
" but as for any attack upon y⁰ fleete, I cannot thinke

[1] Bodl. Libr. *Carte MSS.* 73, f. 596, September 24th.

that they so much desire warr wth us, as unprovoked
as to goe about it[1]." As a matter of fact the Dutch
themselves were almost as much in the dark, and De
Ruyter was only to divulge his orders to two or three
principal officers on strictest secrecy, " aux termes du
serment qu'ils avoient prêté[2] " : he was to co-operate
with the Spanish, not to seize Tangier as many had
feared, but to protect the expected Plate fleet. Though
such were his actual intentions, the danger in the eyes
of the English was that he would seize Tangier before
they had time to occupy it, and for weeks the tension
was acute. Both Sandwich and Lawson had met De
Ruyter's fleet and there was an outward show of
cordiality. Lawson even naïvely asked De Ruyter for
his secret signal " afin qu'en poursuivant les Turcs on
pût se reconnoître de jour et de nuit[3]," but there is
no evidence that the confidence trick[4] was successful.
But with the Dutch fleet an unknown quantity, cruising
now one side of the Straits, now the other, the English
could not but be on tenter-hooks. The Dutch might
at any time be heard of as having seized Tangier,
annihilated one of the smaller English squadrons—
the Dutch numbered 22 ships in September[5]—anything might happen at any time : the air was full of
vague rumours and sudden alarms, and Sandwich was
helpless in his ignorance. That the English were not
the only victims of ' nerves ' is instanced by a letter

[1] *Adm. Libr. MS.* 24, *Duke of York's Letters,* October 21st, 1661
(to Sandwich).
[2] Brandt, *Vie de De Ruyter,* p. 261.
[3] Brandt, *op. cit.* p. 163.
[4] Corbett, *op. cit.* II. 24.
[5] Brandt, *op. cit.* p. 162.

from Tetuan : Sandwich had visited that port to make a trade treaty[1], which simple fact so scared the inhabitants that "now," the writer says, "they are hard at fortifying, even calling in Jew merchants to help[2]." At the beginning of October a more powerful scare than the previous ones sent Sandwich post-haste to Tangier. He had "expectations to have found a fleet of Spanish and Dutch men of Warre before this place, and prepared for all events accordingly," only to find all quiet and "hardly a sail of any kinde in the place[3]."

The situation was now, however, somewhat easier, for in addition to Sandwich's squadron at Tangier[4], Lawson was cruising in the Straits in case of eventualities. The news that De Ruyter had put in to Port Mahon to career still further eased the tension. But until there was an English garrison in Tangier the crisis was not over or the position without danger. A letter written from on board the *Royal James* gives us a glimpse into the thoughts of the English there at the time, and incidentally shows how practical experience brought that appreciation of the strategic value of Tangier which was so lacking in the home diplomatist[5]. "Lord Sandwich," it runs, "is almost sick with staynge for the Garisons, and with fears lest any plott should be

---

[1] Harris, *Sandwich MSS. Journal*, I. 154.

[2] Bodl. Libr. *Carte MSS.* 73, f. 623.

[3] *Hist. MSS. Comm.* 15th Rep. App. pt. 2. *Hodgkin MSS.* p. 161.

[4] He sailed from Lisbon with the *Royal James, Mary, Mountagu, Hampshire, Princesse, Colchester, Forester*, and five small vessels. (Harris, *Sand. MSS. Journ.* I. 160.)

[5] Cf. Lawson on the subject. Sandwich also was always enthusiastic about the possibilities of Tangier (Harris, I. 208).

betwixt ye Spanyards and people of Tanger. Really
ye Garison's stay is very dangerous....This place
makes all the world Jealous. Y^e Spaniard will not
beleeve we shall have it yet, and the Duch make them
beleeve strange thinges ; indeed this place will make
our king feared by all this part of the world[1]." Two
days after this letter was written, on January 14th, 1662,
an opportunity arose which, being taken by Sandwich,
decided the fate of Tangier. Up to that time he had
not received the best of receptions from the Portuguese ; they resented the transfer of their town to the
English[2] and were showing no signs of being over-eager
to hand it over to the prospective English garrison.
On January 14th, however, an ill-judged sortie against
the Moors, who kept the town in a continual state of
semi-siege, threatened to end so disastrously that the
governor was forced to ask for aid from the English.
Nothing could have been better for Sandwich ; and
when he sent, first 80 men, then 120 under Sir Richard
Stayner, to help in the defence of the town, the English
occupation was assured. " Now," wrote Pepys on
hearing the news, " the Spaniards' designs of hindering
our getting the place are frustrated[3]." On January
29th Lord Peterborough and the garrison arrived, and
the occupation was complete. From that time on, the
connection between Tangier and the fleet is conspicu-
ous by its absence. In the early days of the building
of the mole the harbour was inadequate for the protection of a squadron of any size[4], and at no time does any

[1] Bodl. Libr. *Tanner MSS.* 49, f. 139.
[2] Corbett, *op. cit.* II. 27.
[3] *Diary*, February 20th, 1662.
[4] Routh, *Tangier*, 1661–84, p. 79.

attempt appear to have been made to use it as a naval base for the control of the Straits and Mediterranean. On two occasions in particular does this inability or unwillingness to make use of the port as a point whence to control the Straits come into especial prominence. First, in December, 1664, when Capt. Thomas Allin, while waiting for the passing of the Smyrna fleet of merchantmen, chose to ply up and down in the Mediterranean rather than station his small squadron at Tangier and use patrols. On the second occasion the omission had more far-reaching results, for it led to the fatal division of the English fleet in June, 1666, that caused the virtual defeat in the " four days battle."

After the successful occupation of Tangier, Sandwich returned to the less pleasant diplomatic task awaiting him at Lisbon. Haggling over the payment of Catherine's dowry was a lengthy process, and although he could write to Charles that " things have been despatched here with greater haste than this people have been known to make[1]," yet it was the third week in April before he set sail for England with the future Queen on board[2]. The voyage was uneventful, though unpleasant to Catherine who was a bad sailor, and on May 1st the fleet reached Plymouth.

Lawson, in the meantime, had been doing some useful work against the Algerines. "I can conceive yᵗ nothing can be better husbandry than yᵗ it be pursued vigorously[3]," James had written

---

[1] *Clarendon S. P.* III. app. p. 20.

[2] His fleet included the *Royal Charles, Henry, Roy, James, York, Mountagu, Lyon, Princesse, Breda, Dover, Rubye, Pearl, Elias, Dartmouth, Colchester.* (*Sand. Journ.* in Kennett, *op. cit.*)

[3] *Adm. Libr. MS.* 24, *Duke of York's Letters*, February 6th, 1662.

in February, and Lawson had carried out that policy
with such success that by April he had succeeded in
exacting a treaty from Algiers, "they agreeing not to
search our ships[1]." Without Algiers the Corsairs were
but weak, and Tripoli and Tunis soon followed suit in
making treaties with England. At the end of the year
Lawson returned home with the squadron " with great
renown among all men, and mightily esteemed at Court
by all," yet Pepys "found him the same plain man
that he was, after all his success in the Straits, with
which he is come loaded home[2]." In the spring of
1664 he returned again to the Straits with the new
governor for Tangier, the Earl of Teviot. But the lesson
he had taught the Algerines was not yet forgotten and
he had no serious work until the following year when, he
and the fleet having once again returned home in the
winter, the Algerines took the absence of the English
to be a sign of impotence, and returned to their
old habits of preying on English ships. On his return
to the Mediterranean he declared war with Algiers
again, " though they had at his first coming given back
the ships (to the number of eighteen) which they had
taken, and all their men," because they had " refused
afterwards to make him restitution for the goods
which they had taken out of them[3]." The work,

---

[1] Kennett's *Register*, p. 697 (Sandwich's *Journal*).

[2] Pepys' *Diary*, January 5th, 12th, 1663. Clowes, II. 422, says,
after leaving Sandwich in May, 1662, he " took an Algerine pirate of
34 guns; but, ere he was able to effect more, he was recalled to
England, Capt. Thomas Allin...superseding him in command of the
station." Lawson was only recalled permanently, and Allin appointed,
on the eve of war at the end of July, 1664, *vide* p. 91 *infra*.

[3] Pepys' *Diary*, May 3rd, 1664.

however, was unfinished when the imminence of war
demanded his presence at home, and it was his successor,
Capt. Thomas Allin, who finally renewed the treaty of
peace on August 30th[1].

Not one of the most creditable facts in Mediterranean history is the absolute failure on the part of the
Christian European powers to unite in any way to crush
the " Scourge of Christendom," as the Moorish pirates
have justifiably been called. On the contrary, the
Moors knew that to make a good bargain with one power
they could not do better than repudiate agreements
with another, and in 1664 they offered to the Dutch " to
Re-establish all things again upon a good Foot, and
to break the Treaty concluded with the English[2]."
Experience, however, had taught the worth of the
Moors' promises, and the Dutch rejected the offer and
proposed to England, France and Spain, that a quad-
ruple fleet should be made up to destroy the Corsairs
and " utterly ruine their abominable and insupportable
Domination[3]." When that proposal was made an
incident had already occurred which meant an end to
any effective co-operation whatsoever. Lawson's fleet
and De Ruyter's had met ; to a landsman observer it
might have seemed that all the due formalities of a
naval greeting had been gone through—gun answering
gun in the precise proportions laid down by naval
etiquette—but there was a fly in the ointment. De
Ruyter had dipped his flag in salute, but Lawson, while

---

[1] Copy in *Somers Tracts*, VII. 554 ; they are identical with those
made by Stoakes in 1658.

[2] *Life of Tromp*, p. 230.

[3] *Ibid.*

duly answering gun with gun, had not lowered his flag. Lawson sent word to De Ruyter to say that his omission was not intended in the least degree as a slight, but that his orders forbade him to lower his flag to any other nation. De Ruyter was not to be mollified, and parted from the English nursing the incident as an insult to his country, and determined never to lower his flag to them again. He wrote an indignant complaint home recounting the incident and proclaiming his intention. John de Witt, however, had a keener wit than De Ruyter, and was also doing his best to avoid a war which the English seemed intent on launching on him. He sent immediate word that the Dutch flag was to be lowered to the English whenever they met, but at the same time such meeting was to be avoided whenever possible. In other words De Ruyter was to swallow the insult. De Witt was not, however, moved to this order solely by his desire to avoid hostilities ; he gave the ulterior reason in his letter to the Admiral. " L'intention de l'état," he wrote, " a toujours été de ne faire sur ce sujèt aucune distinction de lieux ; mais de faire salue d'une seule et même manière en tous climats indifféremment, afin que les Anglais ne puissent pas alléguer en tems et lieu et inférer de ce qu'on aurait tenu une pratique ailleurs que dans les mers Brittaniques, qu'on aurait reconnu qu'ils auraient un plus grand droit dans ces dernières mers, que dans les autres[1]." Such precautions, however, could not prevent minor disputes arising on the same subject continually, and the ill-feeling produced thereby played its part in the ever accumulating mass of

[1] Brandt, *Vie de De Ruyter*, p. 199.

jealousies and spites that were to cause two more wars before their venom was exhausted.

When one fleet is spending its time avoiding another for fear of being insulted co-operation is scarcely likely, and what further action was taken against the pirates was carried out by English and Dutch independently.

In the summer of '63 Tromp replaced De Ruyter, only to be rejoined and reinforced by him a year later about the same time that Capt. Thomas Allin was sent out to relieve Lawson. In the meantime matters were drifting on towards the inevitable conflict and it was in the Mediterranean that the tension was the keenest. It was there that the only active squadrons of the future belligerents were plying, each ostensibly with the same object in view, each crediting the other with deep-laid plots. The late proceedings of Holmes along the Guinea coast and elsewhere were scarcely calculated to deaden the already smouldering animosities nourished by the Dutch against their would-be trade rivals, and the expectation of reprisals made the English watch the Dutch movements as a cat does its enemy.

It was on August 19th, 1664, that Capt. Thomas Allin[1] on the *Plymouth* sailed from the Downs with a

---

[1] Born 1612, served with Rupert's squadron 1649–50. For details of his proceedings while on this service the best first-hand source is his own personal journal, though for the most part the details with which it is full are more of—doubtful—meteorological than of historical interest. The first lines in a day's note are always on wind and weather—whether a " handsome gale " or what he quaintly calls " very rainy hurry durry weather " ;—in addition to such purely professional matters, the chance of a fight or a lost opportunity of one are put down with evident joy or disgust. A seaman and a fighter, his bare, unliterary journal—often little more than a log·

small squadron, to replace Lawson who was needed
in England in view of the preparations against the
Dutch. Allin's instructions[1] were to consult with Lawson as to the best methods of carrying on the war
against Algiers and of preserving the English trade in
the Mediterranean. In general he was to " contrive
as much as may be to give convoy to his Maj^{ts} Subjects
in all their Trade in those parts,...that the Turkes
may be weary of Warre with his Maj^t and be brought to
a good peace, the obteyning of which " he was " still to
ayme at " ; though no peace was to be made " unlesse
the Shipps of His Maj^{ts} Subjects may passe free from
search or any kind of molestation." He was to draw
the fleet together at times and have scouts watching
De Ruyter so as to be ready for any emergencies against
the Dutch, " but not to act anything against them untill further orders unlesse they shall first have done
some act of hostility."

It was not till near the end of September that he
met Lawson and took over the command of the Mediterranean squadron : he parted from Lawson at Cadiz
on September 28th and notes, " I put up my Flagg
upon the Maynetopp on this morne about 6 aclocke
28 Sept. 1664[2]." Two days before that the English
and Dutch fleets had for the last time before the war
met and parted amicably—De Ruyter bound for
the Guinea coast with a squadron of 12 men-of-war
with " express orders from the States, to sail towards

book—gives a vivid sketch of what the life and work of himself and
his squadron was. (*Tanner MSS.* 296.)

    [1] Bodl. Libr. *Tanner MSS.* 47, f. 193.
    [2] All following extracts are from the journal unless other reference
is given.

Cape Verd and the Coast of Guiney; to reduce the English to reason, and to make them restore by force what they had unjustly usurpt[1]"; Lawson for England in order to do service against the Dutch in the Channel; and Allin to the service in the Straits where his attack on a Dutch fleet proved to be the first open act of war in the second Dutch war. Perhaps it was the knowledge of what the next meeting would be that caused the ironical cordiality of the farewell greetings on both sides. After plentiful saluting and answering, "De Ruyter," says Allin, "came under our sterne and asked me how I did and saluted me with 7 gunnes and dranke to me I dranke to him and answered him 7 he thanked me 3 the which I answered[2], when De Ruyter was clear from the Fleet he shott 7 gunnes to bid Sir John farewell...he answered him 7 and then he shott of 7 more."

Allin did not go direct to Algiers, but cruised along the coast of Spain as far as Carthagena without meeting any Turks or pirates; and it was not till October 31st that he anchored off Algiers, and made efforts to conclude a peace. Possibly the news of Holmes' expedition on the Guinea coast, or more probably Allin's capture of five of their men-of-war, inspired the Algerines with a respect for the English which they had not displayed for the Dutch in their negotiations with De Ruyter in June; anyhow, from the commencement of the negotiations[3], the English representatives met with consideration, and with what was apparently an honest

[1] *Life of Cornelius Tromp.*
[2] The punctuation is Allin's.
[3] Details of the negotiations are in Allin's *Journal*; and *Cal. S. P. Dom.* November 4th. 1664.

desire for peace—accompanied by as honest a determination to obtain it as cheaply as possible. The
Turks refused any compensation for damage and injuries
to trade or for their ill-usage of the consul, and declared
that, as the English prisoners had mostly become the
property of private men, they could not arrange for
their restoration ; even the " mayne Article of nott
medelling or searching our shipps was much debated,
before they would agree with it." However, peace[1]
was finally concluded, and to inform the fleet of the
agreement " instead of 3 gunnes " (as ordered) " they
shott 30 or upwards from all their castles and forts."
A sumptuous present was sent off to Allin—" 300 small
loaves of bread, ten leane small beast, not fitt to eate
and ten as ill sheepe and a dussin Hens." On November
3rd the articles were signed, two Turkish, two English
copies and one French copy. Unsatisfactory though
the terms were in many ways, yet they strengthened
English prestige in the Mediterranean, both by admit-
ting to England the freedom of those seas and by having
a chastening effect on two other trade disturbers—
Tripoli and Tunis.

About this time Allin must have received definite
instructions[2] to seize Dutch men-of-war or the rich
Smyrna fleet that was soon due through the Straits.
He and his captains were spoiling for a fight. On

[1] From Clutterbuck at Leghorn. "The peace with Algiers is
laughed at, no satisfaction being given for any damage sustained,
but if the Dutch war continue, it may prove advantageous, as the
King's ships will have the Dutch only to look after." *Cal. S. P. Dom.*
December 5th, 1664.

[2] Referred to by W. Coventry, *Cal. S. P. Dom.* November 15th,
1664. Clowes, *op. cit.* II. 424, writes as though Allin had no orders
to attack the Dutch.

November 28th at Malaga he was insulted by two Dutch
men-of-war who manœuvred so as to force him to cut
his cable, and jeered him as he left. " I wish he had
indured it to a breech, that we might have had a just
occasion to have done the like to them in the King of
Spayne's Chamber it troubled me much." Though it
was his aim to catch the Dutch in the Straits there is
no sign that he ever contemplated making any use of
the new English station at Tangier. On December
1st he writes, " all the captains very earnest to goe to
sayle for Trafalgar to lay there expecting the comming
of the fleett of Hollanders." A day later in very rough
weather he gave chase to a visionary ' Smyrna fleet '
off Gibraltar, but owing to bad weather, bad piloting,
and darkness, nearly every one of his nine ships ended
the chase on shore ; the *Nonsuch* and the *Phœnix* were
lost, the *Bonaventure* more or less crippled by leaks,
and some of the others damaged to a lesser degree.
Some of the ships grounded twice before getting clear ;
misfortunes that were not improved by the continuance of very stormy weather for more than a week—
before which time Allin had not unnaturally " had
enuffe of it "—or by the fact that when the squadron
got back to Gibraltar again on the 11th the Governor
there refused them assistance. The next day they
received news of the Dutch fleet of 33 sail at Malaga,
and after a council of war renewed their resolve to go
to Trafalgar and wait there, first calling at Tangier
to pick up two other ships of the squadron, thus making
the squadron up to eight sail[1]. In the meantime

---

[1] On the 13th the *Bonaventure* sprung a fresh leak and had to
make for Cadiz.

amended instructions[1] had been dispatched to Allin on
November 21st from England—" notwithstanding any
orders to the contrary...to seize all such ships and
vessels belonged to the United Provinces of the Netherlands as you shall meet with." It is certain, however,
that Allin did not at the earliest receive them for over
three weeks, for on December 17th he complains that
he is " hindered taking a dozen great Dutch ships by
twos and threes, because only allowed to attack their
men-of-war or their Smyrna fleet, and that not in
Spanish ports[2]."

The Dutch[3] fleet had weighed from Malaga on the
16th ; a fleet of about 30 merchant ships, great and
small, convoyed by three frigates under command of
Commodore Brakel. The Dutch account runs thus :
" we made all together towards the Mouth of the
Streights and having passed it on the 28th with some
Merchant Ships separated from us ; the same night
being arrived within 3 miles of Cadiz Bay, Comm. Brakel
gave the signal to anchor ; the next morning at break
of day, we set sail again, and some of our Merchant
Ships were scattered from us : The 29th in the morning
we met 8 or 9 English ships, upon which Brakel advan-
cing towards their Flag, saluted it with some Guns,
but the English Admiral waiting his opportunity till
Brakel came up side by side with him, powered in upon
him a whole Broadside. When we saw that, we repaid
him his change." The Dutch fleet only numbered

[1] Rec. Off. *Adm. Nav. Off. In Letters*, 1664. November 21st.
[2] *Cal. S. P. Dom.* December 17th, 1664.
[3] For this Dutch account cf. *Life of Cornelius Tromp*, pp. 258–9.

14[1] when they came in sight of the English, and before the encounter it was still further diminished by six merchantmen who "contrary to the Orders of their High and Mightinesses, and in contempt of their honour... basely deserted us to Retire into the Road[2]." The fight was sharp but short owing to the weather : Brakel, and Roelofsze on the *Koning Salomo* appear to have met the brunt of the sudden English attack ; Brakel was killed and his ships severely damaged, Roelofsze sank with his ship after an hour's fight. The stormy weather prevented the English from using more than their upper guns, " our ship laying downe side soe much that we could ope noe more ports," and also prevented them tacking to return to the fight. Two of the English ships never came into action, though one of them captured an isolated merchantman—the *Santa Maria* : the only other prize was the *Abraham Sacrifice* taken by the *Oxford*. " What was done we did the most, had God pleased to have sent us fayre weather, we had done great service but it was a frett of wind that we could nott handle our sayles to fight[3]." Such was the somewhat ignominious action by which the English opened the Dutch War : on hearing of the encounter the States General published on January 14th[4] a Declaration of War, ordering the seizure of all English ships ; and though Charles did not officially declare war until March, it was only the season of the year and

---

[1] *Journal,* and *Cal. S. P. Dom.* December 25th, 1664. Cf. Clowes, *op. cit.* II. 423, " thirty merchantmen and three ships of war" at time of action.

[2] *Life of Cornelius Tromp,* p. 258.

[3] Allin's *Journal.*

[4] English (old) style.

T.

a mutual need for preparation that postponed further actions.

During the course of the war the Mediterranean saw but little naval action. Concentration with a view to decisive action was the policy of both English and Dutch, and so thoroughly did the former act up to it that they withdrew Allin and his squadron and left no ships of war in the Straits or Mediterranean. Even Tangier was left to itself to be entirely self-defending : a fact which offers some idea of the completeness of the extinction of the ' Mediterranean policy '—if indeed that policy had even yet penetrated into official circles in England. The Dutch, however, were not the men to allow their policy of concentration to prevent the use of the opportunity thus offered. The three men-of-war that were lying in Cadiz harbour awaiting Allin's departure served as a nucleus for a small fleet— sometimes numbering over a dozen ships—which succeeded not merely in annoying English trade, but also in seriously endangering the safety of Tangier. They made no attempt on Tangier itself, for they " durst not come within reach of the cannon[1] " : instead they contented themselves with "hovering about the Straits mouth, sometimes in and sometimes out, to wait for our merchant ships[2]," and in October they struck a blow which was far more effective than any bombardment promised to be. The victualling ships intended for Tangier had already been long delayed when in September they set sail under the convoy of the *Merlin* and in the company of some fifteen merchantmen.

---

[1] *Hist. MSS. Comm.   Heathcote MSS.* p. 192.
[2] *Ibid.* p. 195.

When off Cadiz this fleet met nine of the Dutch men-of-war. As a result of the pluck and tenacity of the *Merlin's* captain, who " behaved himself bravely with his 'twelve guns'[1]," only four merchantmen and the *Merlin* actually fell into the hands of the Dutch: nevertheless the incident was a serious blow to the garrison, shattered and inadequate as were the victuals[2]. The only step taken by the English government in any way to compensate for the lack of warships in the Straits, was to grant letters of reprisal to privateers, and in the spring of 1665 the State Papers contain references to eleven ships thus licensed[3]. In other words the Mediterranean ' policy ' of England in 1665 was no deep-laid strategic or diplomatic scheme, but a vague idea of ' tit for tat,' of petty private piracy licensed by the State.

So long as the war was confined to England and Holland the English neglect of the Straits and Mediterranean is at least comprehensible, inasmuch as the desired concentration must be in English waters, and Dutch interests in the Mediterranean were comparatively small. With the entrance of Louis XIV into the arena, however, the range of naval action widened, the importance of the ' Gibraltar defile ' begins. The English successes of the first year's war, coupled with the ever growing power of Tangier as a naval station, as the mole stretched out further and the harbour grew, gave Louis a prospect of England supreme at sea holding

---

[1] *Heathcote MSS.* p. 211.   *Cal. S. P. Dom.* November 3rd, 5th, 10th, 14th, 1665.
[2] Routh's *Tangier*, p. 83.
[3] *Cal. S. P. Dom.* January 28th and March 11th, 1665.

the key to the Mediterranean with which she could
lock out all hopes of France's naval growth. Peace over-
tures failed, so in January, 1666, Louis declared war on
England.

The French fleet was divided, part at Toulon under
de Beaufort, part under du Quesne on the west coast.
Colbert's intention was that Beaufort should have
joined du Quesne and if possible united with the
Dutch fleet before the English fleet came out[1]. Precisely at this time, however, England made a move
which seemed to show the fullest appreciation of the
importance of the Straits and Tangier : Sir Jeremy
Smith, a man with a fighting reputation, was sent out
to the Straits with a small but strong squadron. To
all but the English the move seemed brilliant and
deliberate. With Jeremy Smith in the Straits, Beaufort's fleet could not be induced to budge, and in the
meantime the Anglo-Dutch War continued and France
was helpless. And then, as it were to confirm and
strengthen that move, a small additional squadron was
sent out to escort Sandwich to Spain. In reality,
however, Sir Jeremy Smith was sent out primarily to
convoy the Levant ships home, and Sandwich's squadron was sent, not to reinforce but to recall. Smith and
his squadron were recalled and the Straits left open
and neglected at a time when they were the most
important of any of the strategic points in European
waters. In the light of this fact it is difficult to see
how it can be in the least credible that the strategic
value of the Straits ' defile ' was appreciated or at all

---

[1] *Lettres de Colbert*, III. i., February 8th-25th, March 2nd-16th;
cf. Corbett, *op. cit.* pp. 53-5.

understood by the English authorities. It is true that Albemarle was a firm believer in the doctrine of concentration, but his name as a sound strategist would be gone if he had enslaved himself to that doctrine knowing, as we now know and as Colbert then knew, that the mere presence of that small squadron at that one spot could cancel all the naval efforts of France and make her fleet a helpless pawn. This incident was the first of the great lessons that English naval strategists needed before they could see what all Europe already knew. Nor was that the whole lesson. Fate, in the guise of false news of the French approach and an order, perhaps from Charles, to divide the fleet so as to meet Beaufort, was to drive the moral home; the fleet was to meet disaster and suffer heavy loss by reason of a division of forces which could have been avoided by a true comprehension of the fundamental fact lying at the root of what has since come to be known as England's Mediterranean Policy.

CHAPTER V

SECOND DUTCH WAR

1664. *Preliminaries.*

THE occurrences in the Mediterranean and on the coast of Africa were but incidents in a movement that was rapidly and inevitably leading England and Holland into war. At the root of it all was commercial jealousy. The Dutch held the carrying trade of Europe, and the English growth threatened what they pleased to consider as their monopoly. The English too, as Albemarle said, were determined to have a larger share of the trade. " The trade of the world is too little for us two," remarked a naval Captain, " therefore one must down[1]." The Navigation Acts had done their work in irritating the Dutch, if not in actually excluding them in the way intended. Frequent disputes on the vexed questions of the salute and ' Dominion of the Seas ' claimed by England added to the general tension. Goaded as she was beyond all patience, Holland was not over-eager for war, and it was a difficult question how the war could be precipitated and at the same time blamed to her with at least some show of plausibility.

---

[1] Pepys' *Diary*, February 2nd, 1664.

"It seems the King's design," says Pepys, "is by getting underhand the merchants to bring in their complaints to the Parliament, to make them in honour begin a warr, which he cannot in honour declare first, for feare they should not second him with money[1]." The court was 'mad' for the war and the idea was intensely popular in the country. There were not wanting, however, sober opponents of it, and Coventry, "setting aside our ability to goe through with it, or rather taking that for granted (to which possibly some objections might bee made from the posture of His Majesty's stores and treasure)[2]," was of the opinion that the expected trade advantage was of more than doubtful probability, and besides, "it is not a popular discourse, but it is a true one that the crowne may pay too deare for some present advantage to the People." But he was a prophet in his own country and the nation was hurried on into the war. The merchants did not need much encouragement to petition to Parliament for redress for their alleged wrongs—estimated in cash at over 4½ millions, including four millions for the Isle of Poleroon taken by the Dutch nearly 50 years previously. The intentionally truculent representations made to the States on the subject by the English Ambassador, Sir George Downing, fanned the smouldering hatred and gave ample proof of the determination of Charles to force a war.

In the meantime naval preparations were necessary and in May Pepys notes, "Mr Coventry prepares us

---

[1] *Diary*, March 30th, 1664.
[2] Brit. Mus. *Add. MSS.* 32,094, ff. 48–50. Notes against a Dutch war shown only to Lord Arlington.

with expectation of an order for ye very speedy setting
out a squadron of shipps to answer ye Dutch preparations[1]." In July a small fleet was ready—though it
seems to have been little more than a reinforced Summer
Guard[2]—and on July 20th Sandwich hoisted his flag on
the *London* in the Downs, and soon after took his fleet
out into the Channel to practise them. His orders were
to obtain as continual and complete information of the
Dutch fleet as possible, and to "preserve His Majesty's
honour[3]."

The despatch of Sandwich's fleet was in fact a
defensive measure, intended to cover the multitudinous
preparations that were still necessary before anything
like an effective fleet would be ready for offence in the
Channel or North Sea. The Dutch also were for the
time absorbed in defensive measures. With them
safety of trade was the first consideration and they
warned their merchant shipping to sail round the North
of Scotland rather than through the Channel. Tromp
with a squadron of 25 ships was sent to meet and convoy home the incoming East Indiamen[4]. Thus it was
long before any offensive action was taken in home
waters ; apparently neither wished to attack until
their preparations were complete. In August both
England and Holland had a squadron preparing to go

[1] Rec. Off. *Adm. Nav. Off. In Letts.* May 18th, 1664.

[2] It consisted of the *London, Gloucester, Happy Return, Dover,
Kent, Drake, Plymouth, Dreadnought, Crowne, Breda, Guernsey, Lily,
Revenge, Elizabeth, Hampshire, Pearle, Hector,* and *Nonsuch.* Vice-
Adm. was Allin and Rear-Adm. Berkeley. (Harris, *Sandwich Journal,*
I. 214.)

[3] Bodl. Libr. *Carte MSS.* 73, f. 193.

[4] He met them off Fair Isle in August and convoyed them home
without meeting any English. *Life of Tromp,* p. 245.

to Guinea, the latter[1] ostensibly to convoy four West
Indiamen there, the former to follow the latter, convoy
some Guinea ships and presumably to protect Holmes'
conquests. On the 19th, writes Pepys, " Mr Coventry
and Sir W. Pen and I sat all the morning hiring of ships
to go to Guinny, where we believe the warr with Holland
will first begin[2]." On the 20th, Lord Sandwich writes
that he has heard that he is to follow the Dutch fleet to
Guinea, but says he thinks that the fleet " that first
arrives will succeed, and the later one be frustrated
or put to disadvantage ; therefore a squadron should
instantly set out to stop them or sail as soon as they[3]."
This is almost the first authoritative suggestion of
offensive action. The command of the squadron,
however, was finally given to Rupert. " I doubt few
will be pleased with his going," remarks Pepys, " being
accounted an unhappy man " : objections to which
Rupert's hot reply was " God damn me, I can answer
but for one ship, and in that I will do my part ; for it is
not in that as in an army where a man can command
everything[4]." It was not until the beginning of
October that the English fleet for Guinea was ready to
sail. In the meantime it was reported that the small
squadron under Kampden had been increased to 15, and
was to be conducted through the Channel by Tromp
and Opdam[5] ; but it had not sailed when Rupert
weighed from the Hope on October 5th with 12 ships

---

[1] 10 ships under Kampden.
[2] Pepys' *Diary*, August 19th, 1664.
[3] *Cal. S. P. Dom.* August 20th, 1664.
[4] Pepys' *Diary*, August 31st, September 5th, 1664.
[5] It was probably the news of this proposed ' bravado ' that led
to the staying, alteration and increase of Rupert's ' Guinea ' fleet.

bound for Guinea. Rupert never got further than
Portsmouth. He reached there on the 15th and the
squadron stayed there weatherbound.

The following month was one of feverish haste in
naval preparations of every description in England and
Holland. In England one of the main difficulties in
preparing the fleet was lack of men. The press-gang
varied very much in its efficiency in different parts of
the country. In the Eastern counties men were ready
to volunteer to serve if it had not been for the fact that
thus they would have missed their press money. A
letter from Norwich says " By the countenances of the
men they seem very willing to be employed. A company of 40 marched through the town, with drums
beating and other expressions of joy at their taking the
water. There would be volunteers enough against the
Dutch, if they were to be fought at home and not at
Guinea[1]." And from Yarmouth, " The press goes on
hotly along the coast ; throngs are mustering up and
down the streets, frolicking away their press money,
and saying, when their friends try to dissuade them from
going, that they could not serve a better master[2]."
Hull sends 300 men, the full number charged on the
port[3]. But in London and in the South and West of
the country it was a very different matter. In London
and the neighbouring docks, partly owing either to
corruption or sheer inefficiency among the press-masters,
and partly to real lack of the right type of men,
large numbers of landsmen—even apprentices—were

[1] *Cal. S. P. Dom.* October 24th, 1664.
[2] *Ibid.* October 26th, 1664.
[3] *Ibid* November 15th, 1664.

impressed, many of them the merest boys, and complaints
were frequent and urgent. "Most of the pressed men
are fitter to keep sheep than to sail in such great ships[1]";
"pitiful pressed creatures who are fit for nothing but
to fill the ships full of vermin[2]." From Dover comes
the complaint—frequent throughout the country—
that "there are many fit for service, but the magis-
trates will not do their duty[3]." It often happened
that the local authorities in a seaport—being personally
interested in the men and the ships they served—would
give warning of the arrival of the press-gang, and would
even directly oppose it.

In Portsmouth, where the so-called Guinea fleet was
being rapidly increased, the difficulty was paralysing.
Coventry writes for the hastening on of the Thames
ships with as many supernumerary men as possible,
"for here is great want of seamen[4]." At the end of
October an attempt had been made to attract seamen
to the service by the issue of a declaration for the
"encouragement of seamen," settling the proportion
of prize money to be allowed seamen : Coventry orders
its issue to all ports for "it hath much encouraged the
men heere and was receaved with great joy[5]." The
benefit done by it was not, however, very far-reaching,
and the greatest difficulty began to be experienced in
keeping the men when pressed. The Duke of York
went down to Portsmouth and inspected the ships there

---

[1] *Cal. S. P. Dom.* October 21st, 1664.
[2] *Ibid.* December 1st, 1664.
[3] *Cal. S. P. Dom.* November 20th, 1664.
[4] Bodl. Libr. *Rawl. MSS.* A. 174, ff. 491–3.
[5] *Ibid.*

on the 11th of November, and reports[1] that things were
" in pretty good forwardnes excepting the seamen and
somewhat of the victualling[2]," the men either did not
appear after being pressed or deserted after appearance:
" it is grown so comon with them to offend in both
these kinds, that the pressing of men is of little effect,
other than the expending of the King's Treasure " ;
within four days " neere 200 men " had deserted[3].   In
hopes of remedying this he offered a reward of 6d. per
head to people—especially managers of entertainments—
who should secure the return of any such deserters.
This, however, had little effect ; 6d. was not enough.
The only remedy was the vigorous pursuit of runaways
and stern treatment of some as an example.   " Nothing
but hanging will man the fleet " writes Wm. Coventry
three times in three successive letters to Sec. Bennett[4].
Numerous remedies for the lack of men were suggested.
" The King approves your proposal," writes the Duke[5]
to Rupert and Sandwich, " of turning over ye men out
of ye Company's Shipps into ye King's Shipps now
lying in Harbour and securing ye Company's Shipps in
ye Harbour untill a fitter occasion for setting them forth.
I desire you imediately to put it into Execution ;
Leaving on board ye Company's shipps ye officers and
some few men such as you shall judge fitt to Looke to
them and their Lading in Harbour."   It was also

---

[1] *Adm. Libr. MS. 24, Duke of York's Letters*, 1660–6.
[2] One of the first signs of the administrative defect that hampered
the English fatally throughout the war.
[3] *Adm. Libr. MS. 24, Duke of York's Letters*, 1660–6.
[4] *Cal. S. P. Dom.* November 13th, 14th, 16th, 1664.
[5] *Adm. Libr. MS. 24, Duke of York's Letters*, November 2nd,
1664.

suggested that seamen could be obtained from Guernsey and Jersey and " thus French and Flanders seamen
engaged on the King's side who will else be taken by the
Dutch[1]." It was even proposed that possible or useful
men should be sent home from Jamaica[2].

Nevertheless the numbers were increased above the
usual war establishment[3]; order was given that all
the King's ships remaining in harbour were " to be
repaired with all possible speed, and rigged and fitted
forth to sea[4] "; the ships in the Thames and Downs
that were in serviceable condition were to go to Spithead to join the squadron already there. In the
meantime, in the absence of any English fleet in or near
the Downs, the Duke suggested the provision of some
fireships at Dover " that soe in case y[e] Dutch should
come into y[e] Downes with a Fleete opportunity might
be taken in y[e] night of doeing service upon them by
fireships[5]."

Meanwhile the ' Guinea ' fleet got no nearer its
objective. On October 31st Lord Sandwich had
hoisted his flag as joint commander with Rupert; and
Rupert writes that " the ships will soon be in better
condition to meet an enemy, the merchants' goods
being put in good order, and Lord Sandwich's arrival
will hasten forward those that are in port[6]." Early

[1] Cal. S. P. Dom. November 22nd, 1664.
[2] Adm. Libr. MS. 24, Duke of York's Letters, November 17th, 1664.
[3] Rec. Off. Adm. Nav. Off. In Letts. November 17th, 1664. It had previously been lowered below the usual peace rates.
[4] Adm. Libr. MS. 24, Duke of York's Letters, November 4th, 1664.
[5] Adm. Libr. MS. 24, Duke of York's Letters, November 11th, 1664.
[6] Cal. S. P. Dom. October 30th. 1664.

in November the primary objective of Guinea must
have been made secondary to an engagement in home
waters with the Dutch fleet under Opdam, to which end
Spithead was made a rendezvous for the effective
ships in the Thames and Downs. On the 11th and
12th inst. instructions had been given for the seizure
of all Dutch ships, " by force if necessary[1]." On the
11th the Duke of York went to Portsmouth to take
command of the fleet " where his appearance was
useful in forwarding preparations, and delighted the
seamen[2] " : he divided it into three squadrons[3], Lawson and Berkeley as vice and rear admirals of his own,
Myngs and Sansum of Rupert's, and Ayscue and
Tyddeman of Sandwich's squadron : he also had the
men in the Guinea company's ships taken out and put
on the King's ships[4]. Yet the fleet seemed fated not
to sail ; on the 13th it was hourly expected to weigh
anchor, and the decks were cleared for a fight, yet on
the 18th it was still at Spithead and had become by
this time a laughing-stock[5]. On the 19th Coventry

[1] Rec. Off. *Adm. In Letts.* November 11th and 12th, 1664.

[2] *Cal. S. P. Dom.* November 12th, 1664.

[3] Containing respectively 13, 12, and 12 ships (there were also 14
ships not yet ready or assigned to squadrons), Tyddeman was sent to
cruise in the Channel with four or five ships to " teach refractory
Dutchmen their duty." *Cal. S. P. Dom.* November 13th, 1664, and
S. P. Dom. Chas. II, cIV. f. 143.

[4] In pursuance of the suggestion *supra* p. 108.

[5] Earl of Peterborough is " sorry to see the protection designed
for Guinea made the subject of raillery." *Cal. S. P. Dom.* Novembe
18th, 1664. The Duke of York was the mainstay of the preparing of
this fleet ; he was " indefatigable " and Coventry writes, " Those
who know with what earnestness his Royal Highness entered on this
voyage, and how he hastened from London only to be out of impor-
tuning against it, will not easily believe him returning. It is certain

reports that it is " so nearly manned that it may now
be completed from privateers[1]," and on the same day
the ships from the Thames arrived bringing its numbers
up to " 43 of the bravest ships ever seen[2]."

In the meantime Tyddeman and his small squadron
had opened the campaign of attacks on trade which
formed the usual preliminaries of a naval war. He
opened well on the 20th by capturing the greater part
of the Dutch fleet from Bordeaux laden with French
commodities. Once opened, this lucrative campaign
went on apace. The State Papers tell us of 3 prizes
on December 5th, 8 on the 6th, 23 on the 7th ;
indeed on the 10th Col. Walter Slingsby reports that
no less than 150 sail of all sizes have been brought
in between Dover and Plymouth since the commencement. On the 27th, the Duke at length succeeded in
getting his fleet ready to sail, and weighed from Spithead with a fleet of 45 to 46 sail in rough weather--
extraordinarily late in the year for so large a fleet to
set out. Coventry writes of it, "...what weather we
went out in, of wch if you had been a witnesse you
could have judged that lesse resolution or lesse con-
cernment for the King's service then that of his R.H.
would scarce have carryed anybody to sea in such
weather. But it seemed the critical time in wch the
Dutch must pass if they would attempt it at all, and
therefore his R.H. would not be in port[3]." The Dutch
fleet never came out and after five days James decided

nothing under Heaven but the King's commands will bring him back
again."   Cal. S. P. Dom. November 17th, 1664.
   [1] Ibid. November 19th, 1664.   [2] Ibid.
   [3] S. P. Dom. Chas. II. cv. f. 125.

to return to port, leaving a small squadron of eight or nine sail under Sir Wm. Berkeley to sweep the Channel. " Doe what wee could wee have not been able to keepe the fleete together," says Coventry, and it was by twos and threes that it straggled back to port. All energies could now be concentrated on the preparation of the fleet for the coming year. " It cannot but be of great advantage to H.M.'s service," writes James, " that his fleete should be ready before the Dutch," and he gives order that " noe costs may be spared on the King's part that may be conduceing to this service[1]."

1665. The War.

" Englishmen, and more especially seamen, love their bellies above anything else, and therefore it must always be remembered, in the management of the victualling of the navy, that to make any abatement from them in the quantity or agreeableness of the victuals is to discourage and provoke them in the tenderest point, and will sooner render them disgusted with the King's service than any one other hardship that can be put upon them."

Pepys' Naval Minutes.

Such might have been either text or moral of the war, so well is its truth borne out during the course of the war. Indeed, the truth goes even deeper and further than Pepys traced it, for a fleet without food is as immobile as a sail without wind, and time and time again in the war

Preparations. Victualling Difficulty.

[1] *Adm. Libr. MS.* 24, *Duke of York's Letters*, December 16th, 1664.

has the same tale to be told of opportunities missed or left for lack or delay of victuals. Even at the end of 1664 the Duke of York had complained that the fleet had less than the due proportion of victuals[1]; and when in '65 the setting forth of a fleet again became immediate the fatal weakness was straightway brought into strong relief. It was, moreover, a hopeless weakness while the arrangement of the victualling remained as it had been established at the Restoration, when the provision of "all victuals to be provided for His Majesty's ships and maritime causes[2]" had been put into the hands of a single contractor—Denis Gauden. The fault did not lie with him personally; on the contrary, it is very striking to notice how in one complaint after another it is expressly stated that it is not directly against him personally. Of the fleet that went out in April it was written, "noe fleete was ever soe ill supplied for quantities of provision, as, to do the victualler right, none ever better for the goodnesse, against which there is not one complaint[3]." "The victualler is a man of good words, and provides good victuals[4]," writes Coventry at a time when he was nearly frantic with worrying over insufficient victualling. The difficulties were partly inherent in such an attempt to make one man control and arrange the victualling of the whole navy : reliable as he himself evidently was, he could not oversee the work in two or three ports at once : "he usually gave good dispatch, but he could not be in all

[1] Cal. S. P. Dom. November 11th, 1664.
[2] S. P. Dom. Chas. II, Docquet Bk. p. 46, cf. Tanner, Catalogue of Pepysian MSS. p. 152.
[3] S. P. Dom. Chas. II, cxxi. f. 128.
[4] Cal. S. P. Dom. April 15th, 1665.

T.   8

places[1]." It was, however, the financial difficulty
that most hindered efficiency, and afforded Gauden
an unanswerable explanation for most breaches of
contract; he could not keep his side of the contract
unless the government kept theirs, and granted him
"an immediate supply of a considerable sum of
money and a certain weekly payment": he was
not, he said, "in a capacity unless supplied with
money to make the provision necessary[1]." It was
"too much for any one man's purse[2]."

The factor, however, that gives this question the
vital importance—the loss of mobility, the delays and
lost opportunities—is best seen at work, where its
results can be traced down through the whole course of
this war. "The delay in victualling is intolerable,"
comes the complaint early in April. "After all this
expense and pains the fleet is likely to remain unserviceable through defect on the victualler's part....
It will be said that if the victualler send bad victuals
it is his loss, they must be flung overboard; but that
will not repair the King's loss, if his fleet cannot keep
the sea when he has most need of their service." And
pessimistically the letter winds up, "Blind and general
discourses that 'we have a brave fleet and we will
beat them' will not avail, where there is neither money,
victuals nor materials to carry on the war[3]."

On April 20th, the fleet set sail for the Dutch coast,
ill provisioned and ill stored. "Mr Gauden," wrote
Coventry from on board the *Royal Charles*, "hath taken

[1] *Cal. S. P. Dom.* November 13th and 21st, 1665.
[2] *S. P. Dom. Chas. II*, cxxxii. f. 10, September 2nd, 1665.
[3] *Cal. S. P. Dom.* April 4th, 13th, 1665.

care wee shall not be able to stay long abroad, therefore
we hope well of the mettle the Dutch pretend to have,
and they will come immediately out to us[1] " : " If the
Dutch find out our condition as to victuals, they will
play their game very ill if they come out[2]." He was
also much concerned because the men's ' slops ' had
been left behind. " I thinke," he writes, " the health
of the men concerned in their clothes, and men are soe
hard to gett that I should be sorry to loose them so
slightly[3]." As regards the actual manning, however,
things were not so unsatisfactory. " The proportion of
land soldiers is large, yet on the whole the commanders
who had experience in the late Dutch war say that the
fleet is better manned now than then[4]."

The Dutch prohibition of all commerce had shown
their determination that all their force
should be concentrated on their battle
fleet, and that that fleet's primary object should be
" to seek out and destroy that of the enemy[5]." For the
English, prohibition of commerce was not so necessary,
for English trade neither had the volume of that of the
Dutch, nor was it so easily threatened on many of its
routes : nevertheless decisive engagement was equally
the aim of the English fleet. " To try if the Dutch will
come out and venture a battle[6] " was the aim of the
English admiral. Though both belligerents wished for
a decisive battle, there was, however, a difficulty

Strategy of
the War.

[1] Bodl. Libr. *Rawl. MSS.* A. 174, f. 458 (to Pepys, April 21st).
[2] *Cal. S. P. Dom.* April 22nd.
[3] *Rawl. MSS.* A. 174, f. 458.
[4] *Cal. S. P. Dom.* April 18th, 1665.
[5] Corbett, *Maritime Strategy*, p. 158.
[6] *Cal. S. P. Dom.* April 20th

hindering their attainment of that end. The strenuous
efforts that had been made in order to get the fleet out
as early as possible had resulted in James' forestalling
the Dutch, and when the English fleet was at sea the
Dutch were still divided in harbour at the Texel and Vlie.
It was obvious that so long as a united English fleet
was cruising between those places the divided Dutch
squadrons were not likely to come out to be attacked
piecemeal. In other words the presence of the English
fleet was the very opposite to an incentive to the Dutch
to give battle : the very strength of the strategic
position the English held in dividing the Dutch, prevented the attainment of the desired decision[1]. There
was, however, one factor to provoke the Dutch. De
Ruyter—with booty from his tour of reprisal (com-
plementary to that of Holmes)—accompanied by some
merchant ships, was expected home soon : the Dutch
might be enticed out to defend such an important
acquisition of strength. "We thought," says Sandwich, "the hinderinge their trade to come home, the
best provocation to make the enemye's Fleet come
out[2]": and consequently the Fleet was ordered to

[1] Coventry gives some idea of the difficulties by which the English
admirals were faced : he puzzles as to "what to be done if the Dutch
won't come out but send their East India and Smyrna ships to some
foreign port, and then do as they please in the Straits and Guinea,"
and puts the case succinctly—"If we divide our fleet they may
come out and do what they please here ; if we do not, they carry all
before them there" (*Cal. S. P. Dom.* April 28th, 1665); he is
apparently thinking not only of the Texel and Vlie but also of home
waters and the Mediterranean.

[2] *Sandwich MSS. Journal,* I. f. 270 (quoted in Harris, I. p. 289).
Harris gives a detailed account of discussions in council concerning
these questions of strategy : based on the *Sandwich Journal.*

ride at a station some twelve leagues N.W. of the Texel,
while patrols supplied what information could be
obtained. Impatience, however, soon outweighed
strategy, and after two days it was decided to stand in
close to the Dutch coast. On the 28th they rode " so
near the Dutch fleet as to hear their guns fire[1]." For
ten days the English fleet plied up and down along the
coast, having come to none but negative decisions—not
to attack the Dutch in the Texel, not to prevent their
junction " because it would certainely hinder theire
cominge out to engage us which is the chiefe thinge to
be wished for[2]." But now Mr Gauden's care that the
fleet should not stay long out began to have effect :
on May 10th it was decided to return home to revictual
—or rather to make up the stores which had never been
complete—and on the 15th the fleet reanchored in the
Gunfleet. " You will see what a great disappointment
I have had," writes James, " for had he (the victualler)
kept touch I had not been forced to come back, and I
may say I believe never any great fleet ever ventured
to go so far from home and upon an enemy's cost with
so smal a proportion of Drinke, for many of the great
ships had not one days beere on bord when I came in[3]."
In short, the strategic advantage gained by being first
at sea was thrown away by bad victualling, not merely
lost, but thrust into the hands of the Dutch.

Immediately on the return of the fleet preparations
were hurried on and an attempt made to make up the

---

[1] *Cal. S. P. Dom.* April 28th, 1665.
[2] *Sandwich MSS. Journal,* I. f. 275 (quoted by Harris, *op. cit.*
I. 291).
[3] *S. P. Dom. Chas. II.* CXXI. f. 113.

deficiency of beer, food and men. The manning of the
ships did not improve as time went by ; short rations
and shorter pay did not encourage faithfulness, and
desertions were frequent : " sicknesse and the Colliers'
great wages having taken many from us since wee came
in. The colliers give £8 and £9 per voyage, wch is as
much as 7 months pay in the King's ships and may be
performed in a moneth and noe limbes hazarded, the
security against being pressed being added what hopes
is there our men should stay with us or that others
should come to us[1]." Bad weather also hindered the
going out of the victualling ships, and the completion
of the stores proceeded at a very slow rate ; promises
and forecasts remained unfulfilled. " For all they say,
the fleet cannot saile this fortnight, though they knew
the Hollanders were out ; except more victuals come
downe speedily we shall be at a stand[2]." " The delay
of our victuals is the only stop of our going forth to
seeke the Dutch whom we are very willing to meet[3]."

In the meantime, however, the Dutch had come to
sea, and proceeded to make the most of the opportunity
afforded by the absence from the seas of the English
fleet. They had only been out of port six days when
they fell in with a fleet which they at first mistook for
the English fleet : it proved to be an English fleet of
merchantmen from Hamburg laden with the most valuable stores. The mistake concerning nationality had
been mutual, and the man-of-war convoy " mistaking

---

[1] *S. P. Dom. Chas. II*, cxxi. f. 128.
[2] *Ibid.* cxxi. ff. 112, 113.
[3] *Ibid.* f. 128.

the Dutch fleet for the English, fell into it[1]." The
loss was a serious one to the government, depending as
they did so largely upon the Baltic countries for naval
stores, and on receipt of the news the outcry was general.
On the 31st Pepys writes, "to the 'Change, where
great the noise and trouble of having our Hambrough
ships lost : and that very much placed upon Mr Coventry's forgetting to give notice to them of the going
away of our ships from the coast of Holland. But all
without reason, for he did ; but the merchants not being
ready, staid longer than the time ordered for the convoy
to stay which was ten days[2]." However, whatever
the direct cause of the disaster, it was very obvious
that had James not been forced to return for lack of
victuals, the whole thing would never have occurred.
Consequently there was a general demand that the fleet
should put to sea forthwith to meet the Dutch, and on
the 29th, news of the proximity of the Dutch having
apparently been received, the fleet were ordered to be
ready to sail the next morning. It was the King's
birthday, but, writes Sir Thomas Allin, "we were
commanded to fyre noe gunnes only pendants and mast
clothes abroad[3]." Early on the 30th the fleet weighed
from the Gunfleet.

Numerically speaking the rival fleets were evenly
balanced. The English numbered 109
warships, including hired merchantmen,
and 28 fireships and small craft, it carried 21,006 men,
including marines, and mounted 4192 guns. The flag

The two
Fleets.

[1] *Cal. S. P. Dom.* May 29th, 1665.
[2] Pepys' *Diary*, May 31st, 1665.
[3] *Tanner MSS.* 296.

officers and squadrons were : Lord High Admiral (*Red*
Squadron), H.R.H. James, Duke of York, with Sir
Wm. Penn as Captain of the Fleet on the *Royal Charles* ;
White Squadron—Admiral Prince Rupert, Vice-Admiral
Sir Christopher Myngs, Rear-Admiral Robert Sansum ;
Blue Squadron—Admiral Earl of Sandwich, Vice-
Admiral Sir George Ayscue, Rear-Admiral Tho. Tydde-
man ; *Red* Squadron—Vice-Admiral Sir John Lawson,
Rear-Admiral Sir Wm. Berkeley[1]. The Dutch num-
bered 103 men-of-war and 30 small fry, including 11
fireships, carried 21,631 men, and mounted 4869 guns.
It was divided into no less than seven squadrons, the
first, second and fifth of which were commanded re-
spectively by Admirals Opdam, John Evertsen, and
Cornelius Tromp ; Opdam was commander-in-chief.

In morale and personnel, however, a gap widens
between the English and Dutch. The opportune
arrival of the colliery fleet on June 1st had enabled
James to meet the fleet's " only lack—that of men[2] " ;
and colliery ships' men were some of those most sought
after for manning the King's ships. There was no
disaffection among the English. There is no evidence
that there were any serious differences among the flag
officers, while among the lower officers and the men
there were no signs of serious discontent or ill discipline.
Officers and men alike were eager for the fight, " no
rhodomontade but an assurance of beating them[3]."
Moreover, as regards the unity of the fleet, the apparently useless excursion to the Texel in the previous

---

[1] Clowes, *op. cit.* II. 256.
[2] *Cal. S. P. Dom.* June 4th, 1665.
[3] *Ibid.* April 18th, 1665.

month must have been most valuable in securing a
certain amount of cohesion in the fleet, in practising
the amateur tactics of the merchant captains until they
had become adapted to fleet discipline. Sandwich
apparently had the professional fighter's distrust of
the amateur in his attitude towards the merchant
captains, for in the council of war he suggested their
relegation to the rear of the line, saying the King's
captains were " more entire and resolved to aid one
another than it is to be feared the others are[1] " : but
on this occasion his fears were scarcely justified in the
event.

The Dutch fleet on the other hand was in a far less
sound state. Officers and men were in many cases unreliable and disaffection was widespread. The fact
that after the battle four captains were tried and shot
for cowardice—not a usual Dutch failing—and six
others otherwise punished, affords striking evidence of
the morale of the Dutch. Cohesion was almost entirely
lacking. The multiplication of squadrons, the lack of
cordial co-operation between certain of the flag officers,
coupled with the very large proportion of merchant
captains, made any practical unity impossible. " Es
war somit das Band der Zusammengehörigkeit sehr
locker und in Korpsgeist kaum vorhanden[2]."

On the 1st of June, writes Allin, " we spied the
fleett, Captain Lambert first, he fyred a
gun and lett his topgallant sheets fly.
Soe did I and stood for the fleett. They
all wayed and stood off to the S.E. the wind E.N.E.

Battle off Lowestoft, June 3rd, 1665.

[1] *Sandwich MSS. Journal*, I. f. 294, cf. Harris, *op. cit.* I. 299.
[2] Stenzel, *Zeekriegsgeschichte*, III. 151.

fayre weather[1]." Opdam's instructions were to the
" destroying the English at water or at land, wherever
they can meet them[2]," so it is not quite comprehensible why he thus deliberately refused, or at least
postponed, battle, at a time when he held the advantage
of the weather-gauge. On the 2nd, resumes Allin, " we
made sayle towards them but was very little wind all
the forenoone easterly afternoone a fine gale and we
raysed them much, we saw one of their ships blowne up
but it proved a fireship." The fire was caused " by
the Imprudence of him that commanded it, who was
got drunk[3]." The wind veered to S.W., and early on
June 3rd the two fleets were some 14 miles N.N.E. of
Lowestoft, the English having the weather-gauge.

At about 3.30 a.m. the action began, the fleets,
each in line ahead, passing each other on opposite
tacks, S.E. and N.W. The White squadron led the
van of the English, the Duke with the Red was the
centre, and the Blue the rear. Vice-Admiral Myngs
opened the firing, " but very farr off, and soe they fought
the first passe to little or noe puepose, the wind at
S.W.[4]" About 8 a.m., both fleets tacked again and
passed, but again " very farr off that few shott reached,
and those layd at Randum[4]." The Dutch were
endeavouring to win the weather-gauge but the superior
manœuvring powers of the English balked all such
attempts ; particularly did the Red squadron do service
in this direction, guided by the tactical skill of Penn in

[1] Allin's *Journal, Tanner MSS.* 296.
[2] *Sandwich MSS. Journal,* I. ff. 259–263, Harris, *op. cit.* I. 298
[3] *Life of Tromp,* p. 269.
[4] Allin's *Journal.*

the name of James. At the end of the second pass, as
they tacked again, there seemed some chance of the
Dutch getting the gauge, but the position of the Red
squadron prevented[1]; the Duke had gone so far to
windward that supposing they had weathered Rupert's
squadron they would still be to the leeward of James,
and thus between two fires. So they tacked again to
the leeward of Rupert. Thereupon the Duke to prevent a recurrence of the danger tacked into and with
the Dutch[2], and gave order for others to follow suit.
With that move the English line became completely
disarranged, the Dutch could not tack again, and the
battle degenerated into a long straggling *mêlée*. In
the course of this, it is unknown whether by accident
or design[3] Sandwich with his squadron broke through
the Dutch line, a proceeding that must have had a deep
and rapid effect on the already weakened morale of the
Dutch, and soon after it they began to take to flight.
But the fighting in the meantime had been no child's
play. The Dutch flagship with Opdam on board had
been blown up, but before she went she had crippled
the *Royal Charles*, and Lord Falmouth, Earl Muskerry,

[1] *Life of Tromp*, p. 270. " Because the Duke of York's squadron
kept the Weather gage without engaging in Fight, it was impossible
for the Dutch to win that Advantage."
[2] *Sandwich MSS. Journal*, I. f. 297, Harris, *op. cit.* I. 303. " His
Royal Highness, suspecting the enemy would weather our fleet if we
stood on and tacked in our proper berths to make good the like,...
tacked after the enemy, and commanded me to tack." Allin's *Journal.* " His Highness sent me word to stand in, and I presently stood
in soe neere as nott to shoote in vayne."
[3] Harris, *op. cit.* p. 304, apropos of this, gives no quotation from
Sandwich's *Journal* to show that the move was deliberate. Hannay,
Hist. of R. N. I. 341, suggests that some of the Dutch centre flinched
and, lying back, left a gap through which the white squadron came.

and Mr Boyle, a son of the Earl of Burlington, had all
been killed by a single shot at the very side of the Duke.
Vice-Admiral Lawson also was mortally wounded.
Some idea of the *mêlée* nature of the fight may be gained
from the following extract from Sir Thomas Allin's
Journal : " I plyed my gunnes very hard for two houres
uppon Generall Opdam another flagge man and 2 ships
laying on a lyne and a vice Admirall and 4 more 9 in
all, but they payd me handsomely...my masts yards
sayles and hull very much torne. I setting my mayne
sayle to streach ahead from the flagship, cam two new
frigatts or scouts fresh upon me I was forced to take
and receive all to gett off but pay'd the biggest frigatt
(Young Everson) soundly I went and mended what I
could but it was late 3 aclocke before I was fitt to fight,
in that time Generall Opdam's ship blew up...I was
at the taking or beating to yield severall, and at the
beating the fleet together that three gott together and
were burnt by one of our fire shipps, the same formerly
burnt 4 ship all tould of one another. We followed all
night[1]."

The flight and chase were remarkable for two things :
the splendid tenacity of Tromp, who had collected what
ships he could and covered the retreat until his seamen
" openly ascribed to a Miracle the Preservation of his
Ship and Person[2]," thus considerably lightening the
disaster ; and the failure of the English properly to
follow up their victory, which, says Evelyn, " might
have been a complete one, and at once ended the war,
had it been pursued, but the cowardice of some, or

[1] *Tanner MSS.* 296.
[2] *Life of Tromp*, p. 274.

treachery, or both, frustrated that[1]." There seems
little reason to doubt the truth of the strange story told
by Clarendon, supported as it is by the Commons
Journal report of the examination of Harman in April,
1668. Briefly put it is this : during the night after
the fight, when the English were hard in pursuit,
Brouncker, one of the Duke's servants, came up to
Captain Harman saying the Duke had ordered sail to
be slackened; after some demur, and a clever trick on
the part of Brouncker, sail was slackened and the rest
of the fleet followed suit. " The Duchess had given a
strict charge to all the Duke's servants to do all they
could to hinder him to engage too far "—such is Clarendon's explanation of the business. Be the truth of
that as it may, by the time the Duke arose in the morning the Dutch were safe in reach of their harbours and
the English had lost such an opportunity of crushing
the Dutch Navy as they never had before or after[2].
" To confirme the reputation of their victory and to
protect themselves against malice and artifice[3] " the
council of war decided to return to the Downs with
the whole fleet. On June 10th they anchored in Southwold Bay, and on June 18th the fleet was divided
between Osely Bay, Harwich, Chatham and the Nore[4].

The prizes taken from the Dutch numbered about
14 ships, including the *Huis te Swieten*, 70 guns, the

[1] Evelyn's *Diary*, June 8th, 1665.

[2] Allin says : " We stood along and saw them at ancor as many
as could gett close to the Boys...had we had many fyre ships and
gone upon them shooting we had distroyed many of them." *Journal*,
June 4th. *Tanner MSS.* 296.

[3] Harris, *op. cit.* p. 309. *Sandwich MSS. Journal*, I. f. 302.

[4] List of ships assigned to each, *Rawl. MSS.* A. 195, f. 82.

Hilversun, 60 guns, and the *Carolus Quintus* and
Nagelboom, each 54 guns[1] : and in addition at least
12 ships had been sunk or burned. The Dutch had
taken the *Charity.* But two English flag officers and
three captains had been lost : Vice-Admiral Sir John
Lawson, Rear-Admiral Rob. Sansum, Captain James,
Earl of Marlborough, of the *Royal James,* Captain
Kirby of the *Breda,* and Captain Ableson of the *Guinea.*
Apart from these concrete gains and losses this overwhelming victory did not bring much real gain to the
English : owing to the failure to follow it up it was
very far from having crushed the Dutch. Indeed on
the whole it brought rather loss than gain ; it made
the Dutch desperate, and, as Penn said, " the courage
of the Dutch was never so high as when they were
desperate[2]," and it was instrumental in scaring Louis
into joining the Dutch in their fight against the threatened naval predominance of England.

The fight off Lowestoft had given England for the
time being almost undisputed command of the sea and
the Dutch began to entertain fears for two homeward
bound fleets—De Ruyter on the way back with his
booty from the Guinea expedition, and the rich East
India fleet of some 30 sail estimated to be worth many
millions : either or both of which would have fallen an
easy prey to the English fleet. The English designs on
these two fleets were agreeably aided by an
ingenious and opportune suggestion from
Sir Gilbert Talbot, the English envoy at

Bergen
intrigue and
fiasco.

---

[1] Coventry's list in *S. P. Dom. Chas. II,* cxxiii. f. 29, but not
complete
[2] Clarendon, *op. cit.*

Copenhagen. Though the proposal originally came from
Talbot it appears to have met with great approval from
the Danish King, approval that was, however, only
practical as far as the cowardice, tempered by greed,
which was characteristic of that monarch, would allow :
the plan was of the simplest, though the word-play that
accompanied it was often of a wonderful subtlety ; it
was that when the East India fleet, relying on the
neutrality of Denmark, anchored in one of the ports of
Norway—Bergen, in all probability—the English fleet
was to attack it unhindered by the Danish forts; the
price for which abstention was to be a half share in the
spoils. To increase the chances of success and lessen
the danger of any trouble falling on Denmark no
declaration or notice was to be given to the Dutch
ambassador until it was " too late for him to give
advice thereof to that fleete to avoid their coast[1]."
By some delicate reasoning this was " somewhat to
justify the Honour of the King of Denmark to the
world," and was not to " be drawne into consequence
that Denmark consenteth to the violation of their
ports, for it is to be understood but a connivance[2]."
Possibly such subtleties were too much for the Danes—
though it was more probably nervousness and cowardice
wrought up by long suspense ; however, Talbot found
that his statement on June 17th—" all is now well "—
was somewhat premature. The East Indiamen were
long in reaching the coast of Norway and the
Danes' fear of being involved in anything beyond the

---

[1] Bodl. Libr. *Rawl. MSS.* A. 252, Talbot to Arlington, June 17th,
1665.
[2] *Ibid.*

acceptance of a substantial bribe increased in the meantime. "I met with a greate clamour that I went about
to engage this crowne in present warr," Talbot writes
on July 15th[1] ; he could get nothing in the form of a
definite agreement in spite of assurances and promise :
" I am heartily sick with having to doe with a timorous
and unconstant people : For God's sake let me know
what his Majesty will expect from this crowne and I
will put them upon a short categorical answer[2]."

There was, however, no time to wait for a more
definite agreement ; for the East India fleet was by
this time in Bergen and De Ruyter reported off the
Faroes, and on July 20th Talbot sent a messenger
to Sandwich, in command of the English fleet, with
verbal particulars of the arrangement "as being not so
fitt to be putt to paper "—a comment true in more
ways than the one intended. The messenger missed
Sandwich, and on July 24th Talbot wrote[3] explaining
things and how the governor was to "amuse the
Hollanders."

---

[1] He continues : " They made a greate discourse to me how
dangerous it would be for them to engage (in this low condition) to
anything that might provoke Holland against them unlesse they
might be assured that Sweden would stick fast to England and not
make any peace with Holland without the consent of England and
Denmark." July 15th, 1665. *Rawl. MSS.* A. 252.

[2] *Ibid.*

[3] " I have treated with his Majesty of Denmark to give command
to the said governor " (of Bergen) " and all officers under him not to
looke upon you as an enemy when you shall offer any violence to the
Hollanders that ride there.... Therefore you are not to be surprised
if he seem to be highly displeased with your proceeding and that he
make high complaint thereof against you, which nevertheless will
be but in show to amuse the Hollanders and excuse himselfe out-
wardly to the world." *Ibid.* Talbot to Sandwich, July 24th, 1665.

Meanwhile things had not been going too well with the English naval arrangements. The inevitable trouble about victualling and stores which hampered the fleets at every step during this war, was present on this occasion no less than usual ; added to that there was some doubt as to the chief command, and a general atmosphere of haste and doubt resulted badly for the fleet. Apparently there was a suggestion that Rupert should share the command with Sandwich[1], in any case there was a delay in settling the command and a further delay on the part of Sandwich in taking up the command. On Saturday, July 1st, news had been received of De Ruyter's fleet being off Ireland, and at a council of war held at the Nore, at which the King, Sandwich, and Albemarle were present, it was decided to try to intercept it. The command was to be given to Sandwich, whom private affairs claimed till Monday, the 3rd. In the meantime, whether by mistake or for some reason that does not appear, Sir Wm. Penn was given the command and full instructions : the fleet was to sail at the first possible moment to meet the Dutch fleet, to follow them " though they should goe into any Harbour belonging to the King of Denmarke in those parts," and if it was possible " to take or destroy them within those Harbours... nor to neglect the opportunity of doeing it[2]." Sandwich returned on Monday to find Penn in command and *en route* for Sole Bay ; he followed and reached there to find that Penn had taken his orders to hasten out very literally, and that the fleet was just visible on the horizon, bound for the Texel ;

---

[1] *Cal. S. P. Dom.* July 2nd, 1665.
[2] *Rawl. MSS.* A. 468.

picking up Sir Jos. Jordan with five sail more, which
had been unable to get off in such haste, he followed,
and came up with Penn on the 6th, ten leagues off the
Texel. The haste in setting out had been the reverse of
beneficial ; not more than two-thirds of the available
ships were there[1], those that were there were " very
badly furnished with victuals, liquor, yet worse,
wanting 2500 men to what they had last engagement,
some shipps boats and men left ashore for hast of getting
out[2]." Not merely might most of these defects have
been remedied by even a couple of days' wait[3], but also
the fleet might have united with Sir Thos. Allin's
squadron before setting out and thus have been free to
cruise wherever might seem best in order to intercept
De Ruyter[4]. As it was, Sandwich was bound to a
limited cruising ground about the middle of the
Dogger Bank, and it was not until July 17th that he was
joined by Allin and a squadron of above 20 sail. At a
council of war held immediately it was decided, as De
Ruyter was almost certain for reasons both of policy
and weather[5] to make for Holland by coasting along
Norway and Denmark, to override the instructions
directing them to await him about the Dogger[6] and

----

[1] On July 6th the fleet numbered : King's ships, 54; Merchant
ships, 15. *Rawl. MSS.* 468.
[2] *Rawl. MSS.* A. 468 (Sandwich's narrative).
[3] There was a stock of provisions at Harwich.
[4] "...which indigent and disunited condition of the Fleete...
being the Root where unto in all probability may be assigned the
missing De Ruyter on his returne...." *Ibid.*
[5] " The wind was S....improper to bring shipps along for Holland from the North." *Ibid.*
[6] The usual track of ships going to Holland after going round
N. of Scotland.

to make direct for the Naze of Norway with the minor objective of a Flemish fleet of 15 reported at Flackerry.

The event justified the policy entirely, but the previous delays made it of no avail. On the 21st the English were some 30 leagues off the Naze when they had news of De Ruyter at Bergen a week previous to that. As a matter of fact De Ruyter was by that time near the coast of Denmark, and on July 26th, despite a contrary wind, he reached Delf-Zell on the Ems[1], having crept along near the coast the whole way from Bergen. Penn's precipitate start thus lost England a great opportunity of giving a crushing[2] blow to Holland's prestige. There remained the opportunity of striking a lucrative blow at her trade and credit, and if sufficiency of pre-arrangement could give success the attempt deserved to be successful.

Though, owing to his move from the Dogger, Sandwich missed Sir Gilbert Talbot's messenger, yet he had a definite idea of the delicate arrangement with Denmark[3]—though apparently he expected active assistance from the Danes. So when, on the 24th, he received news of the presence at Bergen of the fleet of

[1] De Ruyter's Relation in *Life of Tromp*.

[2] " We thank God for having made us take care to avoid them, since we were in no condition to have resisted them." *Ibid.*

[3] " I was induced to expect the King of Denmark's helpe from the advice of the King my Master, that Sir Gilbert Talbot had written that the King of Denmarke was ready to declare his Treaties broken with Holland, but would be glad to take an advantageous time to say it, which would bee when any considerable substance of the Hollanders was lodged in theire Ports (that then if the English Fleet would attempt them by sea hee would assist and go halfe shares in the prize)." *Rawl. MSS.* A. 468.

28 sail of Straits, French, Portuguese and Dutch ships,
it was immediately decided to detach a squadron of
19[1] ships none above fourth rate[2] ; Sir Thos. Tyddeman
was given command. Calms and north winds, however, hindered their advance and it was July 29th
before the combined fleet reached latitude 58° 46′.

On the next day a further council of war was held
which lasted six hours unbroken : the position, so far
as Sandwich knew it, was a very complicated one—the
only complication of which he did not think (or know)
being the one which finally ruined the enterprise.
There were four main difficulties : " the uncertainty
wee had whether De Ruyter himselfe were within or
noe, which would need a greater force than to attempt
only the Harbour at Bergen " ; the question whether
they could wait for pilots, for they " had not above 3
weekes beene in the Fleetes and scarce any water,
which would necessitate speedily to look for supplies[3] " :
also he was " expecting the whole Dutch Fleete hourely
to give battle with the rest without " (Bergen)[4], and
there was the possibility that the special squadron
might not have completed its task before the rest of
the fleet would have to go " for want of subsistance[5] "
and might so be shut in by the Dutch Fleet from Holland. There appears to have been a stiff debate on
these difficulties, " my Lord proposing what was best
to be acted and pressing to heare every man discourse

----

[1] Eight merchant men-of-war ; five fourth rates ; four fifth
rates ; two fireships. Allin's *Journal, Tanner MSS.* 296.
[2] Not more, owing to lack of room in Bergen roads.
[3] Fleet put on 6s. 4d. short allowances on July 26th
[4] *Rawl. MSS.* A. 468.
[5] *Ibid.*

the point of our condition what was best to be done[1,2]."
While the council was still in progress matters were decided by the arrival of news of nearly 40 sail in or about
Bergen, and it was decided to increase the squadron
to 20 ships, including one third rate. On that evening,
Sunday the 30th, the special squadron for Bergen
parted from the main fleet, Tyddeman being provided
with every scrap of information as regards the nature
of the place which Sandwich had been able to procure[3].

On Monday, the 31st, Tyddeman and his squadron
anchored outside Bergen and sent in a messenger.
The governor received him very favourably, and they
" sailed merrily on with 14 saile and 2 fireships and 4
ketches[4] " and anchored close under the castle. The
governor[5] complained that the English had broken the
treaty by entering the harbour with more than five
ships and " was very tender not onely of his owne, but
his master's honour[6]." As the English representatives[7]

<hr />

[1] *Tanner MSS.* 296.

[2] Penn wanted to go back and lie before Texel to meet the Dutch
Fleet—" God had sent us a wind to make use of." *Ibid.*

[3] " There was scarce a pilot in the fleete that his Lordship could
hear had ever been at Bergen but that he sent for him and discoursed
the matter over with him, and for a whole weeks time the map of this
place, and the discoursing and questioning upon it was his whole
entertainment." Sir Tho. Clifford's account, *Rawl. MSS.* A. 256.

[4] *Ibid.*

[5] Van Steignon. It is interesting at this stage to note the following opinion of this man and his actions—Clowes, *op. cit.* II. 427. " The
governor, unwilling to play the scoundrel upon his own responsibility,
behaved himself like an honest man and fired upon the intruders.''
This was apparently also the Dutch estimate of him.

[6] *Rawl. MSS.* A. 256.

[7] The negotiations were conducted on the English side by
Mr Mountagu (son of the Earl of Sandwich : he fell in the ensuing
action) and Sir Tho. Clifford.

were coming away to the fleet a gun was fired across the bows of the *Sapphire*, wounding one man ; the English, however, took no notice and continued to berth themselves. Fear of reprisals perhaps led the governor to send to ask for further conference, and " now he sung another song... he thought it improper to oppose us[1]." Then ensued a somewhat unedifying contest of haggling over the conditions under which the Dutch ships were to be plundered. The English were in all haste to get to work so as to be clear before the threatened arrival of De Ruyter ; the governor and General Alefeldt[2] on the other hand wished for delay, for they were expecting a Danish fleet of 22 sail by means of which they hoped to monopolise the booty[3] : the English attacking force was also to be limited to six ships. Tyddeman, however, flatly refused to delay, and at daybreak on Wednesday—negotiations had continued throughout Tuesday night—the governor " sang yet another song " : " he confessed ingeniously that the greatest matter that troubled him was the parting with halfe the booty," he said he had orders to secure the whole if possible[4] and suggested the prizes should be sealed up and left at Bergen until advice came from Denmark : the English, however, insisted on division, and so the conferences[5] ended. Meanwhile the Dutch had been

[1] *Rawl. MSS.* A. 256.

[2] Commander-in-chief of forces at Bergen.

[3] This fact Alefeldt let slip to Mountagu.

[4] Clifford remarks on this, " Y[r] Lordship sees this is another straine then his being a man of honour as at his first conference he so much boasted of." *Rawl. MSS.* A. 256.

[5] Among the varying ' songs ' sung and tales told by the Danish Governor and Alefeldt it is somewhat difficult to decide which—if any—had any truth in them, though the last—that they wished for

making the most of their opportunity : on the arrival
of the English they had been "lying one on another,
incapable of execution[1]," but while the negotiations
were proceeding they succeeded in placing four ships
in a line athwart the harbour and constructing some
temporary forts on land.

Sir Thomas Clifford's account of what followed
solves most of the contradictions which appear in other
English and Danish accounts. "At 5 aclocke Wednesday morning wee fell upon the Dutch, with a strict
charge and command to each captain not to fire at the
towne or castle till they fired at us, and for a while the
castle and forts forbore, for neare space of a quarter
of an houre, and our men shot low to the Shipps only
without annoying the towne, and I believe that the
Castle might still have forborne if the Dutch that were
called in there, and the rest of them that had placed
themselves in the towne and about the rocks had not
begunne it, and then it was impossible to hinder our
men from firing at them again. About an hour after
the fight begunne one or two of our Captains say that
the white flag[2] was hung out upon the castle, but the
Revenge being to the leeward and perpetually in the
smoake we could not discerne it, and the captains doe
affirme likewise that all the while the white flagge was
hung out, which was for the space of a quarter of an
the whole prize themselves—seems most compatible with their mode
of conducting negotiations.

[1] *Cal. S. P. Dom.* August 21st, 1665.

[2] Danish King gave account to Talbot " that after agreement
made to leave 6 frigats to keep in ye Hollanders till ye order came,
the Capt. Shott 200 shott from his whole squadron at ye Castle
before ye governor would fire a gunn, nay he hung out his white flag
but all would not doe ; and then he fired...." *Rawl. MSS.* A. 252.

houre, the guns from the castle were still fired at us,
which we suppose to be done by the Dutch that were
called in to strengthen the castle, but being constantly
shot at from thence our men would not be hindered
from answering them and therefore did not cease
firing at them or take any heed to give the Adm. S^{ir} Tho.
Tyddeman notice of the white flag out[1]." After about
three hours and a half the English were forced to
retire : it was a hopeless affair ; the wind was South
and blowing hard almost straight out of the harbour,
thus preventing any use of fireships—for not only
would they have had to be towed in, but also they
would have been dangerous only to the English ships,
which were " moored fast head and sterne quite th'wart
of Harbour[2] "—also the Dutch, as we have seen, had
moved their ships' guns so that they could all be
effective[3] and in addition had landed some 100 pieces
and erected slight forts. Thus in all probability the
wind and the Dutch would have proved sufficient to
defeat the English attempt[4] even had the governor
given or been able to give the passive connivance[5]

[1] *Rawl. MSS.* A. 256.

[2] *Ibid.* 468.

[3] Thus giving nearly double weight to their broadside.

[4] "Against the disadvantage of ye Opposition of Heaven Dane and
Dutch I doe not see what could have been effected." Sandwich's
narrative, *Rawl. MSS.* A. 468.

[5] It is possible that the presence of the Dutch in the town and
forts was not the only reason for the Danish action : about the 20th
of July the French ambassador had been in Bergen and it was
reported that " ye Towne is full of noise y^t ye French King will assist
ye Dutch," and on his return to Copenhagen Talbot says of him,
" M. Terlon is now quite gone from his stile of neutrality and presseth
this king to declare wth France and Holland to force England to
conditions of peace." *Rawl. MSS.* A 282.

expected ; on the other hand had Tyddeman agreed to
wait till the Friday as suggested—which would have
been very dangerous in the light of the information he
had received—he would have obtained that active
support from the governor which would have given
success ; for on that day the belated orders and letter
reached him from Copenhagen bidding him give active
support to Tyddeman—Talbot had at length succeeded
in screwing the Danish King's courage to the sticking
point, just too late. Apart from the underhand
negotiations—the responsibility for which rests on
Talbot—which preceded this expedition, there was
nothing in its failure to discredit Tyddeman or any of
the English ships concerned. Possibly the only just
criticism was that made by one of the Captains concerned (Coleman of the *Hound*), " Teddeman is a brave
man but spent too long in treating with the Dane, who
proved very treacherous[1]."

The English squadron had suffered heavily in the
fight, though it lost no ships except possibly one of
the ketches, and brought off " one though deare bought
prize[2]." Most of the ships were " shattered more in
theire masts, rigging and Hulls then scarce ever shipps
were seene[3] " : the casualties numbered 357, 118 killed
including the Earl of Sandwich's son and no less than
6 captains[4], and 239 wounded[5]. The Dutch claimed

---

[1] *Cal. S. P. Dom.* August 21st, 1665.
[2] *Ibid.*
[3] *Rawl. MSS.* A. 468.
[4] Captains Seale of the *Breda*, Hayward of the *Prudent Mary*,
Utber of the *Guernsey*, Cadman of the *Hambro. Mercht.*, Lawson of
the *Coast Frig.*, Pierce of a fireship. *Rawl. MSS.* A. 256.
[5] *Cal. S. P. Dom.* August 26th, 1665.

to have lost only about 100 killed and wounded ; their masts, sails and rigging were " extreamely endamaged, so that they will take us several days time to repair them[1]."

After he was forced to retire Tyddeman anchored outside the harbour to make what repairs were possible, and in the meantime both he and Clifford wished to have further negotiations with the governor to see if some working agreement could not be arrived at. On Friday, August 4th, the governor sent expressions of regret and goodwill to Tyddeman, and finally on Tuesday, the 8th, at 11 p.m.—in spite of opposition in the fleet[2]— Clifford went to meet Van Steignon " in a sayler's habit, under colour of getting bread and fresh meat," which, he says, " went very much against the haire with me[3]." At the conference the governor informed Clifford that " he was descended of a great race, his ancestors for 700 years gentlemen of the empire, and he would not doe any act that should sully the memory of them, that he was allyed to the Duke of Holstein, prince Palatine, etc., etc.[3] " It is difficult to see what other object he had than that of giving Clifford this information, for he refused any assistance ; and in the meantime the Dutch had moored seven ships in line, triple manned them, and brought 30 guns in each ship to bear on a boom they had built across the harbour—this boom, so the governor stipulated, must not be crossed or broken by the English. Clifford thought the idea was that the

[1] *Life of Tromp.*
[2] " Not one of the captains will heare one word of treating with ye governor." *Rawl. MSS.* A. 256.
[3] *Ibid.*

English were to cripple the Dutch, thus leaving them a
helpless prey for the Danes under the guns of the castle :
however, whatever the scheme was, it failed[1], for on
the 10th Tyddeman, seeing no reasonable chance of
ultimate success and being on short rations, sent a
polite note saying that as the wind favoured a return
to England he had decided to make use of it : he met
Sandwich's fleet off Flamborough Head on the 18th and
on the 21st anchored in Sole Bay.

Sandwich and the main fleet had in the meantime
been seriously hampered by insufficiency of stores.
After they had parted with Tyddeman a gale and very
rough weather from the south had driven them away
northwards until August 4th, by which time the dearth
of provisions made it absolutely imperative for them to
make direct for the nearest place on the British coast
where at least water should be obtainable—a move
which, according to their information, left Tyddeman
exposed to the danger of being overwhelmed by a fresh
fleet under De Ruyter. It was decided to run for
Shetland, and on the 7th the fleet anchored in Bressay
Sound ; whence, having watered[2,3], it sailed on the

---

[1] Van Steignon, however, did his best to make up for his disappointment : he demanded 100,000 thalers from the Dutch ships
as due payment for the protection he had afforded and was affording
them, 3000 he took forthwith and was all but taking more when the
inopportune arrival of De Ruyter forced him to be satisfied with
effusive thanks from the States deputies. He did, however, retain
about 40 guns that had been landed—" sie müssten diese zur eigenen
Sicherheit behalten, da ihnen im Gefecht sehr viele eigene gesprungen
oder zerschossen waren " (Brandt, 318). Cf. note 5, p. 133.

[2] Sandwich complains that it was " very badd," being " redd."

[3] " In meane time I gave myselfe to yᵉ takeing good observation of yᵉ Harbour to give yᵉ King an account thereof and to

13th to reach Sole Bay on the 21st as we have seen.

On Sandwich's arrival at Southwold Bay, every effort was made to prepare the fleet for speedily setting out again, with the hopes of meeting the main Dutch fleet. It was a difficult task : Sandwich needed some 2500 men[1]—he had had to put off over 1000 sick— besides repairs and stores of all sorts, and the recruits sent to him were not only scanty in number, but so unserviceable in many cases that they had to be rejected " rather than pester and increase the sickness of the fleet[2]." Some of the least serviceable ships were sent into harbour and their crews appropriated to other ships. But once again the inadequacy of the victual-ling arrangements hampered the fleet both before and after its setting out, and was largely responsible for the failure to come to any decisive action.

In spite of hindrances, however, the fleet sailed on the 28th, some 110 sail strong. They met with very rough weather and it was not until the 3rd of September that they reached their intended station off the Texel. The same morning they sighted seven or eight sail which they chased, and by sunset had captured them all, including two East Indiamen and four men-of-war[3].

advise in what places it would be usefull to fortifie there." *Rawl. MSS.* A. 468.

[1] *Rawl. MSS.* A. 468.
[2] *Cal. S. P. Dom.* August 25th, 1665.
[3] Two East Indiamen—the *Golden Phœnix* and *Fort of Hunin-gen*; four men-of-war (three of 50 guns, one of 40), the *West-Friesland, Groningen, De Zevenwolden* and *Hope*, one Straits man, one Malaga man, and other small vessels. The English lost the *Hector*, a fifth-rate frigate. *Cal. S. P. Dom.* September 5th, 1665 ; *Rawl. MSS.* A. 195, 185–6 ; *Life of Tromp.*

From them Sandwich heard that " the late storme had
separated theire whole fleete off the Naze of Norweigh
and that they were scattered in the sea round about,"
and that " the greatest Boddy of their Fleet then
together " was some " 80 sayle[1]." In hopes of meeting
this fleet it was decided to tack to the westward, and on
the following morning further reports of them were
received. Then ensued three days' calm, and on the
7th it was decided at a council of war not to stay out
more than four (? 14) days' time[2], owing to increase of
sickness and lack of victuals. On the 9th they fell in
with a further body of over 15 sail of Dutchmen, most of
whom were captured—four men-of-war, one of 20 and
three of 40 guns and upwards, two West Indiamen
and seven or eight fly-boats with provisions for the
fleet[3]. Midday the same day a fleet of about 30 sail,
half merchant, half men-of-war, was sighted on the
weather bow standing for the mouth of the Texel.
Sandwich gave chase and tried to get the weather of
them, but at 4.30 p.m. they were still two leagues off
dead to the windward. The weather worsened, " falling
so thick that wee could not see them and blowing[4] " :
Harman, Berkeley and Jordan nevertheless tacked and
stood with the Dutch, but Sandwich, thinking it unfit
to endanger so large a fleet as his in a night fight off a
dangerous lee shore, called off those that were in chase,
stood away to the westward and finally anchored in

[1] *Rawl. MSS.* A. 468.

[2] *Ibid.*

[3] *Ibid.*: also *Life of Tromp*, p. 317. According to the latter the
Dutch ships were led within reach of Sandwich by the treachery of
a pilot.

[4] *Rawl. MSS.* A. 468.

Sole Bay on the 11th[1]. Thus was another great opportunity lost to the English—the last opportunity that offered that year before bad weather, ill-manning, and ill-victualling forced the fleet into harbour for the winter. Sandwich was very sharply criticised by the inevitable landsman critic on his return for not having made an attempt at this squadron, but his own justification of his caution seems sound[2], and even Harman —who did not return to the fleet from the chase—does not seem to have expected the main fleet to have followed him.

Had the fleet, however, been able to stay out longer, they might have met the main body of the Dutch fleet which did not come to anchor[3] till the 24th, being then not more than 80 sail and very weather-beaten : it is not surprising that the Dutch thought that " the English intended nothing less than a Fight, when they saw so fair an occasion to make a Rich Booty without it[4]." A less cautious and more enterprising leader

[1] *Rawl. MSS.* A. 468 and *S. P. Dom. Chas. II*, CXXXII. ff. 83 and 85. In these two encounters the English lost three captains— Lambert and Langhorne and the Captain of the *Hector*.

[2] " To engage ships promiscuously in the night when neither friend nor foe can be distinguished, may occasion God knows how great damage to a Fleete of 150 sayle and upwards as we all were. Before daylight they would have been in port or have led us ashore to ye ruine of the whole Fleete if wee had persued....It may be remembered wee came ill manned out of Sould Bay, since that wee had 3000 prisoners to guard and theire ships taken manned out of us. And if wee had come to engage wee must have taken men out of the Prizes and destroyed them." (The *Royal James* did so to a 40 gun prize without orders, expecting an engagement.) *Rawl. MSS.* A. 468.

[3] At Goree.

[4] *Life of Tromp*, p. 319.

than Sandwich might have refused to be overcome by
unavoidable difficulties[1], sent home his prizes as weakly
manned as possible, and kept at sea with the rest of
his fleet with the object of engaging the shattered
Dutch fleet at all costs : a decisive blow at that time
might easily have still further weakened the Dutch
prestige and morale, have proved a strong argument in
the winter negotiations, have checked the French alliance with Holland, and possibly have ended the war.

The Dutch were more persistent in their endeavours
to come to some decisive action and on October 11th,
despite continued bad weather, De Ruyter sailed from
the Texel with a fleet of 90 sail of men-of-war. He
cruised at the mouth of the Thames for two or three
weeks, holding a more or less effectual blockade; but with
that insult to the British ' Dominion of the Seas ' he
satisfied himself. " The Dutch have sometimes alarmed
us," writes one Captain Titus, from Margate, " but
never made us a visit. The Body of theire Fleet hath
all this time rode betwixt the Long-Sands Reach and
North Sand Head ; and now and then they send some
shipps on the back of the Goodwins southwards and
sometimes into this Rode. But from hence they have
been Terrified by fower old Dismall Honey-combd Gunns,
w[ch] every time they were shott of more endangered the
gunners than them. They have now left the Coast[2]."

---

[1] Coventry to Arlington : " hopes the fleet is at sea, but unless
the victualler sends supplies they cannot remain long, so that if De
Witt stay any time in Norway, they will be obliged to come back
and lose the opportunity." *Cal. S. P. Dom.* September 2nd, 1665.
Sandwich, however, gives bad weather and prizes as his chief reason
for return.

[2] *Carte MSS.* 223. f. 293.

Meanwhile sickness was ravaging the Dutch. It was estimated that there were 970 sick in the fleet[1], and the number ever increasing. In light of this, the approaching winter, and the fact that the English showed no sign of coming out, it was decided to return to Holland, and on November 1st the fleet set sail eastward. With their departure home ended the naval movements of the year.

In the meantime England was under the spell of that 'visitation' that, for a time, all but paralysed her life. The 'Great Plague' that, during the previous year, had been sapping the very root of Holland's mercantile and naval power, now passed into England. Despite official precautions it crept into England along the lines of the North Sea trade. It first appeared in the East Coast towns and London, and gradually oozed, like a sluggish, deadly tide, westward over England, inevitable, unconquerable.

1666. The War. Plague.

The Navy, however, partly by sheer good fortune, and partly by precautions induced as much by panic as by wisdom, suffered far less than might have been expected, than did the Dutch fleet. This was in part due to the fact that during the worst period of the visitation the greater number of the ships were laid up in harbour unmanned, while the remainder were rigorously kept away from all contact with sources of possible infection. Rather than risk Plague, ships would go without full stores or complement. We hear, for instance, that " several captains refuse to receive clothes, though in great want, for fear of infection[2] " ;

---

[1] *Life of Tromp*, p. 321.
[2] *Cal. S. P. Dom.* October 12th. 1665.

also of "sicke men that are recovered" lying before
the doors of the Navy Office day and night, because,
" having been on shore, the captains won't receive
them on board[1]." Thus for the most part the ships
remained singularly free from the sickness, in striking
contrast to the Dutch—the latter estimated that in
De Ruyter's fleet off the Thames, besides 140 dead and
355 returned sick to Holland, there were at least 970
men sick[2]. There were, of course, exceptions to the
English good fortune: a noteworthy case is that of the
Convertine, a small fourth-rate ship carrying 140 men,
which, in the course of a voyage to Gothenburg, lost 47
men dead, and at her destination had to put 38 ashore
besides 10 other sick who stayed on board[3]. The
Dutch idea that the English were " debarred by a
raging and pestilent distemper from accepting " the
offer of battle[4] was but partially true ; the plague was
but one cause of the lack of men, and, besides men,
stores, victuals, and money itself, were all equally
lacking[5].

The dockyards, however, did not escape from the
pestilence as easily as did the ships, and though in
September Coventry could be grateful that " the yards
have escaped in this very great contagion[6]," yet as
time went on they began to lose their immunity. At
Deptford, Woolwich and Harwich the death-roll was
heavy. Portsmouth remained long untouched—" a

[1] Pepys' *Diary*, September 30th, 1665.
[2] *Life of Tromp*, p.321.
[3] *Cal. S. P. Dom.* December 25th, 1665.
[4] *Life of Tromp*, p. 324.
[5] Cf. List of Shortages, *Carte MSS.* 74, f. 234
[6] *Cal. S. P. Dom.* September 11th, 1665.

strange mercy[1] "—but in the spring of '66 the plague
reached there too, though in a less virulent form.
Thus, further to hinder the supply of victuals and stores,
there was added to the existing lack of money a lack
of men. Beer, almost the most troublesome item of
naval victualling, threatened to be shorter in supply
than ever ; it was reported " on account of the sickness
most of the brewers who supply the Navy have discon-
tinued brewing, and others do not brew half the
quantity[2]." From Gosport comes a typical wail that
" workmen are dispersed, some dead, others shut up,
and others gone away.... Until it please God to remove
the visitation ' the work ' cannot possibly go forward[3]."
The fact that at Portsmouth itself the plague never
got absolutely out of hand was very probably in no
little measure due to the scientific precautions devised
by the energetic Commissioner Middleton when he
enforced the isolation of some of the carpenters and
other dock workers in a kind of quarantine ship, the
Little Francis : " the men are to stay on board it,
to wash themselves and their clothes, and burn rosin
and brimstone for 14 days before they are admitted to
the yard[4]."

In view of this added difficulty in the way of victualling it is surprising to find insufficient
Victuals.   victuals and stores the subject of far
fewer complaints during 1666 than during the previous

---

[1] *Cal. S. P. Dom.* October 12th, 1665.   One physician, no lover of
Portsmouth it would appear, explains it thus : " the air of Portsmouth
is naturally so pernicious to man that the man whose body is able to be
supported in this air is plague free." (*Cal. S. P. Dom.* April 9th, 1666.)

[2] *Ibid.* December 25th, 1665.

[3] *Ibid.* April 24th, 1666.   [4] *Ibid.* April 22nd, 1666.

years. The improvement may be traced very largely
to Samuel Pepys.

As we have already seen, dissatisfaction with the
existing arrangements for victualling was widespread ;
it was recognised that they were hopelessly inadequate :
and, before the end of the summer of 1665, the Duke
of York had proposed that " before the time for the
declaration of victuals comes, some men, diligent and
able in purse, should be joined with the victualler, it
being too much for any one man's purse[1]." A few days
later the King expressed the same desire, also suggesting
that " undertakers be employed in the several ports[2]."
To find men willing to share the thankless work with
Gauden was a difficult, if not hopeless, task. The whole
question was referred to Pepys for enquiry, and his
enquiries impressed him with the truth of " the want
of victuals being the whole overthrow of this yeare
both at sea, and now at the Nore here and Portsmouth
where the fleete lies[3]." Early in October he tendered
his report. Partnership with Gauden had been refused
by those most fitted for it, and the alternative remaining was the appointment of local surveyors of victuals
at each port to check, examine and report. Pepys'
suggestion met with complete approval, " no more
said upon it than a most thorough consent to every
word was said, and directed, that it be pursued and
practised[3]." His personal offer was accepted, and on
October 27th he was appointed Surveyor-General at a
salary of £300 a year. He set about—not over-hastily

[1] *Cal. S. P. Dom.* August 30th, 1665.
[2] *Ibid.* September 7th.
[3] Pepys' *Diary,* October 24th.

—drawing up instructions for his subordinates, thereby
displaying to himself his own ignorance of the subject :
" I am ashamed I should go about concerning myself
in a business which I understand so very very little
of[1]." He was, however, not the man to be hindered
by previous ignorance, and these instructions appear
to have been fairly successful. The State Papers,
which in 1665 teem with complaints about insufficient
victuals, are, during 1666, with few exceptions silent.
In July the Duke of York, who had, however, not been
at sea with the fleet, told Pepys that his victualling
account " was a good account, and that the business of
the victualling was much in a better condition than it
was last yeare[2]." The most striking exception to this
general satisfaction was the letters from the Generals
at sea a month later, in which they, " in very plain and
sharp and menacing terms," complained of short supplies, and " did lay their not going or too soon returning
from the Dutch coast, this next bout, to the want of
victuals[3]." Pepys was certain there was " no reason for
it," and it is evident that the fault lay less with excessive detail and officialdom on the part of the Navy Office
—the admirals complained " that instead of supplies
only accounts are sent[4] "—than with lack of detail and
excess of bluster on the part of the admirals : " there
hath never," writes Sir Wm. Coventry in reply to the
complaints, " been any demand made or any account
stated sent us, which shewed what was wanting, but

---

[1] Pepys' *Diary*, December 1st, 1665,
[2] *Ibid.* July 26th, 1666.
[3] *Ibid.* August 26th, 27th, 28th, 29th, 1666.
[4] *Rawl. MSS.* A. 174, f. 200.

y[e] demands alwayes were to send victual for the Fleet to compleat till such a time.... We had no ground upon which to compute a further supply[1]." There is extant an interesting table of abstracts of the victualling orders and their treatment by the Navy Office which shows very clearly the businesslike methods that characterised the Navy Office in this connection[2].

" 12th October, 1665. Duke orders 35,000 men's victuals for y[e] yeare.

9th October. D. directs at what port it is to be provided at.

14th May, 1666. Admiralls desire hasteing of victuals to them and keeping up y[e] fleete with 4 months victuals.

14th October, 1665. Warrant by Navy Office to Victualler to goe in hand with providing it.

11th October. Let. from Navy Office to Victualler giving same directions.

17th May, 1666. Victualler had pressing let. from Nav. Office to that purpose.

17th May. Nav. Office tells them so and that the want of men in the victualling ships is the only hindrance."

The fact that Pepys was so far successful in dealing with the question of the victualling offers pretty convincing proof of his administrative capabilities, for the prime difficulty of lack of money was, if anything, more persistent and overwhelming in '66 than previously. The national morale had been further shaken by the plague, and official

Money.

[1] Rawl. MSS. A. 174, f. 211
[2] Ibid A. 174. f. 233.

business suffered both by omission and commission :
" nobody minding the publique, but everybody himself
and his lusts[1]." " Want of money in the Navy puts
everything out of order. Men grow mutinous ; and
nobody here to mind the business of the Navy but
myself," writes Pepys[2]. The debts of the Navy were
more cumbersome than ever, and early in 1666, " to
answer a certain expense and debt of £2,300,000[3],"
there was barely £1,500,000, including the Government
grant of 1¼ million ; a deficit of over £800,000. In
October of the same year the deficit was estimated at
£930,000[4]—somewhat of a contrast to the £852,000
estimate of 1664 which " God knows " was " only a
scare to the Parliament, to make them give the more
money[5]."

It was in the face of difficulties such as these that
the preparations for the dispatch of the fleet progressed
during the spring of 1666. The lack of trust in government pay once again hindered the supply both of men
and ships. Merchants had almost to be forced before
they would hire out their ships for the King's service,
and the very close similarity between the proposed
and the ' agreed ' price of hire shows how purely
formal was the ' bargaining[6].' While to meet the old

---

[1] Pepys' *Diary*, October 15th, 1665.   [2] *Ibid.* October 31st.
[3] *Ibid.* February 19th, 1666 : for details cf. *Pepysian MSS.* 2589,
pp. 1–3.
[4] *Pepysian MSS.* 2589, p. 13.   [5] *Diary*, November 25th, 1664.
[6] Cf. List of Hired Merchantmen and prices : *Rawl. MSS.* A. 195,
ff. 82–4. In the autumn of '65 and the spring of '66, 23 merchantmen
of between 3 and 500 tons were hired at an average rate of 9s. 6d.
per ton. Also of smaller vessels between 50 and 100 tons there
were hired, in October three, in November five, in January three,
and in February seven.

grievance of overdue pay and to facilitate manning, the King was forced to ask the East India Company for a loan of "£50,000 with all speed on good security to pay off the arrears of seamen, without which it will be impossible for the fleet to put to sea[1]."

Although the evil effects to health, morale, and discipline, of a delay in harbour were only too well known—"the sickness increases and the ships are pestered with women; there are as many petticoats as breeches on board some of them and that for weeks together[2]"—it was not until May 29th that Prince Rupert and the Duke of Albemarle arrived in the Downs in command of a fleet of 80 sail exclusive of small craft. Rupert and Albemarle were to be in joint command, despite Rupert's dislike to sharing the command and his unpopularity as a leader. Lord Sandwich was now on an embassy to Spain until a scandal concerning the embezzlement of certain rich Dutch prizes had passed over. The question of the advisability of dividing the command of the fleet between two joint commanders was to be brought forward very forcibly by the coming events.

In the meantime, at the beginning of the year, Louis XIV had declared war on England, and for months had been preparing a fleet, at Toulon and Rochelle, which was to unite with De Ruyter and crush England's naval power. On the same day that Albemarle and Rupert had joined the fleet, a rumour, apparently more or less authenticated, reached London to the effect that the united French fleet under

Division of the Fleet.

---

[1] *Cal. S. P. Dom.* April 19th, 1666.
[2] *Ibid.*

Beaufort was already at the mouth of the Channel.
At the time, it was believed that the Dutch fleet was
still in harbour, and while the main fleet under Albemarle was to stay and watch them, Rupert, with 20
ships, was detached to go down the Channel to meet the
French[1]. " A position like that of the English fleet,"
says Mahan[2], " threatened with an attack from two
quarters, presents one of the subtlest temptations to a
commander " : that of dividing his forces ; which,
" unless in the possession of overwhelming force, is an
error, exposing both divisions to be beaten separately."
That statement, however, makes the very common
omission of disregarding the fact that, when the order
was given, the Dutch were believed to be in harbour and
likely enough to remain there while the English were
united and prepared : consequently if Albemarle had
gone with his whole fleet to meet the French he would
have left the Thames open to De Ruyter, and, con-
versely, with all the fleet concentrated against the
Dutch, Portsmouth and the Isle of Wight would have
been exposed to Beaufort.   The division was not a fault
" because it was a necessity[3]."   That this fact was not
unrealised is shown by the promptitude with which,
on receipt of " certaine intelligence that the Dutch Fleet
is come forth," the King gave order " that his fleet
should forthwith bee united " and that Rupert and
Albemarle should meet each other : " pray hasten all

[1] For official narratives concerning the division of the fleet, by
Rupert and by Albemarle, with Coventry's notes, cf. *Brit. Mus. Add.
MSS.* 32,094, ff. 196–204.

[2] Captain A. T. Mahan, *Influence of Sea Power upon History*, p. 118.

[3] Corbett, *Principles of Maritime Strategy*, p. 137.

you can " the orders finish[1]. The true authorship of
the order for division has been the subject of many
conflicting statements. King Charles is on the whole
the most popular scapegoat, but Albemarle and Clarendon have their accusers. Pepys, on the authority of
Sir William Coventry, tells a story about it which at
least equals the others in authoritativeness, and betters
them in point of probability : it rings true of the petty
jealousies which infested the post of Admiral of the
fleet. After saying "that the proposition did first
come from the fleete,...and that there was nothing in
the whole business which was not done with the full
consent and advice of the Duke of Albemarle," "he
did adde (as the Catholiques call *le secret de la Masse*),
that Sir Edward Spragge—who had even in Sir Christopher Myngs's time put in to be the great favourite of
the Prince, but much more now had a mind to be the
great man with him, and to that end had a mind to
have the Prince at a distance from the Duke of Albemarle, that they might be doing something alone—did,
as he believed, put on this business of dividing the
fleete, and that thence it came[2]."

However that may have been, the order to rejoin
reached Rupert too late to enable him to
do more than check the evils done by
division. In the meantime De Ruyter
with a fleet of about 90 sail had come to sea,
and when, early on the morning of June 1st, the
wind, which had been easterly, changed to south-west,

The 4 Days'
Fight. June
1st—4th, 1666.

[1] *Adm. Libr. MS. 24, Duke of York's Letters,* " May 30th, 1666,
12 at night."
[2] Pepys' *Diary,* June 24th, 1666.

he cast anchor about midway between the North Foreland and Dunkirk.   Monk was off the North Foreland
with the greater part of the English fleet numbering
60 sail.   Early the same morning they had weighed
with the flood and were standing for Harwich when
news came of the Dutch.   " About 7 aclocke our scouts
gave ye signall, wch was leting ye top gallan sailes fly
and fireing 2 or 3 guns to let us know they discovered
the enemies fleet to the leeward[1]."   Two hours later it
became known for certain that they were the main
Dutch fleet.   A council of war was immediately called,
at which, largely through the determination of the Duke,
it was decided to attack in the hope that the advantage of the wind and surprise (the Dutch were still at
anchor) would compensate for the handicap of numbers.
After the event Sir John Harman, Rear-Admiral of the
Blue, told Pepys that " at the Council of War before the
fight, it was against his reason to begin the fight then,
and the reasons of most sober men there[2]."   The
decision, or at least the manner of it, seems to have
caused considerable ill-feeling : Penn tells of the commanders saying " that they durst not oppose it at
the Council of War, for fear of being called cowards,
though it was wholly against their judgement to fight

---

[1] *Carte MSS.* 72, f. 37.   The following account is based mainly on
a *Narrative from on board the Royall Charles, Carte MSS.* 72, ff. 37–8 ;
Let. from a French eyewitness, *Carte MSS.* 72, f. 36 ; Allin's *Journal,
Tanner MSS.* 296 ; *Narratives* of Rupert and Albemarle, *Brit. Mus.
Add. MSS.* 32,094, ff. 196–204 ; also *A true Narrative*, publ. by Th.
Newcomb, 1666 ; *Description Exacte*, pp. 142–5, publ. Amsterdam,
1668 ; *Life of Tromp*, pp. 37–40 ; and, of modern authorities, Mahan,
op. cit. pp. 119–23, and Clowes, *op. cit.* II. pp. 169–77.

[2] Pepys' *Diary*, June 11th, 1666.

that day with the disproportion of force[1]." The main objection to giving battle, apart from the disparity of numbers, was that being to the windward was a real handicap. "Le meme vent qui leur estoit favorable pour venir sur nous," says a Dutch account, " estoit si violent qu'ils ne pouvoient pas bien se servir de leur artillerie de Flancs, et facilitoit le moyen au nostres d'employer avec beaucoup d'effect leur batteries basses[2]." Coventry, however, makes note of one very sound justification of the Duke's action—that some of the heavier ships, being slow sailers, " could not avoid fighting[3]." Moreover, the disparity of force was more apparent than real, the English having the advantage in size and guns in proportion to numbers.

At 11 o'clock the Duke gave signal to draw into line of battle, and the fleet stood for the Dutch June 1st. in column. The Dutch in the meantime lay at anchor in a somewhat disordered array : their rear, under Tromp, lay to the S.E. of the centre under De Ruyter, and so considerably to the windward of him ; the van under Evertsen to the N.N.W., and so still further to the leeward of Tromp than was De Ruyter. The wind was high and rising still higher from the S.S.W., and, the sea being lumpy, the Dutch expected the Duke to anchor also ; his attack was a complete surprise: it happened, wrote a Dutch captain, " whilst we were busy in unmooring, and had our Anchors yet but half up ; we were forced to cut our cables in all haste[4]." The surprise, however, proved of but little advantage to the English. Apparently no

[1] Pepys' *Diary*, July 4th, 1666.   [2] *Description Exacte*, p. 142.
[3] *Brit. Mus. Add. MSS.* 32,094, f. 196.   [4] *Life of Tromp*, p. 327.

attempt was made to send fireships among the tempo-
rarily helpless Dutch ships. The column in which the
Duke had chosen to advance was at any time a most
difficult formation to retain and especially so in such
weather ; consequently, by the time he came in touch
with the furthest windward of the Dutch—Tromp's
squadron—the line was in some disorder : the *Swiftsure*
and six or seven of the head of the van being too far
to the windward to engage effectively, and the rear
being somewhat straggling.

As soon as the remainder of the van and the centre
came in touch with Tromp, Albemarle put up his helm and
ran down with the Dutch rear to the S.E. hotly engaged.
The Dutch centre and van, however, being thus left to
the N.N.E. of the English, tacked to the S.W. and
gained the weather-gauge. At the same time a number
of the larger of the English ships had borne away to
the leeward of the Duke, " and not only kept us exposed
to yᵉ enemies shot but to their owne by fireing through
and over us to yᵉ enemie[1]."

After nearly three hours' stiff fighting Albemarle
tacked back to the N.W. Many of his ships must have
already suffered fairly heavily : on his own ship, the
Royal Charles, the " sailes were torne to yᵉ yards in
peeces, and both flag and ensigne shot downe[2]." The
English tacked simultaneously so that the rear became
the van, and their course took them straight into the
midst of the Dutch centre and van under De Ruyter
and Evertsen, which had up to that time been but
slightly engaged. Had the Duke had one fraction of

[1] *Carte MSS.* 72, f. 36.
[2] *Ibid.*

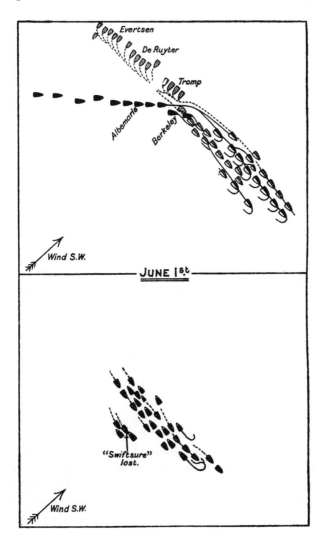

the genius for tactics with which he has been credited, it would be incomprehensible that, having " attacked a vastly superior force in such a way that only part of it could come into action[1]," he should deliberately, after a severe encounter with that part, have turned to meet and engage with the yet fresh remainder. Nevertheless, by tacking simultaneously and to the N.W. as he did, he made certain that his fleet should bear the very fullest brunt of the Dutch attack. The results were somewhat disastrous. The movement threw the new van into confusion and separated Sir William Berkeley still more from the main body : it brought De Ruyter's fresh ships to the windward and left Tromp to the leeward. The English were between two fires, and both to the leeward and the windward some of their ships were isolated, among the latter, in addition to the *Swiftsure*, flying Berkeley's flag, was the *Henry* flying the flag of Rear-Admiral Sir John Harman. Both these admirals put up an heroic fight. The former, though boarded simultaneously from every side, his ship disabled and half his men killed, " yet continued fighting almost alone, killed several with his own hand, and would accept no quarter ; till at length, being shot in the throat with a musket ball, he retired into the captain's cabin, where he was found dead, extended at his full length upon a table, almost covered with his own blood." Harman's fight was no less fierce, but more successful. He was set on by three fireships in succession ; from the first he was freed by " the almost incredible exertions of his lieutenant, who, having in the midst of the flames loosed the grappling-irons,

[1] Mahan, *op. cit.* p. 121.

swung back on board his ship unhurt[1] "; the second
set the sails on fire and caused a panic, only checked by
the Admiral's drawn sword; while the third was sunk
by the ship's guns. Evertsen chose that moment to
offer quarter, but Harman replied with "No, it has not
come to that yet" and a broadside that killed the Dutch
Admiral[1]. Harman was in no further danger, and
succeeded in bringing his ship to Harwich for repairs,
whence he set sail again a day later to rejoin the fleet.
"The undaunted Bravery of that English Rear-Admiral
cannot but be Admired[2]" wrote the Dutch Admirals
in their official report. The losses were by no means
entirely on the English side; besides Admiral Evertsen,
the Dutch had lost several captains and at least three
ships sunk, while both Admiral Tromp and Rear-Admiral
Van Nes were forced to leave their dismasted ships and
hoist their flags on board fresh vessels.

In the meantime Albemarle with the main English
fleet continued on the port tack to the W.N.W., and
after some desultory fighting the two fleets were practically clear of one another by 10 p.m.

After a night of repairing, the English found the
Dutch at daybreak on the port tack and to the windward. Thanks, however, to better seamanship on the
part of his captains the Duke was able soon to obtain
the weather-gauge, and the fleets passed on opposite
tacks, W.N.W. and E.S.E. The English, numbering
44 sail, were in good order, but the Dutch were crowded
and in many cases masked each other's fire. Tromp in
the rear, noticing this, and apparently thinking to

[1] Campbell, *Lives of Admirals*, II. 353–4.
[2] *Life of Tromp*, p. 353.

remedy it, tacked so as to gain the weather of the
English van. It was insubordination, however well

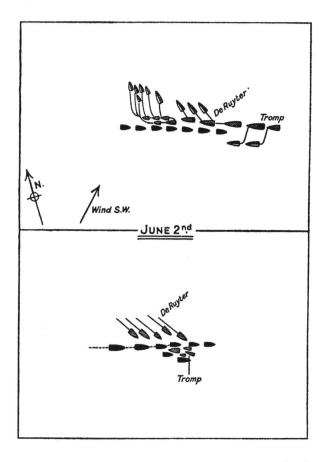

intentioned, and it was made far worse in effect by less
well-intentioned insubordination in the Dutch van,

which, instead of engaging close, stood broad off to the
N. De Ruyter with the centre was forced to do so
also in order to keep his fleet together. In the meantime,
however, " a most horrid noise of both great guns and
muskets " reminded him of the danger in which Tromp,
isolated from his friends and surrounded by the English,
lay[1]. To succour Tromp, De Ruyter came down on
the English on the starboard tack, and they, for fear of
losing the weather-gauge, were compelled to leave
Tromp and continue on their course. Tromp's squadron had suffered heavily ; Vice-Admiral Van der Hulst
had been killed, two ships sunk and three utterly
disabled, Tromp himself once again having to move
his flag.

At the time of the junction between Tromp and De
Ruyter the Dutch were in complete disorder, " all the
ships huddled together like a flock of sheep, so packed
that the English might have surrounded all of them with
their forty ships[2]." Yet Albemarle, having gone about,
appears to have repassed them without making any
serious attack on them, thereby showing a caution in
great contrast to the daring of the previous day.
" Methinks," says a Dutch captain, " he committed
then a strange fault[2]." It is very probable that the
Duke was thinking of the danger which a change of wind
to the N. (the S.W. wind had already dropped almost
to a calm) would bring to his shattered little fleet ; it
is evident also that the discipline in the English fleet
was not all it might have been; consequently, late in
the afternoon, retreat was decided on. "Many of our
shipps being gone, others not doing their duty, and the

<hr>

[1] *Life of Tromp*, p. 355. [2] *Ibid.* p. 347.

Rest much shattered, it was resolved to make a faire
retreate[1]."

The most damaged ships were put in the van, and
" 16 of the greatest ships" were chosen out "to be a
bulwark of the rest and bring up the rear in a breast,
and so he shoved on the other in a line before him[2]."
The retreat was to the W.N.W., and the Dutch followed
in a straggling line without much energy until calm
and nightfall stopped the fight.

The calm lasted till noon on the next day, when a
fresh breeze sprang up from the E. The Duke continued his retreat on the Thames, the Dutch again
following without much display of vigour. About two
hours later Prince Rupert and his squadron of 20 sail
came in sight. " Wee then steered towards the Prince
comforting ourselves wth y[e] thoughts of renewing the
fight by returning on y[e] enemy[3]." About four o'clock,
however, half-a-dozen of the Duke's fleet struck on the
Galloper Shoal. All got off with the exception of the
Royal Prince, and before the other ships could tack to
relieve her she had been surrounded and yielded without a struggle. Probably it was not so much cowardice
as 'nerves' after three days' fighting that was responsible for this incident. The *Royal Prince* was considered
to be the finest ship in the Navy, and Coventry wrote
regretfully : " a little resistance would have preserved
her, and that she was so well able to stand it out. She
was like a castle in the sea, and, I believe, the best ship

---

[1] *Carte MSS.* 72, f. 37; cf. " The Duke had Quite Ruined their
Fleet before y[e] Prince came in if his shipps had don their parts, for
he had but 20 of 57 shipps that stucke to him." *Ibid.*

[2] *Cal. S. P. Dom.* p. xxi.

[3] *Carte MSS.* 72, f. 37.

that ever was built in the world to endure battering; but she is gone and this is an ill subject to be long upon[1]." The Dutch, finding they could not get her off speedily, burnt her. To intercept Rupert, De Ruyter had detached a squadron of over 20, but Rupert, knowing that the Galloper was between them and him, ignored them. There were huge rejoicings on the Duke's fleet to celebrate the reunion. The English decided to renew the action decisively on the following day.

On the morning of the 4th the wind had veered back to S.S.W. again and was blowing hard. The Dutch were almost out of sight at daybreak, but by 8 o'clock the English came up with them and formed up in line, led by Sir Christopher Myngs in the van, " in very good order[2]." Both fleets were now on the starboard tack, the English to the leeward. For two hours the fight ran thus, the English gradually forcing their way into the Dutch line. No less than five 'passes' to and fro were made. Some of the English ships got through to the windward, some remained to the leeward, and gradually all order was lost. The main bodies under De Ruyter and Albemarle retained their positions respectively. In the meantime Myngs with a few ships had headed the Dutch van which was in full pursuit after him. Tromp and the rear had fallen away to leeward and, taking the initiative into his hands more successfully, and so more justifiably than on the previous day, he overhauled the pursuers and brought them back with him to the main action. The main squadrons had, however, been beating to windward,

---

[1] *Cal. S. P. Dom.* 1666, p. xxi.
[2] *Tanner MSS.* 296. Allin's *Journal.*

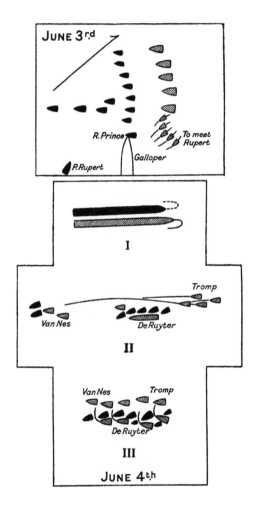

so Tromp found himself to leeward of the English centre. In other words, Albemarle found himself between the Dutch centre and the van and rear, between De Ruyter and Tromp. For a time the situation was critical ; he was surrounded, both his ship and Prince Rupert's were shattered, and ammunition was running short, when De Ruyter made the move which finally broke up the English line. He gave the signal for his squadron to keep away before the wind. This manœuvre took the Dutch windward ships directly through the English centre in a kind of irregular line abreast. It was a shattering blow, but it left the English in the comparative safety of the weather-gauge, for the wind was blowing half a gale. The Dutch " bore away to leeward," writes Allin with an almost audible sigh of relief, " and, glad to part soe, we stood over for the English shoar[1] ": or as the Dutch account has it, " God, after he had so gloriously favoured the Arms of the Victours, was not pleased they should be utterly defeated by the Destruction of their whole Navy, which appeared as unavoidable : For the shattered Remainder of them miraculously escaped by the Favour of a thick Fog[2]."

The fight marks an important development in naval Tactics of 4 Days' Fight. tactics. In it, for the first time, are we able to trace definite and effective tactical manœuvring of squadrons : in it the fight did not commence with manœuvring and end with a *mêlée*. Unavoidably did the lines become confused in the heat of battle, but they always proved capable of reforming. Especially striking is this in the case of

[1] *Tanner MSS.* 296.
[2] *Life of Tromp*, p. 163.

the Dutch, who were confessedly the inferiors of the English both in discipline and handiness ; the manœuvres of their centre and rear squadrons on the first day, Tromp's movements on the fourth day and De Ruyter's breaking through the English so as once more to unite his fleet: it is movements like these, during and after the *mêlée*, which mark the beginning of a new era in naval engagement—an era in which the tactical unit was no longer the ship, but the squadron and the line. The criticism of the Comte de Guiche after witnessing the fight will give some idea of the extent to which the English had developed the new system. " Rien n'égale le bel Ordre et la Discipline des Anglois ; que jamais Ligne n'a été tirée plus droite, que celle que leurs Vaissaux forme, que, lors qu'on en approche, il faut les tous essuier...l'on peut dire, qu'ils vaut bien mieux entrer dans une Flotte d'Angleterre, que de passer auprès ; et bien mieux passer auprès d'une Flotte Hollandoise, que se meler au travers, si elle combat comme elle fit pour lors ; ce qui ne vient que de la lâcheté de quelques-uns, qui s'épaulent tant qu'ils peuvent de leurs camarades. A la vérité," he concluded, "l'Ordre Admirable de leur Armée doit toujours être imité; et pour moi, je sais bien que si j'étois dans le Service de Mer et que je commandasse des Vaissaux du Roi, je songerois à battre les Anglois par leur propre Manière, et non pas avec celle des Hollandois et de nous autres, qui est du vouloir aborder[1]."

The Dutch had won the battle, but it was a Pyrrhic victory; they had lost seven or eight ships, many more utterly shattered ; some 2000 men

[1] *Memoires d'Estrades Comte de Guiche*, pp. 251-2, 266.

killed and wounded; and three flag officers killed, including Evertsen, one of their finest leaders. And that in spite of the fact that for most of the fight they had had the advantage in numbers of nearly two to one. Naturally, the English losses were heavier. Berkeley and Myngs killed, Ayscue a captive in Holland; 12 commanders killed; eight ships lost to the Dutch, including ships of 62, 58, 54 and 40 guns; at least 12 ships sunk or burnt, including the *Royal Prince*; and perhaps 5000 casualties and 3000 prisoners[1].

The fact that the defeat was not a dishonourable one, however, did not prevent the outburst of a perfect fury of recrimination.

Popular feeling.

The unpleasant fact remained that at the end of the battle the Dutch had been left in command of the sea. The gossip with which Pepys fills his *Diary* at this time is of the universal disgust. " Pierce the surgeon, who is lately come from the fleete, tells me that all the commanders, officers and even the common seamen do condemn every part of the late conduct of the Duke of Albemarle: both in his fighting at all, in his manner of fighting, running among them in his retreat, and running the ships on ground; so as nothing can be worse spoken of. Sir G. Carteret...tells me, as I hear from everyone else, that the management in the late fight was bad from top to bottom....There is nothing but discontent among the officers; and all the old experienced men are slighted[2]." Nor was the recrimination

---

[1] *Carte MSS.* 72, f. 70; *Rawl. MSS.* A. 191, f. 108 and Clowes, *op. cit.* II. 277.

[2] Pepys' *Diary*, June 7th, 10th, 1666.

at all one-sided : the Duke professed equal disgust with
his subordinates, and writes " that he never fought
with worse officers in his life, not above twenty of
them behaving themselves like men[1]." The justice of
all these complaints is best proved by the narrative
of the battle itself, and the above-quoted criticism by
the Comte de Guiche offers a suggestive comment on the
whole question.

The general discontent had one salutary effect at
least : there was no exception to the general unanimity
of the opinion that the fleet must get to sea again at
the very first opportunity. As early as the 8th and
9th of June, when as yet only vague accounts of the
battle were to hand, the Navy Commissioners were
arranging and discussing concerning "the haste
requisite to be made in getting the fleete out again, and
the manner of doing it[2]." The business of manning
and victualling was pressed forward with the utmost
energy. For once after a battle the victualling had not
been the subject of complaint, had not been made the
universal scapegoat. There is no doubt that Pepys in
his position as Surveyor must have contributed largely
to the attainment of this satisfactory result, and, as his
Diary shows, he now had a busy time in arranging for
the renewal of supplies. The provision of men was,
however, a more difficult matter, and with increased
urgency came increased licence. Desertion was rife,
every day men came " flocking from the Fleete[3]," and
the provision of substitutes was a difficult problem.
More than ever did the press-gang become no respecter

[1] Pepys' *Diary*, June 7th, 10th, 1666.
[2] *Ibid.* June 9th.   [3] *Ibid.* June 11th.

of persons : " Even our owne men that are at the
Office, and the boats that carry us," writes Pepys, "so
that it is now become impossible to have so much as a
letter carried from place to place, or any message done
for us : nay, out of the Victualling ships full loaden
to go down to the fleete, and out of the vessels of
the Officers of the Ordnance, they press men....
It is a pretty thing to observe that both there (Broad
Street) and everywhere else, a man shall see many
women nowadays of mean sort in the streets, but no
men ; men being so afeard of the press[1]."

An additional incentive to a speedy setting forth of
the fleet was the fear of a French invasion. The Dutch
had come to sea again by the 28th of June, and many
rumours of co-operation between them and the French
were current, of French soldiers waiting on the coast
to be transported, of stores of shovels, pickaxes, wheelbarrows ready to work against English forts, of schemes
of invasion so wonderful as to draw even from Pepys
the epithet " ridiculous conceit."

By July 13th the English fleet was ready to sail,
The new " but for the carrying of the two or three
fleet. new ships, which will keepe them a day or
two or three more[2]." Six days later they sailed from
the Thames for the Gunfleet, leaving Penn behind to
see to the manning of the few ships remaining. Albemarle and Rupert were once again in command, but
some changes had been necessary in the subordinate
commands. The van, the *White* squadron, was under
Sir Thomas Allin, with Tyddeman as vice and Utber

---

[1] Pepys' *Diary*, June 31st, July 6th, *et passim*.
[2] *Ibid.* July 13th.

as rear admirals ; the centre, *Red*, was under Albemarle and Rupert, who were both on the *Royal Charles*
flagship, Jordan vice and Holmes rear admirals ; the
rear, *Blue*, under Sir Jeremy Smith, with Spragge as
vice and Kempthorne as rear admirals. The fleet
seems to have numbered 90 ships of the line and about
17 fireships[1]. The Dutch numbered 98 warships and
20 fireships. It was divided into three squadrons ;
the van under Jan Evertsen and Tjercke Hiddes de
Vries, the centre under De Ruyter, the rear under Tromp
and Van Meppel.

Even at the present time the way out of the Thames
estuary, along the complicated channels past countless
shoals and sand-banks, is a severe test not only of
seamanship but also of local knowledge of sands and
currents ; but in the 17th century the problem of getting
a large fleet of sailing ships safely out to sea was one
fraught with danger, and at no time more so than on
this occasion. The point of the problem was that it
was necessary that either the whole fleet or none of it
should come out of the river. De Ruyter was known
to be cruising off the Naze, and if one part of the fleet
got clear of the sands alone, it would be in danger
of piecemeal destruction by the Dutch, while at the
same time a return into the Channel would be a very
dangerous proceeding. The chart[2] will explain the situation. Rather than risk the dangers of the numerous
little shoals lying at the head of Black Deep the English

---

[1] Contemporary accounts vary largely, as also modern deduc-
tions : cf. Clowes, *op. cit.* II. 279, " 81 ships," and Hannay, *op. cit.*
I. 372, " 92 ships."
[2] At end of volume.

Admirals had decided to take the fleet out by the Swin
channel. But to get safely through the channel to the
open sea, both an ebb tide and a favourable wind were
necessary : moreover, the great length of the column—
perhaps as much as ten miles—added to the difficulty
of the move. On the 19th the fleet reached as far as
the Middle Ground, where, the wind being too much in
the north for further progress, they anchored. For
two days they " couldn't get out for the sands[1]," or
rather, for the wind. At length on the 22nd the wind
shifted a little to the west, and the fleet got under weigh.
The same evening they anchored in the Gunfleet.

Early on the morning of the 25th the English fleet
weighed and bore down on the Dutch in
line abreast to the S.E. The wind was
N.E. but very light and the fleets drew
near but slowly. Probably owing largely to the lightness
of the wind, which would make the heavier ships somewhat unhandy[2], the English line was nothing like so
well kept as it had been in the previous battle when it
had drawn forth so much admiration. " Our peopl
were very slow to gett into a lyne, and some never did,"
wrote Allin, " but shot thorow severall of our ships
contrary to a strict order[3]." The Dutch line was still
worse formed, and was more of a crescent than a

St James'
Fight, July
25th, 1666.

---

[1] *Carte MSS.* 72, f. 41.

[2] Hannay, *op. cit.* I. 373, tells an amusing story of a small yacht
of Prince Rupert's, which on the following day, the wind having
dropped still further, was sent out to mock De Ruyter, stationed
herself opposite the stern of the Dutch flagship and for two hours
pelted away with two little ornamental pop-guns, the huge Dutch
man-of-war being helpless for lack of wind.

[3] *Tanner MSS.* 296. Allin's *Journal.*

straight line. Consequently, when the English bore
up on approaching the Dutch, some ships and some
parts of the line came into action before others. The
van was the first engaged. "We fell to fighting betweene
9 and 10," writes Allin, Admiral of the White. " Sir
Tho. Tyddeman fought bravely upon his party although
the St. George and Ann did him noe service and the
Old James did us as little. The Richard and Martha
went away from us, the Reare Admiral's divisions did us
little helpe. We fell in close and in 4 houres time put
them to beare from us[1]." This virtual desertion on the
part of ships in action had been not one of the least
complaints after the previous battle, and the Duke of
York had ordered that there should in future be an
enquiry into all cases of ships returning to port during
an action, " that soe hereafter it may be looked on as a
certaine thing that every man who returns from y[e]
fleet in an engagement must give an account in publique
of the reasons induceing him to it[2]." This order would
seem to have had some effect, for, besides these cases
mentioned by Allin, there appears to have been very
little complaint of desertions after this fight.

In the meantime the two centres had engaged and
there was some savage fighting. The Admirals on both
sides had to move their flags, the *Royal Charles* being
forced to fall out of the line to refit, and the *Zeven
Proviniën*, De Ruyter's flagship, being completely dismasted in a close tussle with Sir Robert Holmes on the
Henry—which itself fell permanently out of the line.
Between 2 and 3 p.m. the Dutch began to give

---

[1] *Tanner MSS.* 296, Allin's *Journal.*
[2] *Adm. Libr. MS.* 24, *Duke of York's Letters,* July 9th, 1666.

way, and the van and centre made towards the Dutch coast, followed by the English.

In the rear the fight had been more even and pro- longed. Accounts vary considerably as to the course of the action there. Tromp appears to have fought with his usual persistence and individualism. In the first encounter he and Meppel gained somewhat the advantage over the Blue squadron—including the destruction of a 64-gun ship, the *Resolution*—and so far from giving way as their van and centre were doing, they forced Smith to give back. As a result, this part of the action became separated from the main battle : and gradually as De Ruyter gave way further to the leeward the struggle between Tromp and Smith became further and further separated until they were lost sight of by the rest of the combatants. As night came on the main fleets drifted slowly towards the Dutch coast, fighting desultorily, leaving Tromp and Smith hammering at each other well into the night up towards the English coast. The following day opened with an almost complete calm, and only in the afternoon did a wind arise which enabled the Dutch to continue their retreat covered by 20 ships under Admiral Bancker. The same evening they came to anchor off Flushing, protected from the English by shoals[1]. In the meantime Tromp was also in retreat from Smith. In the evening of the 26th the fleet off Flushing heard distant firing and stood out to intercept the Dutch squadron ; but in the night Smith, through fear of the shallow water, lost touch with Tromp, and on the following day the latter slipped

---

[1] Cf chart at end of volume.

in between the shore and the main body of the English. The latter pursued until they found themselves in shallow water, when they were forced to desist. Thus was lost another opportunity of dealing a shattering blow at the Dutch navy. In the late battle, though the Dutch had lost four flag officers—Jan Evertsen, Tjercke Hiddes de Vries, Rudolf Coenders and Govert 'T Hoen—and perhaps 20 ships, the English had only taken four prizes, and lost one ship; here was an opportunity of gaining some more solid glory; the chance of cutting off, of capturing perhaps, the 30 battered ships under Tromp's command. The failure brought a torrent of abuse on Sir Jeremy Smith's head, he being accused of cowardice and incompetence at the very least. The official enquiry into the matter acquitted him, however, of all but a slight excess of caution : " he yielded too easily to the opinion of his pilot, without consulting those of the other ships, muzzled his ship, and thus obliged the squadron to do the same, and so the enemy, which might have been driven into the body of the King's fleet, then returning from the pursuit, was allowed to escape[1]."

The wildest rumours were current in England concerning the victory, and it was long before the accurate facts became public. The following paper belonging to Pepys is a fair example of the more sober of the ' authentic ' accounts that were current after every naval battle. It is endorsed by Pepys, " a copy of what was reade in ye pulpitt at Bow."

---

[1] *Cal. S. P. Dom.* November 3rd, 1666.

"*July* 29*th,* 1666.

" The Dutch totally routed.

14 ships taken.

26 burnt and sunk.

2 flagg shipps taken and out of them 1200 men and what else they would, then sunk them.

Taken in all 6000 men.

Our Shipps have blocked up the Zealanders in Flushing and ride before them.

The Dutch fleete have got into the Texell, we ride before the same.

The Lord Mayor ordereth thanks to be given this forenoone throughout the city[1]."

The Dutch were, for the time being, demoralised. De Ruyter came in raging against the disgrace of the retreat; "severall of my captains and particularly Tromp shall answer for it[2]," he is reported to have said. On his own ship he had lost 200 men, and " the rest tellement intimidé y^t if hee had received another charge hee should not have had a man to fyre a gun, all being resolved to leap overboard and shift for themselves[2]." The whole of Holland was in a panic; the appearance of the English fleet off Scheveling caused tremendous fright at the Hague, and the most amazing rumours concerning invasion became rife.

This was a state of mind that the English did their best to foster. The fleet made a triumphal progress up the entire coast of Holland, capturing ships, scaring the coast towns; on the 6th they were in sight of the Texel. On the 7th, having heard from a Dutch renegade

[1] *Rawl. MSS.* A. 195, f. 202.
[2] *Carte MSS.* 72, ff. 56–7.

of a large fleet of Indiamen lying between Vlieland and
the mainland, a plan for destroying it was evolved at a
council of war. Sir Robert Holmes was to take charge
of a squadron of nine low-rate ships, besides a dozen
fireships and small craft, and to be given 900 men
picked proportionately, 100 from each division of the
fleet: the party to land on Vlie Island and burn and
destroy all that they could, both stores on the island
and ships in the harbour. On the 8th the remainder of
the fleet was drawn up in a line N.E. and S.W. from the
N. of Vlie towards the Texel and at 8 a.m. the expedition stood away towards the shore. After some delay
owing to contrary winds Holmes took his squadron
into Ter Schelling roads on the 9th and there attacked
over 160 merchant ships and two men-of-war lying at
anchor. That afternoon, writes Allin, " we saw divers
smoaks arise upon the land which made us judge that
Sir Robt. Holmes was prosperous[1]." Strict orders had
been given to the men to destroy and not to plunder :
to such effect were the orders obeyed that at least 150
Dutch ships were burnt and utterly destroyed, only some
10 or 11 escaping up a creek. On the following day
the English landed on the island, burnt and sacked the
town—Brandaris—and numerous storehouses. Early
on the 11th, after an attempt on Vlie Island had
been rendered fruitless by bad weather, Holmes came
back to the fleet, he and his men loaded with booty
(despite orders concerning plunder), flaunting captured
Dutch flags. The affair came to be known and referred
to as "Holmes' Bonfire." The loss to the Dutch, both
in money and prestige, was enormous ; the former,

[1] *Tanner MSS.* 296. Allin's *Journal.*

amounting to nearly a million pounds[1], was irrecoverable, the latter they did their utmost to restore by getting their fleet promptly to sea again : nor were they unsuccessful.

With this further success to their credit, however, Albemarle and Rupert were forced back to England by shortage of victuals—though they made the most of their time on their way back by capturing some more Dutch ships laden with stores. As early as August 2nd the men had been put on short allowance, and by the time the fleet reached the English coast on the 17th the shortage of victuals was serious. As a matter of fact victualling ships had already been despatched but, owing to lack of communications and connection, had missed the returning fleet[2].

Meanwhile the Dutch preparations were hastening towards completion, and on the 26th De Ruyter was at sea again and making for the Channel in order to effect the long-promised junction with De Beaufort and his fleet. Two days later the English fleet, under sole command of Prince Rupert, set out to find De Ruyter and to prevent the junction. On the 31st they sighted him off the Long Sand and made all sail for him ; in so doing, however, they became entangled in the Galloper shoals, a number of the ships touching, and had to tack southwards until they were clear, when they stood S.E. by S. At daybreak on the following morning the Dutch were seen off the French coast, and Rupert gave chase down past Calais. Then followed an incident which does not speak very highly for either the daring or

---

[1] *Cal. S. P. Dom.* August 10th, 1666.

[2] For question of victuals see above, pp. 112–14.

generalship of the English commander in letting slip
an opportunity of attacking the Dutch under favourable circumstances and at a critical time. De Ruyter
had driven in close under the French shore, the wind
being N.N.E., when part of his fleet tacked to the north
towards the English. " Our general," writes Sir Tho.
Allin, " tacked also to N. and after then Sir Rob. Holms
and severall others and soe did we nott having eyther
syne to draw into a lyne nor to fall on. The *Guinea*
recd. severall shotts from these ships soe did the
Assurance from De Ruiter. they tacked soe till 6 aclock
and then tacked towards their owne fleett agayne and
then Sir Rob. Holms tacked also and stood into shoare
after them." The rest of the fleet followed suit, and
then, and then only, did Rupert " put out flag of defi-
ance and all stood in to shoare till it was darke and all
bore up and tacked and stopt chase[1]." Why Rupert
should have deliberately refused to engage at the first
opportunity is scarcely comprehensible, for not only
are there no dangerous shoals at any distance off the
French coast at that point, but also had he engaged then
it would have been some way off the coast; the remainder
of the Dutch fleet was still nearer the coast, and, lee-
shore as it was, there was but a very short stretch
before Cape Gris-nez and the practical safety of the
wider channel. Such an opportunity did not occur
again; stormy weather drove both fleets into harbour,
the English to St Helens, De Ruyter to Dunkirk.

For three weeks Rupert held the Straits, Allin being
kept at sea with his squadron, and effectually prevented any junction between French and Dutch—

[1] *Tanner MSS.* 296, Allin's *Journal.*

though it is very doubtful if the union was ever anything more practical than a diplomatic bogey dressed
up for his own use by Louis XIV. Towards the end of
September, however, the Prince was at sea again, and
on the 25th sighted 40 Dutch ships off Dover ; he
drew into line and was " in a handsome posture to windward of them to gayne there van[1]," when the wind began
to rise, and the sea with it. " The Prince tacked to
W. and about 5 ancored in their sight, soe might they have
done to attend fayre weather had they a mind to fight
us but they stood off to the S.E. and S.S.E.[1] "

So ended the naval operations of 1666, and indeed
of the Second Dutch War, for the final act in 1667
which turned a triumph into a tragedy and disgrace
had but little to do with naval action so far as the
English Navy was concerned—wherein lay the tragedy.

In the autumn of the previous year there had
been some talk of withdrawing the main
fleet from service, and in the following
spring sending out only light squadrons and licensed
privateers in order to attack merely the trade of
the Dutch : in 1666 the proposition again came up,
but more forcibly. " It was said that the Dutch
might best be beaten by sending small squadrons
abroad to interrupt and ruine their Trade without
which it would be impossible for them to continue the
Warr or support themselves in Peace[2]." The financial
difficulties under which Charles' government lay lent
additional point to the argument. Charles had taken

1667.

---

[1] *Tanner MSS.* 296, Allin's *Journal.*
[2] *Rawl. MSS.* D. 924, *Continuation of the Dutch War.*

to appropriating for his own purposes—especially the
payment of soldiers—the money voted for the upkeep
of the Navy, and the double prospect of an enquiry
into the past and of increased needs for the future was
specially unpleasant to the son of Charles I. "Parliament," says Pepys, "begins to be mighty severe in
examining our accounts and the expence of the Navy
this war," and strict enquiries began which put not
only Pepys but all the officials and many of the courtiers
"into a mighty fear and trouble[1]."

To lessen the difficulties attending this juncture
Charles adopted a two-fold policy, of peace with Holland and, in the meantime, a reduction of naval ex-
penses to a minimum. The chivalrous conduct of the
Dutch in honouring and returning to England the body
of Sir William Berkeley, who had fallen in the four
days' battle, offered an opening for peace negotiations
between England and Holland. Charles, however,
relying on a breach between Holland and France[2], put
his terms too high, and the negotiations dragged on.
" To justify and maintain this line of conduct he should
have kept up his fleet, the prestige of which had been
so advanced by its victories[3]."

---

[1] Pepys' *Diary*, September 30th, October 2nd, 1666. On October
10th he makes a note of these complaints:

> " They say the king hath towards this war
>   expressly thus much................. £5,590,000
> " The whole charge of the Navy, as we state
>   it for two years and a month, hath been
>   but.............................. £3,200,000
>   " So what is become of all this sum ?   £2,390,000."

[2] Louis XIV had opened a campaign of aggression in the Spanish
Netherlands.

[3] Mahan *op. cit.* p. 131.

At the end of September, when rough weather made
naval action impossible, Rupert was recalled to harbour, and the process of discharging the fleet, beginning
with the first and second line ships on October 2nd, was
begun and carried through. Months later, when this
policy had borne its inevitable fruit, much complaint
was made from English sources of the ' perfidy ' of the
Dutch, who, under cover of the peace negotiations,
had made so base and dishonourable an attack on
England. But really it is difficult to see much deeper
grounds for these assertions than those of injured pride
and dignity. It is obvious that the continuance of the
war in the meantime was a fact perfectly understood
and accepted by the English authorities, and measures
were taken all along the coast for the fortification of
important posts against possible Dutch attacks. In
the light of later occurrences, the measures taken
regarding the Medway have a special interest. As
early as December 27th, 1666, the Duke of York had
given order : " upon considerations concerning y^e
security of his maj^{ts} shipps at Sheernesse, and ye River
of Medway, it hath been thought necessary that a
platforme should be made upon ye point at Sheernesse
for 12 guns to be planted upon[1]." A boom was also
to be set across the river to protect the ships lying
further up stream. Three months later further orders
were given regarding "the Safety of H.M.'s shipps in
the River of Medway " : the complement of the guardships was to be increased, and the ships provided with
grapnels : the *Dolphin* and two other fireships were to
lie inside the chain, while in the upper part of the river

[1] *Adm. Libr. MS.* 24, *Duke of York's Letters,* 1660-7.

the ships, especially the first and second rate, were to
be moored in the safest place : and " besides com-
pleating ye chaine for their further security ye ships
Charles V and *Matthias* may be moored wth in ye chaine
...that they may bring their broadsides to bear upon
ye chaine, and that a competent number of seamen be
allowed to be borne on them[1]." Yet, in reality little
was done. The fort at Sheerness was never completed
—on June 11th, when news of the Dutch fleet in the
Thames had scared people into a panic-stricken energy,
Sir Edward Spragge was sent down to raise the long-
planned fortifications there : but the Dutch arrived
before he did. The chain was scarcely better done : by
May 10th Pett had written to the Navy Commissioners,
" the chain is promised to be dispatched tomorrow,
and all things are ready for fixing it[2] "—it had been
ordered four months previously—and when done it
was only completed in a perfunctory manner and the
Dutch had no difficulty in breaking through it.

While the peace negotiations still hung fire, the
Dutch were steadfastly resolved on the full maintenance
of their fleet, and, if possible, on a revenge for Holmes'
"Bonfire." On June 7th De Ruyter's fleet of 80 ships,
including 15 fireships, was sighted off the North
Foreland : he anchored in the King's Channel that
night. Scouts were sent up the Thames on the following day, and on the 9th a light squadron of 17 men-of-
war and 24 fireships and galleons under Van Ghent set
sail up the Thames with orders to attack the small
English squadron lying in the Hope and also to make

[1] *Adm. Libr. MS.* 24, *Duke of York's Letters*, 1660–7.
[2] *Cal. S. P. Dom.* May 10th, 1667.

a descent on the stores and ships lying up the Medway.

London was seized with a panic only equalled by
that caused by the Fire. " The dismay that is upon us
all, in the business of the kingdom and Navy at this
day, is not to be expressed otherwise than by the condition the citizens were in when the city was on fire,
nobody knowing which way to turn themselves, while
everything concurred to greaten the fire ; as here the
easterly galle and spring-tides for coming up both rivers,
and enabling them to break the chaine[1]." Those
who could began to bundle out of the city with their
most precious belongings. On the other hand there is
a picturesque story reminiscent of, perhaps founded on,
Nero's fiddle, " that the night the Dutch burned our
ships the King did sup with my Lady Castlemayne,...
and there were all mad in hunting of a poor moth[2]."

Prince Rupert went off to Woolwich, the Duke of
Albemarle to Chatham, to attempt to make some provisions to meet the emergency. Sir William Coventry
made frantic appeals for more fireships, and hands were
laid on any and every suitable ship. The fireships
proved of great service ultimately, but the Prince and
Albemarle were too late to be more than onlookers of a
pitiable disgrace. In the Medway the fireships were
unmanned, the guardships half manned, the forts
without guns, and according to some accounts even
the chain was not yet in place. Not merely was the
work not done, but there were no men to do it when Albemarle arrived. Men who had not been paid for months
refused to work in this emergency. Out of 1100 men

[1] Pepys' *Diary*, June 14th, 1667.   [2] *Ibid.* June 21st.

in pay at Chatham Dockyard not more than three
attended to help the Duke in any way.

> " Our Seamen, whom no danger's shape could fight,
> Unpaid refuse to mount their ships, for spite :
> Or to their fellows swim, on board the Dutch,
> Who show the tempting metal in their clutch[1]."

Pepys tells of many Englishmen heard talking on board
the Dutch ships, and crying to their less fortunate
countrymen, " We did heretofore fight for tickets ; now
we fight for dollars[2] ! " ; and there is no doubt that
there was no small number of deserters on board the
Dutch fleet. De Ruyter gained considerable help in
his attack on Chatham from one Captain Thomas Holland[3], an old Commonwealth captain : and there is
also a dramatic story of a cousin of this man going to
De Ruyter after the Medway attack and offering to
lead him up the Thames, and De Ruyter's reply, " If
you are so brave a man as you have represented yourself to be, I will send you back again to your Master the
King, he has now occasion for such valiant men as you
are[4]."

In the meantime Van Ghent had been delayed by
unfavourable wind. On the 10th he had gone up the
Thames nearly as far as Gravesend—the ships at the
Hope having escaped him—but the turn of the tide
and the S.W. wind decided him to drop down again to
Sheerness. Despite a stout resistance by Sir Edward
Spragge, the unfinished fort there caused but little

---

[1] Marvell, *Instructions to a Painter.*

[2] Pepys' *Diary,* June 14th, 1667.

[3] Clowes, *op. cit.* II. 289, says " Dolmar", for which I have been
unable to find any authority.

[4] *Rawl. MSS.* D. 924.

hindrance to the Dutch, into whose hands fell the large magazines of naval stores. The Dutch followed the retiring English up the river without venturing further inland from the water, " because the most part of our Land-Troops were separated from us by the foul Weather, the Generall officers thought not fit to engage themselves too far up the country with so few People[1]." At 6 a.m. on the morning of the 12th, being now accompanied by De Ruyter himself, the Dutch moved up the Medway before a brisk N.E. breeze. About noon their van, led by Van Brakel, reached the chain below Gillingham. Albemarle had had two ships sunk outside the boom, the *Unity* stationed outside also, and two very slight batteries on land at each end of the chain. The sunken ships were not in the channel, the *Unity* was promptly fired by fireships, and the chain snapped as a second Dutch ship crashed against it. A short tussle and the Dutch were swarming up the river in all kinds of craft, from man-of-war to ship's boat. The *Amity*, *Charles V*, *Monmouth* and *Matthias* were soon blazing. Just above these ships lay the *Royal Charles*, the flagship during the last campaign ; she had only 30 guns mounted, so Albemarle had made every effort to get her towed into safety up the river, but mutinous men would not move a finger to help, and Commissioner Pett of Chatham Dockyard had fled nursing his models which he thought more important to the King than aught else. The *Royal Charles* thus fell an easy prey, was converted into a Dutch flagship, and at the present day her stern-piece is displayed in an Amsterdam museum.

[1] *Life of Tromp*, p. 425.

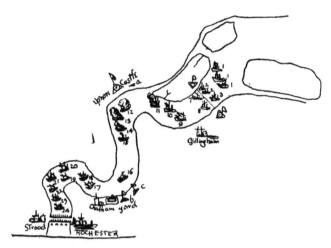

DUTCH IN THE MEDWAY.

"A Scheme of the Posture of the Dutch Fleete and Action at Sheernesse and Chatham 10ᵗʰ. 11ᵗʰ. and 12ᵗʰ. of June 1667, taken upon the place by J. E." (Drawn and sent to Pepys by J. Evelyn, June 20ᵗʰ. The above is a tracing of part of the original in *Rawl. MSS.* A. 195, f. 77–8.)

"1. The 3 Dutch ships wᶜʰ. brake yᵉ chayne.
2. 2 sunk ships without yᵉ chayne.
3. The Unity.
4. The Chayne.
5, 6. Two very slight batteries at each end of the chayne.
7. Chas. yᵉ 5ᵗʰ.
8. The Matthias.
9. The Monmouth as she lay during the Assault.
10. The Royall Charles.

11. Mary
12. R. Oake
13. London   } Burnt.
14. James
15. The Catherine sunke.
16. The Princesse.
17. The Old James.
18. The Guilden Ruiter.
19. The Triumph.
20. The Rainbow.
21. The Unicorne.
22. The Henry.
23. The Helverson.
24. Vanguard sunke.

} As they laye when drawne towards Rochester Bridg.

a. A fort with 8 guns.
b.
c. } Two other batteries with 21 and 16 Guns.
d. A Battery of 60 guns in yᵉ old Dock (not mounted). Note yᵗ. these batteries were not finished til after the fight."

That night the Dutch lay in the Medway between Upnor and Gillingham, they and their handiwork covered by a heavy pall of smoke illumined only by the flickering glow from the burning ships. On the following morning De Ruyter moved further up the river. For a time the garrison at Upnor put up a stout fight, but shortage of ammunition checked them before the enemy would have done so, and the Dutch passed on up to three ships which had been half sunk at the side of the channel; these—the *Royal Oak Loyal London*, and *James*—they fired. Above the latter lay the *Katherine*, sunk in the channel, and, beyond, nine other large ships. However, all but two of the Dutch fireships had been expended and the return passage promised to be dangerous, so no attempt was made against the remaining English ships. The Dutch got away down the river without mishap, taking with them the *Royal Charles* " at a time both for tides and wind when the best pilot in Chatham would not have undertaken it, they heeling her on one side to make her draw little water : and so carried her away safe[1]."

On his return to the Thames, De Ruyter satisfied himself with keeping a blockade, and it would seem that a slight excess of caution on his part lost him a good opportunity of improving on his Chatham exploit. " De Ruyter might have done much more mischief," writes an English contemporary, "if he had immediately after the exployt at Chatham seconded it with another in the Thames : for Gravesend was slenderly provided, Tilbury Fort not erected, and the Dutch having a Spring tyde and an Easterly wind, might soon

[1] Pepys' *Diary*, June 22nd, 1667.

have been pass'd Gravesend, and nothing could have
hindered but that ye Frigatts and Fireshipps might have
come up as high as Woolwich at least, and have fired
all the ships that were afloat and have endangered the
King's Yard and Storehouses[1]." On July 1st he made
a fruitless attack on Landguard fort, and a week later,
being again at the mouth of the Thames, he divided his
fleet into two squadrons ; taking one himself, with
which he cruised down the south coast of England,
and leaving the other in the Thames under Van Nes.

Meanwhile somewhat hysterical preparations had
been in progress in London and Chatham. Fortifications had been hurried on, new forts sprang up, new
guns were mounted. So eager had people been to
block up the fairway in two or three places that in some
cases valuable merchant ships, fully stored victual ships,
effective fireships, had been indiscriminately sunk.
However, the object aimed at was achieved : the stores
and dockyards were safe.

For nearly a fortnight Van Nes cruised off the
mouth of the Thames, mostly in the neighbourhood of
the Gunfleet—and so keeping a small squadron, com-
posed mostly of fireships, securely shut up in the Stour.
On the 22nd, however, he weighed from the Gunfleet
with about 38 sail, including 13 fireships. On the
following day he heard of the presence in the Hope of
five English men-of-war and 20 fireships, and thereupon
pushed up the river. At noon he reached the Hope
and attacked the little squadron there : his success
was very partial, he forced them under the guns of Tilbury and five of their fireships were burnt—the wind

[1] *Rawl. MSS.* D. 924.

being easterly, the English could not make any real use of them—but to achieve so much he expended a dozen of his own. The following day he retired down stream followed by the English, who were now led by Sir Edward Spragge. On the 25th both squadrons anchored at the Nore almost within gunshot of each other.

In the meantime Sir Joseph Jordan had decided to come out from his retreat. For some reason he seems to have come to this decision very suddenly. On the evening of the 23rd he suddenly called in all the seamen, whereupon " ye 4th part of our best men tooke ye opportunity of theire heeles and deserted[1]." That same evening in a very unprepared condition he set sail. Six vessels had to be left behind ; four of them caught up on the following day. On the 26th he came in sight of the Dutch fleet. He arranged his little fleet —seven small men-of-war and 16 fireships—into two squadrons, each led by some of the warships. Spragge's squadron were eyewitnesses of the ensuing fiasco. " Wee were in hopes to see some Bonfires made of the Dutch ships in return to those they had made of ours too lately, but our Expectations were wholly frustrate, for the Dutch manning out all their small craft and Boats, put the Fireships by or cut off their Boats, so that we lost the greatest part of 15 Fireships and not one of them did execution[2]." The fireship crews utterly disgraced themselves ; they practically refused to attack ; two of them, by dint of being pushed on between three of the frigates, attempted to grapple

---

[1] *Rawl. MSS.* A. 195, f. 264.
[2] *Ibid.* D. 924.

one of the Dutchmen but failed to do so ; some of the crews fled from their ships in small boats only to be cut off ; two other crews set fire to their ships when completely isolated, thereby affording a striking display of the badness of the materials, for the ships smouldered for over half an hour before they began to burn properly. One of these fireship captains was afterwards shot, and three others drummed out of the service, for their share in this final incident in the war. Jordan, with his frigates untouched, joined Spragge without any further action. Van Nes, being without fireships, made no more attempts in the Thames, and before another opportunity for an engagement arose the signature of the Treaty of Breda on July 31st put an end to the war.

Such was the last melancholy incident in a melancholy war : melancholy not so much in the practical results—though indeed they form a sorry enough case of lives and money squandered, of good work wasted— as in the pitiful spectacle it affords of good material wasted, ruined; of sturdy, willing seamen become paupers, diseased and mutinous; of volunteers become deserters; of fine old seamen captains displaced by foppish courtier ignoramuses, who, as often as not, owed their preferment to some disreputable intrigue in a disreputable court ; of lack of food and bad food; of lack of pay and pensions; of state money, stores and prizes embezzled by men of every rank, from the King who ' appropriated ' naval money to help pay for his mistresses and his soldiers, to the miserable dock-yard workman, unpaid and half-starved, who ' stole ' 'chips' to help keep his pitiable body and soul together :

in short, it is the spectacle of a great service, of a nation, being rotted to the core by the foul spirit that came into England with Charles II and his court.

Explanations other than these, however, other reasons, had to be given. The people and the Parliament demanded a victim, and in their demands were coming unpleasantly near the true root of all the trouble, when the scapegoat was found and exposed—the unfortunate commissioner of Chatham Dockyard, Peter Pett.

" After this loss, to relish discontent,
   Someone must be accused by Parliament ;
   All our miscarriages on Pett must fall,
   His name alone seems fit to answer all.
   Whose counsel first did this mad war beget ?
   Whose all commands sold through the Navy ? *Pett.*
   Who would not follow when the Dutch were beat ?
   Who treated out the time at Bergen ? *Pett.*
   Who the Dutch fleet with storms disabled met,
   And, rifling prizes, them neglected ? *Pett.*
   Who with false news prevented the Gazette,
   The fleet divided, writ for *Rupert* ? *Pett.*
   Who all our seamen cheated of their debt ?
   And all our prizes who did swallow ? *Pett.*
   Who did advise no navy out to set ?
   And who the forts left unprepared ? *Pett*
   Who to supply with powder did forget
   Landguard, Sheerness, Gravesend and Upnor ? *Pett.*
   Who all our ships exposed in Chatham net ?
   Who should it be but the fanatick *Pett* ?
   Pett, the sea-architect, in making ships,
   Was the first cause of all these naval slips.
   Had he not built, none of these faults had been ;
   If no creation there had been no sin."

                MARVELL. *Instructions to a Painter.*

BIBLIOGRAPHY

THE SOURCES OF ENGLISH NAVAL HISTORY
Sept. 1658—July 1667.

(N.B.   I have marked * works of which I have made special use ; and †, works I have been unable to see, but without which nevertheless the bibliography would be incomplete.)

I. BIBLIOGRAPHY

*Admiralty Library. Subject Catalogue of Printed Books. Pt. I. Historical Section (by W. G. Perrin). London, 1912. 4⁰.

(The most comprehensive collection of Naval Works. Sub-headings—Administration, Biography, etc.)

Bibliothèque universelle et historique. 26 vols. s. 8⁰. Amsterdam, 1686–1718.

British Museum. Subject-Index of modern works added to the Library. 1881–1910. Ed. by G. K. Fortescue. 5 vols. la. 8⁰.

—— List of Books of Reference in Reading Room. Vol. II. (Under Bibliography, Navy, England.) la. 8⁰. 1910.

—— *Class Catalogue of MSS.

*Cambridge Hist. of Eng. Literature. Vol. IV. (Bibl. to Chaps. IV and V, "The Literature of the Sea" and "Seafaring and Travel.") la. 8⁰. Camb., 1909.

*Cambridge Modern History. Vol. IV. (Bibliography to Chap. XVI.) Vol. V. (Bibliography to Chap. IX.) la. 8⁰. Camb., 1906–8.

(With the exception of Dewar's Sources, these last three are the only recent attempts at an adequate naval bibliography of the period.)

Courtney, W. P. Register of National Bibliography, with selection of the chief bibliographical works and articles publ. in other countries. 3 vols. 8⁰. London, 1905–12.

*Dewar, A. C., Lieut. Sources of Naval History in the seventeenth century.

(Publ. as pamphlet for the International Historical Congress, London, 1913. The only comprehensive naval bibliography of the period; but somewhat loosely arranged, and not without errors.)

Dictionary of National Biography. la. 8⁰. London, 1885 etc. (See short bibliographies at end of bio- graphical notices.) (See also § VII, Biography.)

Langlois, C. V. Manuel de Bibliographie Historique. 2 Fasc. Paris, 1901–4. 8⁰.

(1ᵉ Fasc. Éléments de bibl. génér., et Instruments de bibl. histor.)

Lasteyrie, Robert de. Biblio. génér. des travaux hist.

et archéolog. publ. par les sociétés savantes de la France. (In progress.) 4º. 1888 etc.
(There is no corresponding publication in England.)
Le Long, Jacques. Biblio. hist. de la France, conten. le catalogue des ouvrages impr. et MSS., qui traitent de l'hist. de ce royaume. 5 vols. Fol. Paris, 1768–78.
*London Library, Subject-Index of. s. 4º. 1909.
(Under Navy, England, Netherlands, etc.)
*Lowndes, Will. The Bibliographer's Manual of Eng. Lit. (New ed. by Bohn.) 6 vols. s. 8º. London, 1864.
Monod, Gabriel. Biblio. de l'hist. de France. Catalogue jusq. 1789. 8º. 1888.
Pepys, Samuel. A descriptive catalogue of the naval MSS. in the Pepysian Library at Magdalene Coll., Camb. (Navy Records Soc. Publ.) (In progress. Vols. I–III published.) 8º. [London], 1903 etc.
—— Bibliotheca Pepysiana: a descriptive catalogue. (In progress. Published: Part I, "Sea" MSS.— Part II, Early printed books.) s. 4º. London, 1914.
*Revue Maritime et Coloniale. Table des matières, 1861–88. Paris, 1870–80–89.
(Reference to numerous articles bearing on this period. Unfortunately does not appear to have been carried up to date.)
Sonnenschein, W. S. Biblio. of History and Historic Bibliography.
(Sections from "The Best Books" and "The Reader's Guide," Class F. 23, 24, 30.) London, 1891–5. (Rather popular.)
Stolk, Abraham van. Atlas van Stolk: Katalogus der Historie-Spot-en Zinneprenten betrekkelijk de geschiedenis van Nederland. (In progress.) 8º. Amster., 1895 etc.

II. STATUTES, ETC.

*Acts and Ordinances of the Interregnum. Ed. C. H. Firth and R. S. Rait. 3 vols. 8º. London, 1911.
*Statutes of the Realm. 1660–7.
Raithby, John. Statutes relating to the Admiralty, Navy, Shipping and Navigation of the U.K. from 9 Hen. III. to 3 Geo. IV. inclusive. 4º. London, 1823.

Also, for Treaties, Dumont, Jean, Baron de Carlscroon. Corps universel diplomatique du droit des gens; contenant un recueil des traitez d'alliance, de paix, etc., faits en Europe depuis le règne de Charlemagne. 8 vols.; Supplément, 5 vols. La Haye, Amsterdam, 1726–39.

Parliamentary Journals, etc.

Parliamentary History. Vol. IV. 1660–88.
Journals of the House of Lords. Vols. IX, X. 1660–6, 1666–75.
*Journals of the House of Commons. Vol. VIII. 1660–7.

III. NAVY LISTS

Apart from mere lists of fleets or squadrons, the first 'Navy List' is probably :

Gloria Britannica, or the Boast of the British Seas, containing a True and Full Account of the Royal Navy of England, shewing where each Ship was Built, by whom, and when, its Length, Breadth, Depth, Draught of Water, Tons, the number of Men and Guns, both in Peace and War, at Home and Abroad, together with every Man's Pay, from a Captain to a Cabin-Boy, truly calculated and Cast up, for a Day, a Week, a Month, and a Kalendar Year, or 13 months and 1 Day. Carefully Collected and Digested by a True Lover of the Seamen. 1689.

Miscellaneous Lists

1. *Contemporary.*

*Pepys, Samuel. Sea Commission Officers. My Naval Register relating to the three following Particulars, viz. 1. The Execution of the Office of High Admiral. 2. The Flag Officers charged with the Fleets ; and 3. The Commanders and Lieutenants of all single ships...between May 1660, and...Dec. 1688. Begun and closed with particular lists of the Officers actually in Commission at each of the said periods.

(Pepysian Library, 2941. See also " Catalogue of Naval MSS. in the Pepysian Library," Vol. I. Nav. Rec. Soc.)

*Pepys, Samuel. A Register of the Ships of the Royal Navy of England from...May 1660, to...Dec. 18th, 1688.

(Pepysian Library, 2940. See also "Catalogue of Naval MSS. etc.")

2. *Later compilations.*

(*a*) Officers.

Admirals and Captains, A List of, who have lost their lives in the Service, from 1665 to 1801. (See Schomberg's " Naval Chronology," Appendix, Vol. v.)

Captains, A List of, who have served in the Royal Navy of Great Britain, from the year 1653 to 1802. (See Schomberg's " Naval Chronology," App., Vol. v.)

Chaplains of the Royal Navy, 1626–1903. (Comp. by A. G. Kealy, Chapl. R.N.) 12º. Portsmouth, 1903.

Jackson, Sir Geo. Naval Commissioners, 1660–1760. Compiled from the Original Warrants and Returns ; by the late Sir G. Jackson, Bart. With Historical Notices by Sir G. F. Duckett, Bt. 8º. London, 1889.

Noblemen and Gentlemen, A List of, who have been raised to the dignity of Admirals in the R. Navy of England and Great Britain...from 1660 to 1801. (See Schomberg's " Naval Chronology," App., Vol. v.)

Secretaries of the Admiralty, Clerks of the Acts, etc. Comp. by Col. Pasley. (See H. B. Wheatley's " Sam. Pepys and the World he lived in," 5th ed., London, 1907, p. 266 etc.)

(*b*) Ships.

See *Clowes' " Royal Navy," Vol. II, for Navy at Restoration.

See Oppenheim's " Administration of the R.N." for Commonwealth and Protectorate Navy.

Charnock's " Marine Architecture " and Derrick's " Memoirs " also contain useful lists

IV. MANUSCRIPTS

(a) LIBRARY AND PRIVATE COLLECTIONS

1. *Admiralty Library.*
   - *6. Orders and Instructions. 1658–60.
   - 8. Orders and Warrants. 1658–60.
   - 19. Duke of York's Instructions. 1660–2.
   - 20. Duke of York's Instructions. 1662–6.
   - *23. Orders of the Duke of York. 1660–5.
   - *24. Duke of York's letters. 1660–8.
   - 150. Index of Orders. 1660–1741.

These are all in MS., and with the exception of the last-named are copies, apparently made piecemeal contemporaneously. Many of the originals of Vols. 20, 23 and 24, are among the Admiralty Papers at the Record Office.

2. *Bodleian Library, Oxford.*

The most important collections in the Library dealing with this subject are four volumes of Sandwich Papers and Letters among the Carte Papers, and twenty-six volumes of Pepys Papers (besides many other volumes that were originally his property in the Rawlinson collection); seven volumes of Sir Thomas Allin's papers and journals in the Tanner collection are also of interest and have not previously been thoroughly examined. There are numerous naval papers scattered throughout these three collections.

Catalogues. Catalogi Codicum MSS. P. 4. Cod. Th. Tanneri. P. 5. Codd. Rawlinsoniani. 4°. Oxf.

—Calendar of Carte Papers (in MS.).

There are occasional naval papers of the period in all the volumes undermentioned, details being given in cases of special interest or value.

Tanner MSS.
   - 45. Administrative reform, 1665–6 etc.
   - 47. Tangier and Mediterranean.
   - 48, 49, 51, 93, 114.
   - 292.
   - 294, *296. Sir Thomas Allin's papers. Journal 1660–7 in 296.
   - 297.

Rawlinson MSS.

A. 58, 59.

    63, 64. Numerous letters from Opdam, etc. to U. States.

    66, 67. General, concerning Sound negotiations, 1658–60.

    *170–195 incl. Pepys Papers, of which the following contain matter dealing with this period :—

        *174, 175, 176, 177, 181, 183, 184, 185.

    187. Victualling and arrears of pay.

    191, 192, 193.

    *195. " in and about the time of the 1st Dutch War 1665–68, designed for the most part for a collection, as I remember, towards the history thereof." Especially 1666–7.

    197. Register of Ships.

    199.

    209, 212, 216.

    *252
    *256 } Bergen.

    448. Report on Striking the Flag. 1661.

B. 451, 455.

    *457. Answer from Pepys for Commiss. of Navy to observations upon Dutch War and the management thereof.

    463, 465, 466.

    *468. Sandwich's narrative of Bergen.

C. 381. Mediterranean.

    423. Tangier (see also Pepys' shorthand notes and journal 1667–83, C. 859).

D. 916. Tangier.

    919.

Carte Papers. (Sandwich Papers.) 72, *73, *74, *223

    Also occasional papers in other volumes, see MS. Calendar (arranged chronologically).

Clarendon Papers, The, contain occasional papers of naval interest, but are not yet calendared beyond 1663 ; they are, however, arranged chronologically.

3. *British Museum.*

A. General Treatises.

Add. MSS. 9335. Hollond's Discourses on R.N.
    Slingsby's Discourse.
    11,602. Rich. Gibson Collection. Incl.
    papers on Gentlemen in Navy.
    11,684. Rich. Gibson Collection. Incl. Eng.
    Safety at Sea and Exam. of Dutch action
    at Chatham.
    30,221. Sir Ph. Meadowes, etc., on Dominion
    of Sea (f. 13).

B. Lists of Ships, etc.

*Harl. 1247. Numerous lists, 1658–66 (ff. 46, 51, 52, 55).
Stowe 428. 1658–9.
Harl. 7464. 1660–91.
Add. 36,781. 1661 (f. 101).
Stowe 432, 433. Ships, complement, building. 1656
    and 1662.
Sloane 4459. 1665.
Egerton 2543. 1666 (ff. 144–56, 179–81).
*Add. 32,094. 1666 (ff. 101–2, 116, 118, etc.).

C. Orders and Instructions.

*Add. 36,782. Register of Orders in Council, Warrants,
    etc., of Adm. and N. Board. 1660–6.
Stowe 430. Register of Instructions, etc. 1661–92.
Harl. 7464. Establishment of R.N. Jan. 1662. (Also
    Add. 9311.)
Harl. 6287. Ditto, with reflections thereon (1668).
Stowe 142. Instruct. from Jas. D. of York regarding
    Impressment. 1665.

D. Miscellaneous collections of Naval Papers.

Harl. 1509, 1510 } on Prizes.
Lansdowne 194 }
Add. *9311. 1660–5, miscell.
    9315. Warrants.
    9317. Chatham Chest.
    9328. Miscell. 1663–.
Harl. 6287. Incl. Pepys on Victualling and Pursers
    (" New year's gift ") [also Lansd. 253, ff. 280–94].

Sloane 1709. Incl. case of Surgeons in R.N. (f. 279).
Lansd. 1215. Incl. paper concerning half pay
(f. 19).
Add. 34,353. Striking flag.
    18,986. Misc. 1659–.
   *22,546. Misc. 1659–.
Stowe 325. Proposals for Maritime Insurance, 1661
(f. 184).
Harl. 6277. Charge of Netherlands war, Sept. 1664—
Sept. 1666.
Egert. 2543. Minutes by Nicholas of Adm. Commiss.
meetings. Oct. 1664—Jan. 1665.
Egert. 2618. Sandwich to Albemarle regarding Texel
fight. Sept. 1665.
Add. 27,999. Bergen (Talbot).
Add. 37,425. Report on June 3, 1665.
Stowe 744. Dutch War, 1666.
*Add. 32,094. Dutch War, etc.
Harl. 7010. Accts. of June ⎫ of Rupert and Albe-
  1–4, 1666,   ⎪ marle. For narratives
Lansd. 777. Accts. of June ⎬ concerning division of
  1–4, 1666,   ⎪ fleet on June 1, see Add.
Add. 4107. Accts. of June ⎭ 32,094, ff. 196–204.
  1–4, 1666,
*Harl. 4888. Acct. of Division of fleet in 1666.
Add. 29,597. Articles against Sir Jas. Smith for action.
Aug. 1666.
Egert. 928. Minutes of council of war under Allin. 1667.
Harl. 7018. Complaints against Pet. Pett. 1667.

4. *Historical Manuscripts Commission.*

3rd Report, Appendix. Northumberland, D. of, MSS.
of, 1872. (A few papers belonging to, and dealing
with, Prince Rupert and his naval command.)
*4th Report, Appendix. Bath, Marquis of, MSS. of,
pp. 229–37, 1874 (very slightly calendared but containing much valuable material: Sir W. Coventry's
papers, including letters on naval administration,
letters from Pepys, Holmes, Talbot, Tyddeman,
Clifford, dealing with Bergen, Holmes' expedition

(1664), etc. Also Coventry's Discourse on the management of the Navy. Notes by C. of Councils of War).
Some more naval papers in this collection are still
more scantily indexed in the 3rd Rep. pp. 180–200.
5th Report, App. I. Sutherland, Duke of, MSS. of,
pp. 150–78, 1876. (Many letters concerning Restoration, only introducing Navy indirectly.)
　　Malet, Sir A., MSS. of, pp. 314–5. (Coventry
papers: outbreak of war in 1664–5, letters from and
to Albemarle before the four days' fight, 1666.)
11th Report, App. V. Dartmouth, Earl of, MSS. of,
1887. (Much naval matter for 3rd Dutch War and
after, but little before. Duke of York's Orders:
see " Fighting instructions." Details of four days'
fight, 1666.)
12th Report, App. VII. Le Fleming, S. H., MSS. of (at
Rydal Hall), 1890. (Large collection of news-
letters covering the period.)
13th Report, App. II. Portland, Earl of, MSS. of (at
Welbeck), pp. 100–7, 1893. (Orders to Sir Wm.
Penn, 1666–7 ; many of these have been published
in the " Professional Life of Penn.")
14th Report, App. IV. Kenyon, Lord, MSS. of, pp. 67–
79, 1897. (A few papers dealing with the " warr
with the Duchy," 1664–7. List of ships, officers,
salaries.)
15th Report, App. II. *Hodgkin, J. E., MSS. of,
pp. 153–68, 1897. (Valuable collection of Pepys
papers, including letters from the Mediterranean from
Lord Sandwich and others.)
15th Report, App. VII. Somerset, Duke of, MSS. of,
1898. (Sailing orders on various occasions to Capt.
Seymour of the " Pearl," 1664–8.)
[1]*Heathcote, J. M., MSS. of (at Conington Cas.), 1889.
(Fanshaw papers: dealing with negotiations with
Portugal, state of Tangier from the time of the
English occupation, movements of English fleet in
the Mediterranean, letters from Allin and Lawson.)

---

[1] It is difficult to know in what order to tabulate the publications of the Commission, as the official order appears to vary.

5. *Pepysian MSS. at Magdalene College, Cambridge.*

The bulk of the Naval MSS. in the Pepysian Library belong to the period of his secretaryship, but there are ten volumes of "Miscellanies," comprising copies of miscellaneous papers dealing with naval matters, which Pepys intended to use as material for his projected naval history. A volume entitled "Naval Minutes" also contains many interesting opinions and facts noted by Pepys. See the printed Catalogues of the Pepysian MSS. (page 195).

488. King James II's Pocket-book of Rates and Memorandums.
1490. Papers concerning the enquiry of 1686, including Pepys' "Memoirs relating to the State of the Royal Navy." [The "Memoirs" have been printed (see page 208).]
2242. Papers concerning the enquiry into Naval Administration in 1668, including Pepys' report thereon.
2554. Mr Pepys' Defence of the Navy. 1669.
2589. Expense of the Navy from 1660 to 1666.
2611. Penn's Collection (including Instructions, 1653–65).
2801. Instructions for Fighting.
*2866. Naval Minutes. (These are odd notes of facts, opinions or arguments to be noted, questions to raise or answer, all with a view to the projected history; but their very informality and personal character give them additional value in showing the contemporary view of many and various matters.)
2867. Naval Precedents.
*2870–79, inclus. Miscellanies, especially
2871. Many details of distribution of ships.
2874. Report on Striking of Flags.
2879. Collection of papers concerning Rights of Search and Trinity House, etc.
*2940. Register of Royal Navy Ships, 1660–86.
*2941. Register of Sea Officers, 1660–88.
("MS. Naval Register relating to the three following particulars, viz.: 1. The Execution of the

Office of High Admiral ; 2. The Flag Officers charged
with the Fleets ; and 3. The Commanders and
Lieutenants of all single ships employed in the
service of the Crown between May 1660...and
December 1688, etc.")

6. *Printed Calendars.*

*Clarke Papers (Camden Society Publ.). 4 vols. s. 4º.
London, 1891–1901.

*Hyde, Edward, Earl of Clarendon, Calendar of State
Papers of, preserved in the Bodleian. 3 vols.
8º. Oxford, 1869–76. (Papers dealing with pre-
Restoration Royalist intrigues.)

*Thurloe, John, State Papers of. Ed. by J. Birch.
7 vols. Fº. London, 1842.
(Originals in Bodleian. Many of naval interest :
especially Baltic expedition in 1659.)

(b) STATE PAPERS

1. Calendars of State Papers preserved at the Public
Record Office.

(a) *Domestic Series. Ed. by M. A. E. Green.
Commonwealth. 1658–9, 1659–60. la. 8º. London,
1885–6.
Charles II. 1660–1, 1661–2, 1662–3, 1663–4, 1664–5,
1665–6, 1666–7, 1667. Also Addenda
1660–70 in volume 1670. la. 8º. London, 1860 etc.

These contain the great mass of the existing information
about the Navy of the Restoration ; official and private
letters from officers on service, official correspondence from
and to the Navy Office, News-letters, etc. Many are not
fully calendared—notably papers dealing with Allin and
Holmes—but sufficient information is given to be an
adequate guide to the original papers.

(b) Colonial Series.
America and W. Indies. Ed. by W. Sainsbury.
1574–1660, 1661–8. la. 8º. London, 1860, 1880.
(Including many papers dealing with the expedi-
tions of Holmes and Harman, especially the latter.)

(c) Treasury Books. Ed. by W. A. Shaw. 1660–7. la. 8°. London, 1904.

2. *Admiralty Papers (see List of Admiralty Records, Vol. I, Pub. Rec. Of. Lists and Indexes, No. XVIII, F°. London, 1904).

Secretary's Dept.

Adm. Sec. In-Letters.
Ad. I. 5246. Copies of Orders in Council. 1660–88.
Out-Letters.
Ad. II. Orders and Instructions. 1665–79.
Index and Compilation.
Ad. X. 10. Abstracts of Captains' Services. 1660–1741.
Ad. VII. 549. List of Captains and Ships (1660–1737).

Accountant General.

Accounts. Various.
112. Victualling Accounts. 1657–8.
B. Books 24–44. 1655–68.
Treasurer's Ledgers 1–11. 1660–8.
Miscellanea. Various.
119. Prices of Stores, 1660–1720.
132. 1658–1730. Register of Orders to Yards.
136. 1658–1765. ,, ,, ,,
139. 1662–1731. Orders from Navy Board (Abstracts).

Navy Board.

In-Letters.
*1–14. 1660–7.
2066. 1660–1700. Abstracts of letters from Admiralty.
2507, 2533, 2538–9. 1658–1768–9. Standing orders to Yards.

Miscell.

3117. 1660–7. List and Descriptions of Ships.
3537–8. Miscellaneous.

Victualling Dept.

Accounts 47, 48. Sea and Harbour Victualling.

Chatham Chest.
    2.   1656–7.   Accounts.
  128.   Miscell.   Orders, etc.

V. PRINTED AUTHORITIES, CONTEMPORARY

(a) GENERAL

Aitzema, Lieuwe van, Saken van Staaten Oorlogh, in ende omtrent de Vereenigde Nederlanden. 6 vols. 4º. The Hague, 1669–72.
    (To 1669.)

Baker, Sir Richard. A Chronicle of the Kings of England (up to 1661. Detailed account of Restoration). Fº. London, 1670.

Basnage de Beauval, Jacques. Annales des Provinces-Unies, depuis les négociations pour la paix de Munster. 2 parts. Hague, 1719. Fº.

Burnet, Gilbert. History of my own Time. 2 vols. 8º. London, 1723–34.—Ed. by M. J. Routh. 6 vols. 8º. Oxford, 1833.—Pt. I. (Chas. II), ed. by A. Airy. 2 vols. 8º. Oxford, 1897–1900.
    (Hostilely criticised by many, especially Ranke and Swift : memoirs rather than a history. Nevertheless a cardinal authority, " conspicuously and honourably fair in tone though frequently inaccurate in detail " (Airy).)

Clarendon, Edward Hyde, Earl of, Life of, by himself : in which is included a continuation of his History of the Rebellion. 3 vols. 8º. Oxford, 1759.

Heath, James. A Chronicle of the late Intestine war... to which is added a brief account of the most memorable transactions in Eng., Scot. and Ireland and Foreign Parts from 1662–1675, by J. Philips. Fº. London, 1676.

*Kennett, White, Bp of Peterborough. A Register and Chronicle, ecclesiastical and civil,...with proper notes and references towards discovering and connecting the true history of England from the Restoration of Chas. II. Fº. London, 1728.
    (Only one volume—Jan. 1660 to Dec. 1662—compiled with extracts from newspapers, tracts, etc., also from Sandwich MS. Journal.)

Whitelocke, Bulstrode. Memorials of the English Affairs;
or an historical account of what passed from the
beginning of the reign of King Chas. I. to King Chas. II.
his happy restauration. F⁰. London, 1682.
(Very little naval matter. Parliamentary debates on
the Baltic.)

(b) MEMOIRS, LETTERS, etc.

Blencowe, R. W., Sydney Papers, ed. by, consisting of
a journal of the Earl of Leicester and original letters
of Algernon Sidney. 8⁰. London, 1825.
(Letters from A. Sidney while ambassador in Baltic
in 1659; see also Sydney Papers below.)
Burton, Thomas, Diary of, 1656 to April 1659. 8⁰.
London, 1828.
(Parliamentary debate on Baltic question.)
*Estrades, Godefroi Comte d'. Lettres, Mémoires et
négociations de M. le Comte d'E., 1663–8. 5 vols.
12⁰. Brux., 1709.
—— Ambassades et négociation de M le Comte d'E.,
1637–62. 2 vols. 12⁰. Amsterdam, 1718.
—— Sale of Dunkirk...in the year 1662, taken from the
letters, etc., of the C. d'E. by E. Combe. 12⁰. London,
1728.
(Estrades was largely responsible for the conduct
of the French side of the negotiations for the purchase
of Dunkirk.)
Evelyn, John, Diary of. To which are added a selection
from his familiar letters...Ed. by W. Bray. New
editions with life and preface by H. B. Wheatley
(4 vols.), and Austin Dobson (3 vols.). London, 1906.
(Very little of naval interest in the Diary. A great
contrast in interest and value to Pepys' Diary. Evelyn
also proposed to write a naval history but never got
beyond the introduction. See below, page 217.)
*Fanshaw, Sir Richard, Bart. Original Letters of his
Excell. Sir R. F. during his Embassies in Spain and
Portugal...etc. (1664–5). 8⁰. London, 1701. (F. was
ambassador to Portugal 1662–3, and Spain 1664–5,
when he was superseded by Sandwich.)

*Gramont, Armand de, Comte de Guiche. Mémoires...
    concernant les Provinces-Unies. 12º. London, 1671.
    (Eye-witness's account from Dutch side of the four
    days' battle.)
*James, Duke of York, [James II]. Memoirs of English
    Affairs, 1660–73. 8º. London, 1729.
    (Largely naval, including many of D. of York's
    orders.)
Ludlow, Edward. Memoirs, 1625–75. Ed. by C. H Firth.
    2 vols. 8º. Oxford, 1894.
    (Ludlow was in exile from 1662 till his death. Some
    account of Republican intrigues with Dutch by an
    " honest dull man.")
*Pepys, Samuel. Diary of, 1660–71. Ed. by H. B. Wheatley.
    9 vols., and Suppl. vol. (Pepysiana). 8º. London,
    1893–9.
    (Absolutely invaluable as giving public and official
    contemporary opinion. His professional position in
    the Navy Office enabled him to give an unofficial view
    of the inside of naval administration, the more valuable
    because unconsidered.)
—— Memoirs of the Royal Navy, 1679–88. Ed. by
    J. R. Tanner. s. 8º. [Oxf., 1906.]
[Sydney Papers.] Letters and Memorials of State. Ed.
    by A. Collins. 2 vols. Fº. London, 1746.
    (Collections of Letters, etc., of the Sidney family
    from Elizabethan times ; Ewald's life of Alg. Sidney,
    and Blencowe's collection largely drawn from this.
    Baltic negotiations, 1659.)
Temple, Sir Wm., Bart., The works of. 2 vols. 4º.
    London, 1750.
    (Including: Vol. i. Life of Sir W. T., by a particular
    friend.
      Observations upon the United Provinces, in-
    cluding " Of their Government," " Of their People
    and dispositions," " Of their Trade," " Of their
    Forces and Revenue," etc.
      Vol. ii. Letters from Sir Wm. T. concerning the
    1st Dutch War begun May 1661.
      Letters to Sir Wm. T.. etc.

Temple was envoy and ambassador at the Hague
1665–8. He arranged the secret Treaty between the
Bp of Münster and Charles II. The letters include
some from Arlington, Sandwich and Coventry.)

(c) TECHNICAL

Binning, Thomas. A Light to the Art of Gunnery wherein
is laid down the true Weight of Powder both for Proof
and Action, of all Sorts of Great Ordnance. Also the
True Ball, and allowance for Wind, with the most
necessary Conclusions for the Practice of Gunnery...etc.
London, 1676.

Bond, Henry. The Boatswain's Art : or the Complete
Boatswain. Wherein is shown a true Proportion for
the Masting, Yarding, and Rigging of any Ship...etc.
(21 pages.) 8⁰. London, 1670.

Bourne, William. The Safeguard of Sailors : or, a Sure
Guide for Coasters. Describing the Sea Coasts of
England, Scotland, Ireland, France, Flanders, Holland,
Jutland, and Norway. With directions for bringing a
ship into the principal Harbours. 1677.

Bushnell, Edmund. The Complete Ship-Wright. Plainly
teaching the Proportion used by Experienced Ship-
Wrights, according to their Custom of Building.
Also, a way of Rowing of Ships, by heaving at the
Capstane, useful in any ship becalmed...1st ed. 8⁰.
London, 1664.

(48 pages, with diagrams and one plan.)

Childe, L. A Short Compendium of the new and much
enlarged Sea-Book, or Pilot's sea Mirror : containing
the distances and thwart courses of the Eastern,
Northern, and Western Navigation. 1663.

(Copy in the Brit. Mus. contains an advertisement
list of works on Navigation.)

†Dassie, F. L'Architecture Navale, contenant la Manière de
construire des navires etc. 4⁰. Paris, 1677.

(Plans, pictures, and explanations of technical
terms.)

Elton, Richard. The Complete Body of the Art Military,
in three books by R. Elton. F⁰. London, 1668.

*Fighting Instructions, 1530–1816. Ed. by J. S. Corbett. (Navy Records Soc. Publ. 29.) 8º. London, 1905.

(Traces evolution of naval tactics ; development of fighting in line. " Sailing Tactics was a purely English art.")

Hayward, E. The size and Length of Rigging for all His Majestie's Ships and Frigates,...proportions of Boatswains' and Carpenters stores...for 8 months sea service. Fº. London, 1660.

*Hoste, Paul; L'Art des Armées Navales ; avec la Théorie de la Construction des Vaisseaux. 2 vols. Fº. Lyon, 1727.

(An English translation and Adaptation by Lieut. Chr. O'Bryen. 4º. London, 1762.)

(The standard authority on naval tactics for nearly a century. Valuable accounts of actions in the war of 1665–7 used as illustrations and examples. With over 130 engravings illustrating tactical evolutions.)

*Oeconomy of H.M. Navy Office, The, containing the several duties of the Commissioner and Principal Officers thereof. Being the first Rules established for them by the Duke of York. 12º. J. Browne, London, 1717.

(These are little more than a re-issue of the regulations of the Earl of Northumberland in 1638, with a few minor alterations and a letter of the Duke of York prefixed.)

Vervolgh op het bootsmans praetje van het schip Hollandia. s. 4º. 1672.

(d) TRACTS AND PAMPHLETS

In British Museum.

*(1) *Thomason Tracts* (see special Catalogue, Lond., 1908, 2 vols.; none later than 1661) including:

1659. Feb. 8. English Fleet designed for the Sound. (669, f. 21.)

,, Nov. 29. Monk to the Navy (Thro' V. Adm. Goodson). (669, f. 22.)

1659. Dec. 28. Lawson's letters to Mayor of London and Commissioners of the Navy. (669, f. 22.)

1661. Jan. 17. Orders and Instructions for paying off the Navy. (E. 1075, f. 29.)

(2) *Miscellaneous Tracts, English.*

1659. Nov. 4. Letters from Commanders and Officers of the Fleet to Gen. Monk. Pub. by S. Griffin. London. (1093, c. 37.)

1660. A List of all the Ships and Frigots of England. (Baltic fleet, 1659.) M. Simmons. (103, 1. 54.)

1664. A Brief Relation of the Present state of Tangier. (583, c. 8.)

„ An History of the Transactions betwixt the Crown of England and the States of the Netherlands, since they first began to be a Republique, to this day. Tho. Mabb. London 56 pp., s. 4⁰. (8122, d. 93.) (A rabid justification of England. Another copy with different title-page: " The English and Dutch Affairs displayed to the life." 1103, f. 12.)

1665. A List of H.M. Fleet as divided into Squadrons. (190, g. 13.) (227.)

„ Copy of a Paper presented to the King... by the Spanish Ambassador. (Portuguese marriage and Span. claims on Tangier. 190, g. 13.) (379.)

* „ Instructions to a Painter for the drawing of a picture of the State and Posture of the English Forces at sea...in the conclusion of the year 1664. London. (1871, e. 9.)

„ Relation de ce que l'on a appris jusques à présent du Combat Naval sonné le 12, 13 et 14 de juin, 1665. (An ingenious tale of English fireships disguised as flagships, etc.) Quil. Scheybels. Bruxelles. (807, c. 28.)

1665. A Royal Victory obtained against the Dutch
Fleet, June the 2nd and 3rd, 1665. (A song.)
F. Coles. London. (Rox. iii. 240.)

„ Gratulatory Verse upon our late glorious
victory over the Dutch. By the Author of
Iter Boreale (R. Wild), London. (1871,
e. 9.) (17.)

„ Joyful News for England, or, a Congratulatory
verse upon our late happy success in firing
150 Dutch ships in their own harbours.
Fo. R. Head, London. (Lett. iii. 95.)

*1666. A True Narrative of the Engagement Between
H.M. Fleet and that of Holland, begun
Jun. 1st, 1666 at Two aclock in the after-
noon. Publ. by command. Th. Newcomb.
London. (816, m. 26.) (13.)

„ The Victory over the Fleet of the States
General obtained by H.M. Navy Royal in
the late engagement begun the 25th of
July inst., as it came from his H. Prince
Rupert and H. Grace the Duke of Albemarle. Publ. by Command. Tho. Newcomb. London. (816, m. 23.) (14.)

1689. Observations concerning the Dominion and
Sovereignty of the Sea. Sir Philip Meadows.
47 pp. London.

Also a volume of " Tracts relating to the Navy " (533,
d. 2) consisting of a number of tracts of 1693–1702 ; including " Piracy Destroy'd ; or, a short Discourse shewing
the Rise, growth and causes of Piracy of late " (London,
1701), and " An historical and Political Treatise of the Navy:
with some Thoughts how to Retrieve the Antient Glory of
the Navy."

The Harleian Miscellany of pamphlets and tracts
selected from the library of Ed. Harley, 2nd Earl
of Oxford. 10 vols. 4o. London, 1808–13. (Index
in Vol. x.)

The Somers collection of Tracts ; arranged by W. Scott.
13 vols. 4o. London, 1809–15. (Vols. vi, vii and

VIII contain numerous tracts dealing with civil and ecclesiastical questions of the period, but none are of direct naval interest.)

3) *Dutch Tracts.* (8122, ee. 7 and 8.)

"Traktaken betreffende Engelsche Staatszaken," of which Vol. VII, 1661-5, and Vol. VIII, 1666-73, contain many tracts of interest, of which the following are the more important :

Vol. VII. 1661-5.

2. t'Samen-Spraeck tusschen een Portuguees ende een Spanjaert, ober het befloten Houwelijck van den Herst. Koninck van Engelant met de Tochter van den Hertogh van Bragance. Brugge. 1661.

3. Raets-vraginge van den K. van G. Brittainen van sijnen Broeder den Hertogh van Jorck, of het Houweljek met de Princes van Portugael. (From English.) 1661.

12. Twee Memorien van de Herre Downing...overgegeven aen de Herrn Staten Generael. Den 3 end 8 Aug. 1661.

13. Vervolgh Schryvensnyt Engelandt aenzen Nederlants Coop Man...ontrent den torstand van de Engelish en Hollandtsche Tractaten. Enckhuyschen. 1661.

17. Historisch-Verhael van de vrye Nederlandsche extraordinare Ambassade by den Koninck van Brittangien vervolght 't zedert den 27 Jan. 1662. 2 parts. Rotterd. 1662.

24. Naer der Klagh-Vertoogh aen de H.M. Heeren Staten Gener. wegens de Bewinthebberen vande Gener. geoctro. W. Indische Comp., ter sake vande on wettelljcke...proceduren der Engelsche in Nieu-Nederland. (Nae de Copye.) 1664.

25. Den Toestant der Swevende Verschillen, tusschen de Oost, ende West-Indische Compagnien, van Engelant, ender van de Nederlanden. (Nae de Copye.) 1664.
(Negotiations from Oct. 18, 1663, to Feb. 3, 1664.)

26. Advys ende Antwort van haer H.M. Heeren St. Gener. op het sentiment ende verklaring van de H. Downing... ontrent de twee Schepen Bon' Avontura, en Bon' Esperance. Gehonden in 's Gravenhage, den 10 Junij, 1664. Leyden, 1664.

27–29. (Correspondence between Eng. and Netherlands July 13—Dec. 20, 1664.)

30. Klachte der W. Indesche Compagnie, tegende O. Indische Comp....voor-gevallen in een Dialogue... Middelburgh, 1664.

32. Memorie van de Bewint-Hebberen der W. Indische Comp. ter Kamer van Amsterdam... Nessens een be-eedigde verklarung van And. C. Vertholen Schipper op het Schip de Eendracht. Amsterdam, 1664.

34. (Dutch Trans. of Coventry's account of June 3, 1665.) Antwerp, 1665.

35. Lyste. (Large sheet-list giving fleet that left Texel 22nd and 23rd May (n.s.), and those that returned after the battle of June 3–11. " Lost or missing—16 and one yacht.") 1665.

36. Hertoge van Jorck... Generale Instructie voor ...gevonden in 't Schip de Charity of Liefde, genomen by Cap. de Haen. Haarlem, 1665.

38. Neerlander en Engelsman. t'Samen spraek overden Zee-Strijt den 13 Junij, 1665, lest voorgevallen, 1665.

39. Autenticq Verhael, van al 't geene, guepasseert is, in, ende ontrent 's Landts Vloote, 't sedert ...den 13 Jun. tot. den 13 Aug. 1665. (54 pp.)
(Including details of Dutch inquiry into the conduct of the fleet on Jun. 3–13, 1665.)

40. Zee-Journal, ofte Autentijcq Verhael, Uyt d'annotatien vande Heeren haer Hoo. Volm. inde Vloot...aen-gaende al het... geschiet is van den 13 Juny to den 6 Octob. 1665. (68 pp.) Amsterdam, 1665.
(Including Dutch version of Bergen affair.)
41. Den Engelsen Blixem, Welck is de Zee... mitsgaders nader openbaringe van der Engelsen Handel ende wandel. (Dutch side of the English Dominion question: cf. "An History of the Transactions," above, page 211.) 1665.
42. Brief van Johan Valkenburg... (Large sheet.) 1665.
(Published by order of the States and distributed throughout the Fleet.)

Vol. VIII. 1666–73.

3. Oprecht...Verhael, van 't gene is geremarcqueert onder het bloedigh gevecht,...voorgevallen op den 11, 12, 13 en 14 Junius, 1666. Middleburgh, 1666.
4. Een vonpartijdig...Verhael...(identical with above). Rotterdam, 1666.
5, 6, 7. Een trouw verhael...in 't Neder. Duyts vertaelt; op dat de Nederlanders en alle andere mogen sien, de versiede Logenen, daer de Engelse haer behelpen, oomme haer gepretendeere Victorie staende te honden. (Trans. by different printers of the English "True Narrative of the Engagement" (see above, page 212); publ. by command of the States Gen.) Rotterdam and 's Gravenhage, 1666.
8, 9, 10, 11. Verhael van 't gepasseerde inde Zeeslach Tusschen de Vlooten van Engelandt ende van de Ver. Neder...opgestelt...in date den 24 Junij, 1666...Naer een curiens examen vande Hooft-Officieren, Commandeurs

en Capiteynen der voorsz. vloot. 's Gravenhage, 1666.
(French trans. of this in "Description exacte,"
see below.)
13, 15. Het Engelsche Verkeet-bert, gespeelt op
de Vlaemse Kust. (2 parts.) Velissingen,
1666.
(A discussion between numerous persons about
the four days' fight.)
16. Brieven aende H.M. Staten Gener. van De
Ruyter, Tromp, en Meppel. Schiedam, 1666.
(Aug. 5–7, 1666. Account of sea-fight, Aug. 5.)
17. Journal van den lesten Uyttoch, Zee Slagh,...
geschiet den 4 Aug. 1666. 1666.
(42 pp. 12º, includes above letters.)
18–20. Den Oprechten Hollandsen Bootsgezel...
geveest zijnde in de Laatste Zeeslag. (2 parts.)
Rotterdam, 1666.

(e) MISCELLANEOUS

Burchett, Josiah. A Complete History of Transactions
at Sea to conclusion of the last War with France.
Fº. London, 1720.
(Not in detail before 1688. Not reliable; e.g., Allin
and Smyrna fleet.)
Churchill, Awnsham and John. A Collection of Voyages
and Travels by A. and John Churchill. 6 vols. Fº.
London, 1744–6.
Colliber, Sam. Columna Rostrata, a critical History of
English Sea-Affairs. 8º. London, 1727.
*Description exacte de tout ce qui s'est passé dans les
guerres entre le Roy d'Angleterre, le Roy de France, les
Estats des Provinces Unies des Pays-Bas, et l'Evesque
de Munster. Comm. de l'an 1664 et finissant avec la
conclusion de Paix faite à Breda en l'an 1667. (241 pp.)
s. 4º. Amsterdam, 1668.
(A moderate account from the Dutch point of
view. Full and valuable accounts of various actions.)

Evelyn, John. Navigation and Commerce, their origin
and progress. 8⁰. London, 1674.
(Intended as an introduction to a history of the
Dutch War. Suppressed by order of the King on
first publication.)
*Hollond, John. Second Discourse of the Navy, 1659.
Ed. by J. R. Tanner. (Navy Records Soc. Publ., No. 7.)
8⁰. London, 1896.
(Victualling, pay, etc.)
*Manley, Sir Roger. The late Warres in Denmark. F⁰.
London, 1670.
(Contains report made by Meadowes on his return
to England from his embassy in Denmark during the
Baltic expedition of 1659.)
Molloy, Chas. De Jure Maritimo et Navali: or a treatise
of Affairs Maritime and of Commerce. First ed.
8⁰. London, 1676.
(Chapters on "The Right of the Flag, as to the
acknowledging the Dominion of the British Seas,"
"Dominion established by Treaties of Alliance,"
"Salutations of Ships of War, and Merchantmen,"
etc., in Book I.)

(f) *NEWSPAPERS

The principal newspapers, under various changing
names, during the period were:

Up to April 1660:

Mercurius Politicus,
Publick Intelligencer.

Later:

Mercurius Publicus,
Parliamentary Intelligencer,
The Monthly Intelligencer,
London Gazette,
Current Intelligence.

(For history of the Press during the period see Kitchin,
George. Life of Sir Roger Lestrange. 8⁰. London, 1913.)

VI. PRINTED AUTHORITIES, LATER WORKS

(a) GENERAL, AND ENGLISH AND DUTCH NAVIES

Allen, J. Battles of the British Navy. 8º. 2 vols.
  (Bohn's Illustrated Library.) London, 1852.
      (This, in company with Du Sein, Yonge, etc., has
  been largely superseded by the works of Clowes and
  Hannay and Rittmeyer, *q.v.*)
Campbell, John, LL.D. Lives of the Admirals: containing
  an accurate naval history. New edition, revised.
  8 vols. 8º. London, 1817.
      ("Naval History of Chas. II," and "Memoirs" of
  Monk, Mountagu, Rupert, Ayscue, Lawson and Spragge.)
*Clowes, Sir W. Laird. The Royal Navy. A history from
  the earliest times to the present day, by W. L. Clowes,
  assisted by Sir C. Markham, Capt. A. T. Mahan, Mr T.
  Roosevelt, etc. 7 vols. la. 8º. London, 1897–1903.
      (The standard English Naval history. Vol. II.
  Ponderous and rather unequal: uses strange and
  arbitrary distinction between "major" and "minor"
  operations. The operations in the Mediterranean are
  "minor." Illustrations of prints and medals, but no
  maps beyond diagrams. No bibliography. Note Navy
  List of 1660   Some of the omissions, *e.g.* Restoration,
  Administration, are supplied by Hannay, *q.v.*)
Derrick, C. Memoirs of the Rise and Progress of the
  Royal Navy. 4º. London, 1806.
      (Useful lists and notes about Shipbuilding.)
Du Sein, A. Histoire de la Marine de tous les peuples.
  2 vols. 8º. 1863–79.
Eardley-Wilmot, Rear-Adm. Sir S. Our Navy for a
  Thousand Years. Fourth ed. 8º. London, 1911.
      (Popular.)
Entick, John. A New Naval History. Fº. London, 1757.
Firth, C. H. The Last Years of the Protectorate, 1656–8.
  2 vols. 8º. London, 1909.
      (A general history, including, however, the financial
  decay of the Navy before the death of Cromwell.)

Gardiner, S. R. History of the Commonwealth and Protectorate, 1649–60. 3 vols., and Suppl. chapter. 8º. 1894–1903.
(The standard general history of the period. Unfortunately, owing to author's death, never completed beyond 1656.)
*Hannay, David. Short History of the Royal Navy. Vol. I. 1217–1688. 8º. London [1898].
(On main points not so "short" as Clowes. Note specially administration and development of naval strategy after the Restoration.)
*Jonge, J. C. de. Geschiedenis van het Nederlandsche Zeewezen. 6 parts. 8º. The Hague, 1833–48. (Second ed. 1858–62.)
(The standard Dutch Naval history. From 1665. Good bibliography and valuable lists.)
Lediard, T. Naval History of England, 1066–1734. 2 vols. Fº. London, 1735.
(One of the better early histories; quotes largely from original sources; spends most of his footnotes in controverting Rapin—which, at times, is enlightening.)
Moreau, César. Chronological Records of the British Royal and Commercial Navy. Fº. 1827.
*Rittmeyer, Kontre-Adm. Rudolph. Seekriege und Seekriegswesen in ihrer weltgeschichtlichen Entwicklung. 2 Bde. 8º. Berlin, 1907–11.
(Combines De Jonge and Clowes; discussions on Strategy and Tactics; good critical bibliography of general works: maps and illustrations.)
Robinson, Comm. C. N. The British Fleet, the growth, achievement and duties of the Navy of the Empire. 8º. London, 1894.
(Note Customs, personnel and social side of Navy, 150 illustrations, prints, etc.)
Stenzel, Alfred. Seekriegsgeschichte...mit Berücksichtigung der Seetaktik. 5 vols. 8º. Hanover, 1911.
(Much space devoted to discussion of the tactics of the Dutch Wars. Very few references. Rather fond of comparing seventeenth century politics with those of

present day—substituting England for Holland, and Germany for England.)

Wheatley, H. B. Samuel Pepys and the World he lived in. Fifth ed. 8º. London, 1907.
(Chapter on Navy, p. 128, and following.)

Yonge, C. D. History of the British Navy from the earliest period. 2 vols. 8º. London, 1863.
(Cf. Allen, above, page 218.)

(b) Special Subjects

(1) English and Dutch

Anderson, R. C. Naval Wars in the Baltic, 1522–1850. 8º. London, 1910.
(Little about the Baltic expedition of 1659.)

Beaujon, A. Overzicht der gesch. van de Nederlandsche zeevisscherijen. 8º. Leyden, 1885.

*Corbett, Julian. England in the Mediterranean: a Study of the Rise and Influence of British Power within the Straits, 1603–1713. 2 vols. 8º. London, 1904.
(Only complete work on subject; fairly detailed account 1662–7. Not many references and no bibliography.)

Davis, Lt.-Col. J. Hist. records of the Second Queen's Royal Regiment. 6 vols. la 8º. London, 1887–1906.
(Full account of Tangier, 1663–. Good bibliography.)

Edmundson, Rev. George. Anglo-Dutch Rivalry during the first half of the Seventeenth Century. 8º. Oxford, 1911.
(Origin of the Dutch Wars.)

†Japikse, N. De Verwikkelingen Tusschen de Republiek en England van 1660–5.

Jurien de la Gravière, J. P. E. Les Anglais et les Hollandais dans les mers polaires et dans la mer des Indes. 2 vols. s. 8º. Paris, 1890.

Lopez de Ayala, Ignacio. Historia de Gibraltar; documentos ineditos perteniendos a la ciudad de Gibraltar. 4º. Madrid, 1782.
(Eng. trans. London, 1845.)

Lord, W. F.   England and France in the Mediterranean, 1660–1830. 8°. London, 1901.
  (Very scanty before 1800, mostly Napoleonic. No references, and arrangement peculiar.)
Low, Charles R.   History of the Indian Navy, 1613–1863. 2 vols. London, 1877.
*Routh, E. M. G.   Tangier; England's lost Atlantic outpost, 1661–81. 8°. London, 1912.
  (Full references and bibliography; numerous illustrations from old prints.)
*Tanner, J. R.   Navy of Commonwealth and First Dutch War. (See Chap. xvi in Cambridge Modern Hist., Vol. iv. Cambridge, 1906.)
*Tanner, J. R., and C. T. Atkinson.   Anglo-Dutch Wars. (See Chap. ix in Camb. Modern Hist., Vol. v. Cambridge, 1908.)
  (The best summary of the period. Bibliographies at end of respective volumes.)

(2) *Other Nations*

Chevalier, E.   Histoire de la Marine française jusqu'au traité de paix de 1763. 8°. Paris, 1902.
Fernandez Duro, C.   Armada Española desde la Unión de los Reinos de Castilla y de León. 9 vols. la. 8°. Madrid, 1895–1903.
Guérin, Léon.   Histoire Maritime de France. 6 vols. Nouv. éd. la. 8°. Paris, 1851–2.
La Roncière, Charles de.   Histoire de la Marine française. 4 vols. 8°. Paris, 1899–1910.
  (Vol. iv, pub. 1910, only goes to 1642. A standard work.)
Mitchell, J.   History of the Maritime Wars of the Turks. (Trans. from Turkish of Haji Khalifeh. Oriental Trans. Fund.) 4°. London, 1831.
Sue, M. J. Eugène.   Histoire de la Marine française, 17e siècle (1653–1712). 5 vols. 8°. Paris, 1835–7.
†Tuxen, J. G.   Den Danske og Norske Sömagt fra de aeldete Tider ind til voge Dage. laere Skildringer. Kjöbenhavn, 1875.

(c) TECHNICAL

(1) *Strategy.*

*Colomb, V. Adm. Philip Howard. Naval Warfare, its ruling principles and practice historically treated. Second ed. la. 8º. London, 1895.
(Standard work. Dutch wars treated from strategic standpoint; accounts of actions: chapters 2, 3, 4, and references passim.)

*Corbett, Julian. Some Principles of Maritime Strategy. la. 8º. London, 1911.
(Treated historically: references to Dutch Wars passim.)

*Mahan, Capt. A. T. The Influence of Sea Power upon History, 1660 to 1783. 8º. London, 1889.
(The classic of naval strategy: cf. later works on subject by other writers. Detailed accounts of actions. Maps.)

Maltzahn, V. Adm. Baron Curt von. Naval Warfare: its historical development from the age of the great geographical discoveries to the present time. (Trans. from German by J. C. Miller.) 8º. London, 1908.
(Short (152 pp.) but clear general view of development of naval strategy.)

*Rittmeyer, Kontre-Adm. R. Seekriege und Seekriegswesen. Bd. I. 8º. Berlin, 1907. (Discusses strategy of Dutch Wars.)

Rodenberg, Carl. Seemacht in der Geschichte. la. 8º. Stuttgart, 1900. (33 pages.)

Stenzel, A. Seekriegsgeschichte. Vol. II. 8º. Hanover, 1911. (Strategy of each campaign.)

Thursfield, James R. Nelson and other Naval Studies. 8º. London, 1909.
(Including "The Dogger Bank and its Lessons," "The Attack and Defence of Commerce.")

(2) *Tactics.*

Castex, Lieut. R. Les Idées Militaires de la Marine du xviiiᵉ siècle. De Ruyter à Suffren. 8º. Paris, 1911.
(Chap. I on seventeenth century, including critical paragraph on Hoste, "Le Théoricien du xviiᵉ siècle.")

*Rittmeyer, Kontre-Adm. R. Seekriege und Seekriegswesen. Bd. i passim. 8º. Berlin, 1907.

Stenzel, A. Seekriegsgeschichte. Vol. ii passim. 8º. Hanover, 1911. (Discussions of tactics of each engagement.)

(3) *Hydrography*.

The charts in use in the English Navy appear to have been small sheets of Dutch publication—or English copies of Dutch originals. Pepys notes "that Ashley's Books of Maps were never printed but once. And never looked after: whereas yᵉ Dutch Waggener has been continually kept in print and sold under many names over all yᵉ world in diverse languages, and continually prefered and used by us, notwithstanding Ashley's pretence to have corrected him."

Wagenaar, Luke. The Mariner's Mirror. 41 charts. la. fº. 1588.

(*d*) ADMINISTRATION

(1) *General*.

*Charnock, John. An History of Marine Architecture. Including an enlarged and progressive view of the Nautical Regulations and Naval History,...especially of Great Britain, etc. 3 vols. 4º. London, 1800–2.

Marsden, R. G. The High Court of Admiralty in relation to National history, etc., 1550–1660. (Transactions of Roy. Hist. Soc., 1902–3.)

*Oppenheim, M. A History of the Administration of the Royal Navy and of Merchant Shipping in relation to the Navy, from 1509–1660. 8º. London, 1896.

(Note especially victualling, pay, morale. Plentiful figures, lists and references.)

Raithby, John. The Statutes relating to the Admiralty, Navy, Shipping, and Navigation of the United Kingdom from 9 Hen. III. to 3 Geo. IV. inclusive. With notes, referring to the subsequent Statutes, and to the decisions in the Courts of Admiralty. 1164 pp. 4º. London. 1823.

*Tanner, J. R. Administration of the Navy from Restoration to Revolution. (Intro. to A Descriptive Catalogue of the Naval MSS. in the Pepysian Library at Magdalene College, Cambridge, Vol. I. Navy Records Soc. Publ. 1903.) Also in Eng. Hist. Review, XII, XIII, XIV.
(Forms a continuation to 1688 of Oppenheim's work.)

(2) *Shipbuilding.*

Arenhold, Kapt. L. Die historische Entwicklung der Schiffstypen vom römischen Kriegsschiff bis zum Gegenwart. la. 4°. Kiel and Leipzig, 1891.
(Includes 30 engravings showing development of ships and armament.)

Charnock, John. An History of Marine Architecture. 3 vols. Illus. 4°. London, 1800–2.

Derrick, Charles. Memoirs of the Rise and Progress of the Royal Navy. 4°. London, 1806.
(Useful notes about shipbuilding, and lists: references.)

Steinitz, F. The Ship, its origin and progress: with plates and flags. 4°. London, 1849.
(Numerous plates illustrating development of ship building; also a slight naval history—scanty on Dutch Wars.)

(3) *Personnel.*

Hannay, D. Ships and Men. 8°. London, 1910.

Robinson, Comm. C. N. The British Tar in Fact and Fiction...with introductory chapters on the place of the sea officer and seaman in Naval history and historical literature. Illus. 8°. London, 1909.
(Studies of the sailors of the Commonwealth and Restoration; uniforms, customs; songs, etc., many reproductions of old prints.)

(e) MISCELLANEOUS

(1) *Articles in Reviews,* etc. (The following does not pretend to be in the slightest degree even a representative list.)

American Historical Review, July, 1909. "The English Conspiracy and Dissent," by Wilbur C. Abbott. (Navy and Restoration.)

English Historical Review. *Vols. XII, XIII, XIV. "Administration of the Navy from Restoration to Revolution"; by J. R. Tanner. (Publ. in Vol. I of Catal. of Pepys MSS.)

Marine Rundschau. 1901, p. 117; 1902, p. 265; 1903, p. 463; "De Ruiter," Kapt. Gudewill. Jan. 1911. "The North Sea: Its History, Politics, and Geography." (Trans. and reprinted in Roy. United Serv. Instit. Jour. 1911.) Cf. Inhaltsverzeichnis zu den Beiheften zum Marine Verordnungsblatt und der Marine Rundschau, 1872 bis 1902.

Mariner's Mirror, The: Journal of Soc. for Nautical Research. 3 vols. 8°. [London?], 1911–13.

Nauticus. Jahrbuch für Deutschlands Seeinteressen. Berlin. 1900. Number contains articles on "Entwicklung der englischen Seemacht," and "Blüte und Verfall der holländischen Seemacht."

Revue Historique, XXV, 28. "Études Algériennes; la course, l'esclavage et la rédemption à Alger," H. D. de Grammont.

Revue Maritime et Coloniale.

1864, Vol. XII, 565. "Le personnel de la Marine Militaire et les classes maritimes sous Colbert et Seignelay." (de Crisenoy.)

1875, Vol. XLIV, 165. "Les écoles d'hydrographie au XVIIe siècle."

1879, Vol. LXIII, 448, 666. "Les Ingénieurs de la marine sous Colbert et Seignelay" (1664–90).

1884, Vol. LXXXII, 137. "Combat naval entre les Hollandais et les Anglais, le 11, 12, 13 et 14 juin, 1666. Relation inédite."

1885, Vol. LXXXV, 497. "Batailles Navales au milieu de XVIIe siècle."

Vol. LXXXVI, 74.

1888, Vol. XCIX, 577. "Tourville et la Marine de son temps."

(2) *Mercantile Navy and Commerce.*

†Baasch, E. Hamburgs Konvoyschiffahrt und Kon-
voywesen. Ein Beitrag zur Geschichte der Schiffahrt im
XVII. und XVIII. Jahrhundert. la. 8º. Hamburg, 1896.

Blackmore, Ed. The British Mercantile Marine: a short
historical review, including the rise and progress of
British shipping and commerce. 8º. London, 1897.

Cornewall-Jones, R. J. The British Merchant Service,
being a History of the British Merchant-Marine from the
earliest times to the present day. 8º. London, 1898.

East India Company. An Historical Account of the inter-
course between the inhabitants of Great Britain and
the people in the West Indies, containing likewise a
compleat history of the East India Company from its
erection under Queen Elizabeth. (In Harris, Voyages,
1764. Fº. Vol. I, pp. 873–934.)

——— Dutch, History of the Rise, Progress, and Establishment of the. (In Harris, Vol. I, pp. 914–48.).

Oppenheim, M. Administration of the Royal Navy and
of Merchant Shipping, 1509–1660. 8º. London, 1896.

(3) *Other Miscellaneous Works.*

*Firth, C. H., ed. Naval Songs and Ballads. (Navy
Records Soc., Vol. XXXIII.) 8º. [London], 1908.

Hawkins, Edward. Medallic Illustrations of Great Britain
and Ireland, to death of George II. Ed. by A. W.
Franks and H. R. Grueber. 2 vols. 8º. London, 1885.

Mayo, J. H. Medals and Decorations of the British Army
and Navy. 2 vols. 8º. 1897.

VII. BIOGRAPHY

(a) CONTEMPORARY

(1) *Collective.*

*Bos, Lambert van den. Leben und Thaten der durch-
lauchtigsten See-Helden, und Erfinder der Lande
dieser Zeiten, anfangdend mit Christopher Columbus
und sich endend mit dem hochst berühmten Admiral
M. A. de Ruyks. 2 parts. Sultzbach, 1681.
(Includes Opdam, Tromp and De Ruyter.)

(2) *Individual.*

De Ruyter

*Brandt, Gerrit. La Vie de Michel de Ruiter; où est comprise l'Histoire Maritime des Provinces Unies, depuis l'an 1652 jusques à 1676. F⁰. Amsterdam, 1698.

(Original in Dutch, 1687. French trans. by son of author.)

(Exhaustive and calm account from the Dutch side. One of the chief contemporary authorities.)

De Witt

Hoeven, Emanuel van der. Leeven en dood de doorlustige heeren gebroeders C. de Witt en J. de Witt. 4⁰. Amsterdam, 1705.

Monk

Gumble, T. Life of Gen. Monck. s. 8⁰. London, 1671.
Skinner, T. Life of Gen. Monck, from an original MS. of T. Skinner; ed. by W. Webster. 8⁰. London, 1723.

(MS. of *circa* 1680 ? Detailed accounts of actions of 1665.)

Münster, Bp of

Life and actions of C. Bernard von Galen, Bishop of Münster. London, 1680.

Rupert

Historical Memoirs of the Life and death of Prince Rupert. Pub. by Th. Malthus. s. 8⁰. London, 1683.

Tromp

*La vie de Corneille Tromp. (Author unknown.) 8⁰. Hague, 1694.

(Though anonymous, this is—in company with Brandt's De Ruyter, *q.v.*—the chief contemporary authority dealing with the war from the Dutch side. Detailed eye-witness's accounts of actions.)

(b) LATER

(1) *Collective.*

*Campbell, John, LL.D. Lives of the Admirals. New edition, revised. 8 vols. 8º. London, 1817.
(Includes Monk, Mountagu, Rupert, Ayscue, Lawson and Spragge.)

*Charnock, J. Biographia Navalis, or Impartial memoirs of the lives and characters of Officers of the Navy of Great Britain from 1660 to the present time. 6 vols. 8º. London, 1794–8.
(Vol. I. 1660–7.)

Cust, Gen. the Hon. Sir Edward. Lives of the Warriors who have commanded Fleets and Armies before the Enemy, 1648–1704. 2 vols. Illustrations. 8º. London, 1874.

De Liefde, Jan. Great Dutch Admirals. s. 8º. London, 1873.

*Dictionary of National Biography.
(See under Sir Tho. Allin, Sir Wm. Berkeley, Sir Wm. Coventry, Cromwell, Sir Rich. Fanshawe, Sir Rich. Goodson, Sir John Harman, Sir Rob. Holmes, Sir Phil. Meadows, Gen. Monk, Edw. Mountagu, Sir Wm. Penn, Sam. Pepys, Peter Pett, Prince Rupert, Sir Alg. Sidney, Sir Rich. Stayner, Sir Tho. Tyddeman.)

Laughton, J. K. Studies in Naval History. Biographies. 8º. London, 1887.
(Du Quesne and Colbert.)

See biographical notes on Penn, Coventry, etc., in Wheatley's "Sam. Pepys and the world he lived in." 8º. London, 1907.

(2) *Individual.*

Cromwell, Rich.

Guizot, F. P. G. Richard Cromwell and the Restoration of the Stuarts. Trans. by J. Scoble. 2 vols. 8º. London, 1856.

De Ruyter

Grinnell-Milne, G. Life of Adm. de Ruyter. 8º. London, 1896.
(A popular life.)

†Klopp, Dr O. Leben und Taten des Admirals de Ruiter.
8º. Hanover, 1852.

De Witt

*Lefèvre-Pontalis, A. Jean de Witt, Grand pensionnaire
de Hollande. 2 vols. 8º. Paris, 1884.
  (Eng. trans. by S. E. and A. Stevenson. 2 vols.
  8º. London, 1885.)
  (One of the chief modern authorities.)
Simons, P. Johann de Witt und seine Zeit. Übersetzt
von F. Neumann. 2 parts. Erfurt, 1835–6.
  (Trans. from Dutch edit., pub. Amsterdam, 1832–
  42.)

Du Quesne

Jal, Auguste. A. du Quesne et la Marine de son Temps.
2 vols. 8º. Paris, 1873.

Evertsen

Jonge, J. C. de. Levens-beschrijving van Johan en
Cornelis Evertsen. The Hague, 1820.
  (See also his "Geschiedenis van het Nederl. Zee-
  wezen" above, page 219.)

James II

Clarke, J. S. Life of James II, collected out of memoirs
writ of his own hand. 2 vols. 4º. London, 1816.

Monk

Corbett, Julian. Life of Gen. Monk. (Eng. Men of Action
Series.) 8º. London, 1889.
Guizot, F. P. G. Memoirs of George Monk, D. of Albe-
marle. Trans. and edit. by J. S. Wortley. 8º.
London, 1838.

Mountagu

*Harris, F. R. Life of Ed. Mountagu, 1st Earl of Sandwich.
2 vols. 8º. London, 1912.
  (Containing the most recent results of research into
  naval history of this period. Much new material from
  the Sandwich MS. Journal, etc., at Hinchingbrooke:
  full of references, but no complete bibliography and
  no maps.)

Münster, Bp of

Brinkmann, C. Charles II and the Bp of Münster, 1665–6. (Eng. Hist. Review, Vol. XXI, 1906.)

Penn

*Penn, Granville. Memorials of the Professional Life and Times of Sir Wm. Penn. 2 vols. 8º. London, 1833. (A standard authority on the period: impartial: prints many valuable papers, orders, etc.)

Pepys

Smith, J. The Life, Journal, and Correspondence of Samuel Pepys,...deciphered by Rev. J. Smith. 2 vols. 8º. London, 1841.
   (Sandwich correspondence starting June 1661 in Vol. I.)
Wheatley, H. B. Samuel Pepys and the World he lived in. 5th ed. 8º. London, 1907.
   (Slight sketch of development of Navy under Pepys.)
*—— Pepysiana. (Supplementary vol. to Diary.) 8º. London, 1899.
   (Chap. on Navy Office, etc.)

Rupert

Warburton, Eliot. Memoirs of Pr. Rupert and the Cavaliers, including their private correspondence. 3 vols. 8º. London, 1849.
   (Note Rupert's declaration as to division of the Fleet in 1666, Vol. III.)

Sidney, Algernon

Ewald, A. C. Life and Times of Algernon Sidney, 1622–83. 2 vols. 8º. London, 1873.
   (Cf. Sydney Papers, above, page 208.)

INDEX

CAMBRIDGE UNIVERSITY PRESS

THE ROYAL NAVY
By JOHN LEYLAND
Cambridge Manuals Series.   Royal 16mo.
Cloth, 1s 3d net.   Leather, 2s 6d net.

" *The Royal Navy*, by John Leyland, is one of the latest volumes in The Cambridge Manuals of Science and Literature, and one of the best.   It sketches lightly, but accurately, the history of English Sea Power from the days of Offa, Alfred, and Canute, to those of Nelson, and shows with great clearness how the growing greatness of our Empire has always depended upon her command of the sea.   The book is absolutely free from technicality and statistics, but the great principles it enunciates are illustrated throughout most conclusively.   It is a book well worth reading in the circumstances of to-day."—*Methodist Recorder*

NAVAL WARFARE
By J. R. THURSFIELD, M.A.
Cambridge Manuals Series.   Royal 16mo.
Cloth, 1s 3d net.   Leather, 2s 6d net.

" It is not too much to say that the editors of The Cambridge Manuals of Science and Literature have done a service to the nation in commissioning Mr J. R. Thursfield to write this little treatise.   In a short but interesting introduction Rear-Admiral Sir Charles Ottley sets forth the title of Mr Thursfield to speak with authority upon a theme at once so great and so technical, and gives the high sanction of his approval to the contents of the book.   In these days, when the Navy—what it stands for and is designed to do—is constantly and rightly in the thoughts and on the lips of all classes, not only at home but in the great Dominions also, a clear, readable, concise, and authoritative exposition, which all can understand, ought to be widely read and should do much good....Every one who desires to understand the inwardness of the strategical and technical questions involved in this naval conflict should read Mr J. R. Thursfield's excellent little treatise."—*Times*

THE MODERN WARSHIP
By E. L. ATTWOOD, M.Inst.N.A.
Cambridge Manuals Series.   With frontispiece and 17 figures.
Royal 16mo.   Cloth, 1s 3d net.   Leather, 2s 6d net.

" Mr Attwood sets forth in a clear and lucid manner some of the elementary principles governing warship construction....The author concerns himself mainly with the capital ship, telling us something of hull construction, including watertight subdivision, engines, boilers, auxiliary machinery, and general equipment.   He also touches lightly on such theoretical aspects of his subject as 'Stability and Rolling,' and the question of power in relation to speed, with some interesting notes on experimental work with wax models at the Government tank at Haslar.   The concluding chapter deals with the cost of warships....The diagrams supplied are simple and appropriate."—*Athenæum*

NAVAL COURTS MARTIAL
By DAVID HANNAY
With frontispiece and 6 plates.   Demy 8vo.   8s net.

" Mr David Hannay has turned his attention to a practically unexplored field of naval lore in the shape of the court-martial records.   He entitles his work *Naval Courts-Martial*, and has set out to present from this point of view some picture of what the old Navy was like down to the end of the Napoleonic wars.   The result is a book which cannot fail to be of absorbing interest to every student of naval history."—*Army & Navy Gazette*

MILITARY HISTORY
By the Hon. J. W. FORTESCUE
Cambridge Manuals Series.   Royal 16mo.
Cloth, 1s 3d net.   Leather, 2s 6d net.

" Packed into a small space you will find Mr Fortescue offering any number of common-sense observations on war in general and on our British wars in particular.... Mr Fortescue is a historian who has the courage of his opinions as well as a thorough grasp of his material."—*Sunday Times*

I

CAMBRIDGE UNIVERSITY PRESS

THE CAMBRIDGE
NAVAL AND MILITARY SERIES

General Editors:

JULIAN S. CORBETT, LL.M., F.S.A., and H. J. EDWARDS,
C.B., M.A.

Ocean Trade and Shipping. By DOUGLAS OWEN,
Barrister-at-Law, Lecturer at the Royal Naval War College.
With 7 illustrations. Demy 8vo. 10s 6d net.

Naval and Military Essays. Being Papers read in the
Naval and Military section at the International Congress of
Historical Studies, 1913. Demy 8vo. 7s 6d net.

THE CAMBRIDGE MODERN HISTORY

Planned by the late Lord ACTON, LL.D. Edited by
Sir A. W. WARD, Litt.D., G. W. PROTHERO, Litt.D., and
STANLEY LEATHES, M.A.

In twelve royal 8vo volumes. Bound in Buckram.

Vol. I. THE RENAISSANCE.	Vol. VII. THE UNITED STATES.
„ II. THE REFORMATION.	„ VIII. THE FRENCH REVOLUTION.
„ III. THE WARS OF RELIGION.	„ IX. NAPOLEON.
„ IV. THE THIRTY YEARS' WAR.	„ X. THE RESTORATION.
„ V. THE AGE OF LOUIS XIV.	„ XI. THE GROWTH OF NATION-
„ VI. THE EIGHTEENTH CEN-	„ ALITIES.
TURY.	„ XII. THE LATEST AGE.

Price for the complete text in 12 volumes, £7 10s 0d net.
Separate volumes, 16s net.

SUPPLEMENTARY VOLUMES

(1) Genealogical Tables and Lists and General Index. Price
16s net.

(2) Atlas. Price 25s net.

The complete work in 14 volumes is sold for £8 15s 0d net.
It may also be obtained in the Roxburgh style, in brown Persian
sheepskin, with brown cloth sides, price £9 net; in Three-quarter
green Morocco, with large leather corners and cloth sides, price
£11 net; and in Full rose-red Morocco, price £15 net.

Cambridge University Press

Fetter Lane, London: C. F. Clay, Manager

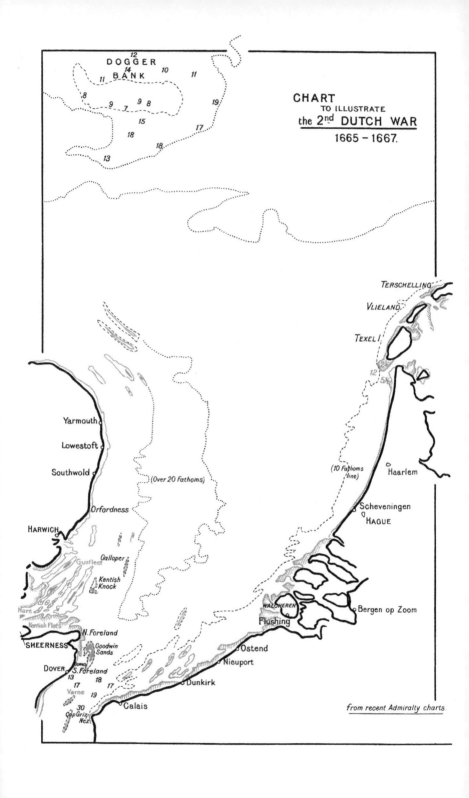

DOGGER BANK

CHART
TO ILLUSTRATE
the 2nd DUTCH WAR
1665 – 1667.

TERSCHELLING
VLIELAND
TEXEL I.

Yarmouth
Lowestoft
Southwold
(Over 20 Fathoms)
Orfordness
HARWICH
Galloper
Kentish Knock
Nore
Kentish Flats
N. Foreland
SHEERNESS
Goodwin Sands
DOVER S. Foreland
Varne
Calais
Cap Griz Nez

Haarlem
Scheveningen
HAGUE
(10 Fathoms line)

WALCHEREN
Flushing
Bergen op Zoom
Ostend
Nieuport
Dunkirk

from recent Admiralty charts

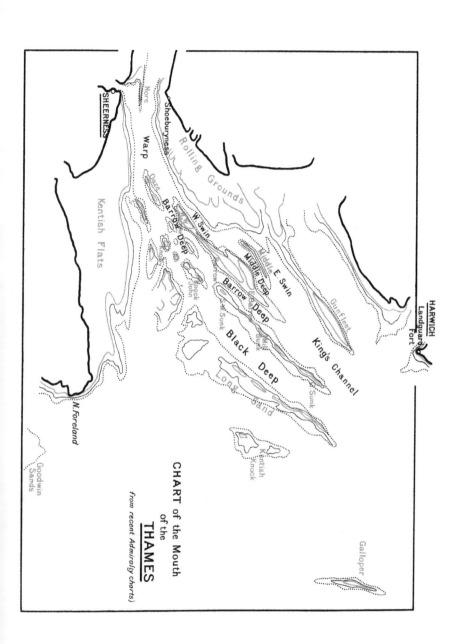

CHART of the Mouth
of the
THAMES

from recent Admiralty charts)

www.ingramcontent.com/pod-product-compliance
Ingram Content Group UK Ltd.
Pitfield, Milton Keynes, MK11 3LW, UK
UKHW010340140625
459647UK00010B/722